The Politics of the Encounter

EST. 75 1938
YEARS
THE UNIVERSITY OF GEORGIA PRESS 2013

The Politics of the Encounter

URBAN THEORY AND PROTEST UNDER
PLANETARY URBANIZATION

ANDY MERRIFIELD

THE UNIVERSITY OF GEORGIA PRESS
Athens and London

Publication of this work was made possible, in part, by a generous gift from the University of Georgia Press Friends Fund.

Set in Minion and Trade Gothic by Graphic Composition, Inc., Bogart, GA.
Manufactured by Sheridan Books, Inc.
The paper in this book meets the guidelines for
permanence and durability of the Committee on
Production Guidelines for Book Longevity of the
Council on Library Resources.

Printed in the United States of America
17   16   15   14   13   P   5   4   3   2   1

Library of Congress Cataloging-in-Publication Data

Merrifield, Andy.
    The politics of the encounter : urban theory and protest under planetary urbanization /
Andy Merrifield.
        pages cm. — (Geographies of justice and social transformation ; 19)
    Includes bibliographical references and index.
    ISBN-13: 978-0-8203-4529-1 (hardcover : alk. paper)
    ISBN-10: 0-8203-4529-6 (hardcover : alk. paper)
    ISBN-13: 978-0-8203-4530-7 (pbk. : alk. paper)
    ISBN-10: 0-8203-4530-X (pbk. : alk. paper)
    1. Sociology, Urban. 2. Urbanization. 3. Social justice. 4. Lefebvre, Henri, 1901–1991. I. Title.
HT151.M445 2013
307.76—dc23
                                                                    2012046528

British Library Cataloging-in-Publication Data available

To the memory of Herbert Muschamp, 1947–2007

At every moment of the encounter, I discover in the other another myself: You like this? So do I! You don't like that? Neither do I!

Roland Barthes

Yet is no body present here which was not there before. Only is order othered.

James Joyce

CONTENTS

The Personal and the Political

A Different Kind of Blue

The late Herbert Muschamp, onetime columnist at the *New York Times*, once suggested my and Henri Lefebvre's work on the city sprang from a variation of what psychoanalyst Melanie Klein called "the depressive position." Muschamp was one of America's most influential (and controversial) architectural critics, a brilliant, exuberant urban commentator, a chip off Lefebvre's own block. He and I became friends in 2002, around the time of the publication of my books *Metromarxism* and *Dialectical Urbanism*, although after I'd relocated to France it was more often a fellow-traveler kind of thing, a friendship across a divide of water, ideology, and time. When I asked Muschamp to write a foreword to my book on Lefebvre, he happily complied. It was in that foreword that he embarrassingly threw me into the same bag as our greatest philosopher of the city, the French Marxist Lefebvre.

Muschamp died from lung cancer in 2007. He was fifty-nine. His death created a gaping hole in U.S. urbanism. A rare voice was silenced, a cosmopolitan and romantic voice for whom the city meant, above all, *freedom*—political and sexual freedom.[1] Muschamp was pained whenever he saw those freedoms taken away. He loved New York yet wasn't afraid to condemn the city, to correct popular misconceptions: that it was an island off an island, imagining itself a liberal stronghold when, Muschamp insisted, the record strongly indicated the reverse. New York had given us Rudolph Giuliani's chronic hostility toward the First Amendment; fake premodern architecture and other monstrosities "designed" to make land pay; new magazines featuring cover stories on assorted religious crazies; and a host of other Red State (Republican) backlashes against 1960s sensibilities. Muschamp never got over the jingoistic (and bottom-line) fiascoes of post-9/11 Ground Zero or the idiocies of the Bush years.

His loss was personal for me as well, a loss of a supporter and source of inspiration. Yet when Muschamp was alive I'd never reflected too much on his allusion to Melanie Klein. I'd likely smiled or laughed when I first read it. Muschamp's writing could be fun as well as instructive in its humor, lighter touch, depth, and profundity. With hindsight and age, now that he's gone, I can see

he was right on both counts—right about me and Lefebvre. The city we hate
is also the city we love. A sort of negative attachment gets played out; it is the
business of the city, Muschamp said, to offer something for everyone to hate,
"even to present itself as completely hateful to some people most of the time."[2]
He'd spotted it in me, and he'd spotted it in Henri Lefebvre. Muschamp knew,
as I did, that biography and criticism often meant disguised forms of autobiog-
raphy, indirect ways to voice your own opinions through other people, through
"authority figures." My book *Henri Lefebvre: A Critical Introduction* had been
written in a Savoyard mountain village next to a huge slither of rock called
Le Vuache in the pre-Alps. I'd quit New York a few years earlier, fled and downsized to the countryside where I thought I needed to be, where I thought I could
draw breath and gather myself up again. I'd been pushed, of course, because of
New York's exorbitant cost of living, but I'd jumped, too, out of the city and even
out of academia, making the leap by my own volition.

Henri Lefebvre himself had spent his last years in a small Medieval town at
the foot of the Pyrenees where he'd stomped around as a kid. Guy Debord likewise eloped from Paris, settling in a lost and lonely Auvergne, where he lived
like a reclusive monk behind a high stone wall; he even developed a penchant
for wearing traditional smock blouses. (I'd been fascinated by Debord's wall and
his fleeing from Paris in the 1970s, and I wrote a book about it that mirrored
my own urban flight.) Lefebvre and Debord penned some of the most beautiful
lines ever written about Paris; but they also laid into the city, its politicians and
planners, its bureaucrats and entrepreneurs, doing so with a spleen that made
Baudelaire seem mild-mannered. Here, then, was Klein's (and Muschamp's) depressive position thesis getting worked through, channeling itself dialectically.

That depressive position was most personally articulated in *The Wisdom of
Donkeys* (2008), my attempt to evoke the delights of rural life, of going slow and
appreciating nature, of returning to tradition and going backward toward some
saner, calmer antiquity—with my long-eared companion (donkey) in tow, or
leading the way. At the time, the Bush administration was in full force; the
world was at war and I wanted no part of it; I was with an animal who was the
epitome of peace. The world was obsessively high-tech and moving nowhere
very fast; here was a low-tech beast who dawdled and made steady progress.
Urbanization was carpeting over the whole world with concrete, polluting our
atmosphere, bombarding everybody with endless noise; here I breathed in clean
air on quiet pastures of tender green. Politicians and financial bigwigs pushed
everybody about; this animal took no shit from anyone.

So, for almost eight years, I lived out a surreal French rural idyll, and capped
it off with a book about donkeys, trying to convince myself I could make peace

and quiet work. I was wrong: going backward, or moving forward very slowly, doing it noiselessly, was really slow death, a death of the creative spirit. After finishing *The Wisdom of Donkeys*, I recognized pretty soon that I needed *speed*, a fast life, a noisy life again; I needed to move forward headlong to embrace the future. I needed the *magic* potion of being among people again, lots of people, of being out on busy streets somewhere. What emerged from that desire was *Magical Marxism* (2011), my attempt to conjure a spell-like potion and to somehow tap it politically. Almost all of *Magical Marxism* was written in São Paulo, Brazil, in the Dom José cafe in Jardim Paulistano, at the junction of ruas Arthur de Azevedo and Oscar Friere near the city's Hospital das Clinicas. Whenever I lifted my head out of the text, I could watch a vast metropolitan world go by. During that Brazilian sojourn, I joked how I once lived in a village of nineteen people (summer population!); here there were some nineteen million people and yet I felt more at home, was more existentially at ease, had a more intimate sense of belonging.

There was another reason I went to São Paulo: I'd hoped to find firsthand the crazy Latin American intensity I'd imbibed within the pages of Gabriel García Márquez's *One Hundred Years of Solitude*. (True, this wasn't Caribbean Colombia, but then García Márquez always said there was only one other place on the South American continent that felt and thought like his native coastal region: Brazil.) After a while, I knew this magic existed nowhere in the objective reality of São Paulo, with its gridlocked streets, crumbling infrastructure, and grinding poverty that afflicted the bulk of its millionfold denizens. The only magic I could find was the *subjective* magic I mustered inside my own head, in occasional mad leaps of the imagination. This wasn't so much idealism as *really* making the mind work, making it come to life, putting it into practice. (A lot of people in São Paulo, and in the world, did just that, hence *Magical Marxism*'s subtitle: *Subversive Politics and the Imagination*.) Nonetheless, there was something subtle at play, too: somehow, somewhere, actually being in a city, being "big urban" again, helped that magic come, helped it incubate and gurgle in a giant melting pot. Its vaporous gases wafted over me amid the throng as I universally communed with the glorious turmoil of the crowd.

Strangely, *Magical Marxism* makes short shrift of the city and its problems. It isn't an urban book, and it tackles the link between politics and the city only sketchily, only in its conclusion, via the "Right to the City" (RTTC) movement. Moreover, with hindsight now, what little I said there—between *Magical Marxism*'s drafting and its eventual publication—seems ill-conceived and problematic. But why does the city as an explicit object of political analysis figure so little, and so problematically, in a book written almost entirely in one of the world's largest metropolises? A decade prior, I'd feted a distinctively *Metro-marxism*, an unashamedly urban Marxism, suggesting that some of the most innovative Marxism had been carried out by certain urbanists and that some of the most innovative urban studies had been done, and continues to be done, by certain Marxists. Now, circa 2011–2012, just as statisticians tell us that for the first time in human history the balance has tilted, that the majority of the world's population now lives in cities (not in the countryside), I'd somehow made a bizarre ontological leap. I'd gone from the metro to the magical; from a jazzy, speeding Forty-second Street cityscape to a spooky, ostensibly bucolic scene straight out of *As You Like It* (one of Shakespeare's most unsettling political comedies), replete with fairytale fawns and donkeys, fluttering butterflies, and Nietzschean night owls in broad daylight.[3]

Why the shift in context? And just what *is* the context of magical Marxism? How and where, if anywhere, does the city fit in? At first, I wasn't sure, and began thinking that maybe it didn't fit in, that global Marxist politics would have to move beyond a city politics—that the city wasn't, in fact, necessarily a privileged terrain for political struggle, especially given new social media like Twitter and Facebook. I know now—or think I know—that this isn't the case: the city, somehow, is important, virtually and materially, for progressive politics. And yet, how so? And what, precisely, is this "somehow"? Searching for answers to these questions is what prompted the present book. I had a hunch that the answers would take me beyond the "depressive position," beyond my own urban ambivalence—who *isn't* ambivalent about cities, anyway?—and that it would involve a whole problematization of the concept of "the right to the city." Intellectually, I needed to be back in the city, needed to reclaim it *personally*; I also needed to reclaim that terrain *politically*. Near the end of *Magical Marxism*, I'd written loosely, over-rhetorically, about the right to the city as a global "cry and demand." (The phrase is Lefebvre's, from *Le droit à la ville*.) Lately, I'd said, the right to the city bore the acronym "RTTC," an unofficial planetary charter, proclaiming the right to the global city, the right to any city, and the right to every city for its citizens. RTTC, I reckoned, are the "normative letters"—after James Joyce, one of my heroes—of a potentially revitalized Left that might equally mean *Here Comes Everybody* (HCE). Again, the term is Joyce's,[4] because this is the banner now taken up everywhere around the world, wherever people come or wherever the effects of a decomposition of work and a decomposition of living space strike. RTTC are the normative letters of planet urban, our planet, *the* social environment to which everybody is coming and that everybody is somehow shaping.

As a political manifesto, though, what does the right to the city *really* signify? What would it actually look like? Would it resemble the Paris Commune, a great festival of merriment, of people storming into the center of town (when there was still a clear center), occupying it, tearing down significant statues, abolishing rents for a while? If so, how would this deal with the problem Marx identified? How would it deal with the central banks and all those flows of capital and commodities? And why should taking over the city necessarily prevent these transactions, this trade, anyway? Right to *what* city? Does it mean the right to the metropolitan region, to the whole urban agglomeration, or just the right to the city's downtown? And if power—particularly financial power—is global, does this not render any singular demand hopelessly archaic? Does it still make any sense to talk about right to *the* city, as if this was something monocentric and clear-cut? These thoughts had occurred to me more than once while wandering around São Paulo, around its grungy old downtown near Praça de Sé, near São Paulo Cathedral, or around its *new* glitzy, Manhattanized downtown along Avenida Paulista, which feels like midtown Park Avenue. (Miesian Seagram buildings are everywhere.) In São Paulo, centers are all over the place and move about at speculators' whims. If there is a center to reclaim, it's hard to know which one.

São Paulo's streets, like many in burgeoning, developing-world megacities, are brimming with both life and death, with under- and overworked bodies; they're full of unemployed, subemployed, and multiemployed attendants, people cut off from a "traditional" rural past yet excluded from the trappings of a "modern" future, too. For these urban dwellers, "the right to the city" serves no purpose either as a working concept or a political program. It remains at a too-high level of abstraction to be anything that is *existentially meaningful in everyday life.* Put a little differently: The right to the city politicizes something that is *too vast and at the same time too narrow,* too restrictive and unfulfilling, too empty a signifier to inspire collective retribution. At least this is my working hypothesis, the thesis I want to explore in the discussion that follows.

The other thing that's become evident is how "the right to this and that" has been proclaimed so frequently by leftists, in so many different walks of life, in so many arenas, that the concept is now pretty much a political banality. For rightists, the "rights" issue undergirds a lot of conservative thinking about personal responsibility and individual freedom. Be it Tea Party or Tory Party, the Right on both sides of the Atlantic now defiantly champions rights, peddling the right of (wealthy) citizens to challenge public service providers and to contest, opt out, and attack any state action that isn't in some way geared toward bolstering private enterprise. Even Lefebvre's sacred urban right now figures in the mainstream's arsenal, reappropriated and defanged as it is in the

UN-Habitat's 2010 Charter and World Bank's manifesto for addressing the global poverty trap.

Before long, I began to think the unthinkable, or at least began to probe the unthinkable: maybe, just maybe, "rights" isn't the right clarion call for progressives. Maybe the right to the city isn't the *right* right that needs articulating? Saying this in no way denies the role of people fighting to maintain affordable rents in cities, to keep their neighborhoods mixed and relatively democratic, and to ensure that public spaces stay open and that gentrification doesn't displace all but the superwealthy. But what it does mean is that to bundle these multiple struggles together, and then to file them under the rubric "RTTC," is to render them as somehow vacuously abstract, suggesting far too vast a political understanding and far too narrow an existential need. It's too vast because the scale of the city is out of reach for most people living at street level; it's too narrow because when people do protest, when they do take to the streets en masse, their existential desires frequently reach out beyond the scale of the city itself and revolve around a common and collective humanity, a pure democratic yearning.

Soon I began saying the unthinkable. I began to air publicly the problems I had with the right to the city; soon I began participating again in academic conferences and professional colloquiums. Gradually, ideas for this book took shape and were worked through orally with criticism and debate. Meanwhile, dramatic things were happening in the world, from Cairo's Tahrir Square to Madrid's Puerta del Sol, from Athens's Syntagma Square to street riots in Tottenham, London, from occupations near Wall Street to those outside St. Paul's Cathedral—the city had seemingly become the critical zone in which a new social protest was, and still is, unfolding. Right to the city or something else? And if something else, what else? Either way, the global sway of Wall Street's and the City of London's decision makers has, at last, been called into question, contested by collective bodies in the public realm. This has come at a time when an inexorable shift of the human population into urban agglomerations has occurred and the city-region is now viewed as the fundamental unit of economic development and potential environmental collapse. It is all politically stimulating, yet theoretically tricky to unravel or figure out.

Soon, too, the problematization of the right to the city, both intellectually and politically, led me to believe that a similar problematization of the city and "urban question" was necessary, an interrogation of the whole role of the city as a theoretical and political object, the site and stake of global social struggle. And here, unsurprisingly, staple reading once again (once again!) seemed to point me, lead me back, to Henri Lefebvre—back only in order to go forward. But beyond mere prescience, what is the real relevance, the real application, of Lefebvre's work? Does it help us unravel the sociospatial complexities of *planetary urbanization* (*planétarisation de l'urbain*, Lefebvre's term) and help us tackle the political exigencies of urban society? Do his insights let us puzzle our way through the practical and abstract geographical problematic of urbanization?

The present book applies itself to such questions, taking leave from where Lefebvre left off, working through the man while trying to move beyond the man. In particular, I want to rethink urban theory in the light of what's unfolded across planet Earth since *The Urban Revolution* and to reconceive urban politics, especially as it relates to the right to the city. I want to mobilize Lefebvre's specifically urban writings, to use and apply him, and maybe sometimes even to abuse him, but always propelling him beyond himself, into the realm that he'd mischievously termed the "virtual object," which is to say, our real world today, two decades on since his death.

There are two interrelated themes in this book that warrant spelling out; Lefebvre can only propel us part of the way along this analytical and political highway. The first is a shift from the question of cities to a prioritization of urban society and, especially, of *planetary urbanization*. This spells more, I hope, than mere semantics. Indeed, it's an appeal to open up our perceptual parameters, to stretch them out, to initiate a perspectival shift from how we've traditionally seen cities. In fact, it marks a call to abandon the term "city" itself, to give up the ghost of thinking in terms of absolutes—of entities with borders and clear demarcations between what's inside and what's outside. It suggests, instead, something new, something futuristic, something that embraces urban becoming. It suggests something akin to Fredric Jameson's advocacy for a new "cognitive mapping," a new way to reposition how we look at ourselves and our world, one that helps us come to terms with the "hyperspace" of late capitalism on the global stage.[5] Jameson invoked city planner Kevin Lynch, whose *Image of the City* (1960), Jameson reckoned, limited itself to the problems of city form, of city imageability, especially lack of it. Yet, for Jameson, this idea of imageability, of cognitive mapping, of finding one's sensory and perceptual bearings, becomes "extraordinarily suggestive" when projected onto some larger conceptual and political terrain, and maybe—though Jameson never says so—projected onto the plane of planetary urbanization. Perhaps a new cognitive map is more pressing than ever before, offering a new way to conceive a *theoretical* object that is no longer a *physical* object, and a new way of reclaiming a *nonobject* as a *political* object. How to give form to a reality that is now seemingly formless? And how to recenter oneself on a planet in which urbanization creates a decentered polycentricity?

In a way, Lefebvre proposed the like in *The Urban Revolution*, a position dramatized by his appeal in the first chapter to move "From the City to Urban Society." The shift is profound and disconcerting in equal measure; one, I will argue, on a par with what Einstein did in the physical sciences, and one that requires *daring* to come to terms with its analytical and political implications. In this respect, my friend Herbert Muschamp still proves helpful in any conceptual reframing. In the foreword he wrote to my book, Muschamp thought Lefebvre in *The Urban Revolution* had "pulled the plug on formalism."[6] "That was his decisive contribution," Muschamp said, "to those who regard buildings primarily as pieces of the city, not as autonomous works of art." Muschamp hastened to add that this disconnect represented an expansion of aesthetic values, not a denial of them. "What Lefebvre rescinded," said Muschamp, "was the equation of aesthetics with the simplistic brand of formalism promoted by New York's Museum of Modern Art." Muschamp had in mind the doyen of American high-modernism, Philip Johnson, who espoused such a brand of architecture, one that was about the moving and shaping of geometric forms in two or three dimensions. All else was sociology, not architecture, said Johnson. Because Muschamp had abandoned formalism, his writing, Johnson concluded, with typical certitude, "isn't about architecture, of course."[7]

But Lefebvre's rejection of this sort of formalism—of the specific credence that a work's artistic value (be it a painting, a building, or even a whole city) is determined by its form—could only give rise to another sort of formalism whose critical test is whether it emphasizes an aspect of the truth or whether it can create a new truth. We might remember that there's nothing formless as such about Lefebvre's conception of space; he was keen to emphasize that space is global, fragmented, and hierarchal in one fell swoop. Its mosaic is stunningly complex, punctuated and textured by centers and peripheries all over the place, yet it is a mosaic in which the "commodity-form" gives this patterning its determining definition. The "commodity-form" of space is thus bounded, even if its "value-form" is somehow boundless. The "commodity-form" vis-à-vis the "value-form" is the key distinction Marx makes at the beginning of *Capital*. It was one way, after all, in which he could talk about how things have particularity and generality *at the same time*; they have intrinsic form yet are also extrinsically formless. Although Marx applies these analytical and methodological insights to understand time, to figure out the link between labor-time and "the immense accumulation of commodities," Lefebvre raises the stakes of the game to talk about the immense accumulation of *space*, about how space, too, is Janus-faced, both in form and formlessness.

In a text like *Le droit à la ville* [*The Right to the City*], Lefebvre recognizes how the city takes on the form of a supreme work of art, a supreme oeuvre, perhaps our greatest to date; its form is there before us and is made by us. From this standpoint, the city is at once an artistic "object" and a "nonobject," since its "content" comprises social and spatial relations; sociological, political, and economic phenomena, in other words, whose form is characterized by an apparent formlessness. Of course, form and content are part and parcel of Lefebvre's belief in dialectical logic as opposed to formal logic, even if the latter is the basis of the former.[8] Yet when Lefebvre in his opening salvo to *The Urban Revolution* moves from "the city" to "the urban society," he's urging us to abandon not form but the standard formal frame, to reposition ourselves and redescribe what we see the way a Cubist artist might have seen it. There, to be sure, formalism plays a key role in creating shapes and forms, images and movements that let us glimpse new contents or contents that we were never able to fully grasp. (Think of Picasso's *Guernica*.) Lefebvre's shift from "cities" to "urban society" marks, too, a shift from the concrete to the abstract—and from the absolute to the relative—toward the theorization of what both Marx and Lefebvre call a *concrete abstraction*. Such is the shift I plan to mimic, to shed light on, in my journey from the city question to the question of planetary urbanization. In short, I will try to develop another kind of formalism, another way of seeing, derived from abstract expressionism.

Pulling the plug on a certain kind of formalism opens the doors—or stretches the perimeters—for us to invent a different formalism, to conceive and cognitively map the process (read: content) of contemporary urbanization, to see it analytically as a form of abstract expressionism, as fractal geography. What I suggest here is that radical politics must likewise open up its horizons, understand itself through its own formalism, through its abstract expressionism becoming one day concrete. Hence the second major theme of the book, really *the* major theme (as its title implies), is a shift in political priority from the right to the city to *the politics of the encounter*. I want to suggest that "the encounter" can inspire another way of conceiving political engagement within the urbanization of the world. Lefebvre himself, remember, said the city is the supreme site of encounters, often chance encounters, especially chance political encounters. But why not posit the power of encounters as the stuff that percolates through the whole social-urban fabric, through the entire zone of possible militant praxis? This is the sense in which I will try to move Lefebvre *beyond* Lefebvre, staking out the contours of the encounter and showing how encounters happen when an affinity "takes hold"; when a common enemy is identified; when common notions cohere and collectivities are formed; and when solidarity takes shape, shapes up.[9]

Consequently, if the urban process is a form that is formlessly open-ended—as I will posit it here—any transformative politics presumably needs to be likewise. If one loses the right to the city, then one might gain a capacity to forge a politics based upon the encounter; a more free-floating, dynamic, and relational militancy, to be sure, "horizontal" in its reach and organization, yet one more apt for our age of diffusive metropolitanization, one more attuned to a political landscape in which new social media have become subversive weaponry. I still like to think that this present offering has something in common with *Metromarxism*: both are *pro*-urban books, and both endorse the coming of urban society—even if this latest text expresses more reservations about the reality of an *undemocratic* urbanization of the planet. Like Marx's analysis in the *Communist Manifesto*, the logic of this capitalist urban expansion has positive and negative implications and is both progressive and retrogressive for life on Earth, the best and worst of times. In the *Manifesto*, Marx welcomed the technological and social development of the productive forces and the rise of urbanization for its "civilizing" tendencies and cosmopolitan ambitions, for its ability to rescue people from the "idiocy of rural life." Marx was correct to see urbanization in this perversely positive light, even if there have been a few twists and turns in the capitalist drama since his heyday. This book will delve into a few of them, emphasizing the things Marx saw as well as those he was never quite able to see.

Perhaps above all else, *The Politics of the Encounter: Urban Theory and Protest under Planetary Urbanization* is a book that tries to move forward, tries to be futuristic, and tries to trace out the method Lefebvre himself called *transduction*. Transduction isn't fact-filled empiricism nor is it induction; it is a theoretical hypothesis that's more than deduction as well, since it supposes an incessant to and fro between concepts and empirical observation, between what is and what might be, between what is already here and what might be here more in the future—for better and for worse. My intention isn't to brandish lots of empirical data to prove my case; it's more to develop another "structure of feeling" for coming to terms with planetary urbanization, for representing it in the mind's eye, and for seeking at the same time to establish political representation. What I hope to offer is a book of *ideas*—ideas that I'll draw not only from Lefebvre but also from art and science, from politics and literature. These ideas may help us crystallize what a practical and dynamic politics of the urban can do against the blinding glare of twenty-first-century capitalist urbanization.

My futuristic thinking in *The Politics of the Encounter* has been partly energized by science fiction, including the sci-fi imaginary of one of the maestros of the genre, Isaac Asimov. Lefebvre got me going with Asimov; he made an almost throwaway comment in *The Right to the City*, alluding to Asimov's *Foun-*

dation series, and a giant planet completely urbanized, Trantor, whose whole surface was a single city, with forty billion inhabitants. Here we are 22,500 years into the future; yet, Lefebvre wonders, "Is there any need to explore so far in advance?" Isn't this profile unfolding "before our very eyes"?[10] I became absorbed by Asimov's *Foundation* saga and some of his brilliant ideas around "psychohistory," and I wanted to bring these ideas into dialogue with Lefebvre around planetary urbanization. I first tested them out at a conference on Lefebvre in September 2011, at his old university, the University of Paris X Nanterre, now the Université Paris Ouest Nanterre La Défense. These ideas were politely received, if not altogether understood by the French contingent, who sometimes had a hard time lifting their heads out of their texts and even greater difficulty moving Lefebvre along, doing something *with* him, mobilizing him, moving beyond the great man himself. It was as if they were paralyzed by his indomitable authority, by his *maître* status, terrified to move beyond anything but exegesis, beyond what Lefebvre said, beyond what Lefebvre meant. (It's not only a French defect: the Anglo-Saxon Lefebvrian cottage industry is almost as culpable.)

Somehow it was all *un*-Lefebvrian. He, remember, had once grumbled about the great interpreter of Hegel, Alexandre Kojève, because the latter was happy just to know what Hegel said, happy just to explain Hegel's contradictions, happy to explain Hegel's unhappy consciousness. But Kojève did nothing with these contradictions, Lefebvre said, didn't bring them to bear on current contradictions, on what is happening now, in the present, and on what might happen in the future. Ditto the French Lefebvrian Left, who seemed not only trapped within Lefebvre but also trapped within a politics and urbanism that smacked of a past Golden Age when *soixante-huitards* took to the streets and reclaimed the center—when there still was *a* center to reclaim. Long ago, Lefebvre warned about the pitfalls of the same old same old, about a business-as-usual Marxism, about business-as-usual beliefs in the hallowed "working class" coming to our rescue. Lefebvre was a perpetual invoker of the new, a kind of Miles Davis of social theory, who refused to stand still or play those old notes—that old kind of blue.

During the 1970s Lefebvre invoked a conceptual opening up and rethinking of politics and urbanism because this was the only way to confront a concurrent opening up and opening out of the world. He saw this in motion in Paris in the 1950s and 1960s, especially under Pompidou's post-1968 regime (1969–1974), where policies of decentralization, modernization, and recentering the old urban core became de rigueur. (Much of this urban transformation took place under Lefebvre's nose when he was teaching at Nanterre; the campus itself was gouged out of Paris's western periphery, behind La Défense. If you wanted to figure out what was happening to cities, Lefebvre said back then, "you had only to look outside the faculty window."[11]) By the time he'd visited Los Angeles in the 1980s, Lefebvre knew that the future of the urban was more like the reviled Californian metropolis than the glorious City of Light: inevitably polycentric, centers here and there, stretched and torn up, sprawled and ghettoized. Urban processes were decoupling from their traditional city forms, from internally coherent historical cities with cores that went back to the Middle Ages. The fastest-growing cities now bear no relationship to cities of old and have no concern for quaint historical continuity.

And speaking of quaint old Paris, during the Nanterre conference the organizers put me up in a miserable hotel in the Latin Quarter, along rue Cujas, close to a tiny cinema that, in the early 1970s, Gérard Lebovici had bought exclusively for the replaying of Guy Debord's obscure movies. But that was another age, one I'd once labeled a sentimental age, an age of sentimental urbanism.[12] For a while, I'd thought this might be the way to go, an urban equivalent of walking with a donkey; but, again, I was wrong, and I still am wrong, this isn't the way to go; it's an age best forgotten, one that we should leave behind, rebuilt with something newer and fresher, with something more open, airier, and brighter. This is the urbanism and politics of the future: embracing the future, embracing full-on its perils as well as its possibilities, knowing all the while there is no going back, no search for lost time, no quest for lost space, no fleeing from the giant megacities, no breaking them up into smaller units as Marx and Engels implied a Communism of the future should achieve.

In a weird kind of way, this dangerous embrace of the future was something I'd seen and heard on French TV the evening after my presentation at Nanterre. Returning to my hotel room in the evening, merry from a few *coups*, on Canal+ was Murray Lerner's 2004 documentary about Miles Davis, *Miles Electric: A Different Kind of Blue*. The subject matter was the legendary jazz trumpeter's electric phase from the late 1960s to the early/mid-1970s and his passionate embrace of electricity, of electric guitars and synthesizers, of Fender Rhodes pianos and electric trumpets. It was Miles moving with the times, Miles shaping the musical and historical times, dialoguing with rock and roll, with Sly Stone and James Brown, with Jimi Hendrix, appearing at rock concerts like the 1970 Isle of Wight festival, bringing to the world brilliant, innovative masterpieces like *Bitches Brew* (still one of the biggest-selling jazz albums on record). "This was everything I imagined a future music could be," said arranger Paul Buckmaster of *Bitches Brew*. Here were formless notes, long pieces that seemed to be going nowhere (critic Stanley Crouch thought this was "bullshit"). Formless just like contemporary urbanization, but somehow just like any contemporary politics of urbanization should be, too: long notes being blown, spreading horizontally, diffusing across the planet, perhaps not even going anywhere at first, yet drifting toward a future fusion, embracing electronics and electricity, letting them light up and connect our world, letting them play a different kind of blue. . . .

This book was no solo flight, even if the bulk of it was written alone in Bean café at Liverpool's Brunswick Dock. I've had a lot of help along the way, and I've done a lot of talking as well as, I hope, my fair share of listening. Much of the text was spoken before being written, and the written form has been tailored and tweaked *after* its oral public airings. Special thanks go to Louis Moreno, whose ongoing dialogue with me around these themes continues to prove inspirational and good fun. Bob Catterall, too, at CITY journal has been unfailing in his friendship and support for my work, even if sometimes we've fought over its meaning. Hats off to Derek Krissoff for initially commissioning this project for the University of Georgia Press and to Regan Huff for most ably seeing it through to fruition. Mazen Labban and Nik Heynan did brilliant jobs reading and evaluating an earlier version of the manuscript, proffering pages of generous comment and incisive criticism; the present text bears their talented stamp. Thanks must likewise be extended to a whole host of others who, in their differing ways, perhaps not even realizing it, somehow, somewhere, contributed toward this book: Pushpa Arabindoo, John Berger, Marshall Berman, Neil Brenner, Andrew Harris, David Harvey, Corinna Hawkes, Maria Kaika, Roger Keil, Esther Leslie, Peter Marcuse, Diana Mitlin, Daniel Niles, Miguel Roblas-Duran, Christian Schmidt, Ed Soja, Erik Swyngedouw, Jane Wills, and the "Open Space" crew at the University of Manchester, especially Lazaros Karaliotas, Brian Rosa, and Ioanna Tananasi. I am also grateful to the editorial board of the *International Journal of Urban and Regional Research* (IJURR) for inviting me to give the 2011 Association of American Geographers Annual Lecture at Seattle, where ideas for this book were initially tested. Finally, my gratitude goes to the Leverhulme Trust for giving me the freedom and money to shape up the many words that follow.

The Politics of the Encounter

CHAPTER ONE

The Final Frontier

Planetary Urbanization

Thus the heavenly spheres that encompassed the world and held it together did not disappear at once in a mighty explosion; the world-bubble grew and swelled before bursting and merging with the space that surrounded it.

Alexandre Koyré

If we cannot produce a new theory, and I agree it is not easy, we can at least find new words. . . . If we find new words we can hope to produce a framework of understanding. Without a framework, any means of instrumentality are futile.

Rem Koolhaas

I. Perspective and Prospective

Near the beginning of the "Perspective ou prospective?" chapter of *Le droit à la ville*, the Marxist urban studies godfather, Henri Lefebvre, alludes to the godfather of science fiction, Isaac Asimov. The comment is barely a paragraph long and Lefebvre doesn't elaborate. Yet even in its brevity Lefebvre's remark is intriguing, and it has intrigued me for a while now. In this opening chapter, I want to begin to develop what Lefebvre means here, at least what *I think* he might mean. Specifically, I want to use him for framing the theoretical and political dilemmas that confront progressives in our age of planetary urbanization. For in "Perspective ou prospective," Lefebvre projects the urban trajectory of his day—1967, the centenary of Marx's *Capital*—22,500 years into the future, into the sci-fi imaginary of Asimov's magisterial *Foundation* series. The drama focuses on the giant planet-city Trantor with its 40 billion inhabitants, a thoroughly urbanized society of dazzling administrative and technological complexity, dominating a vast galaxy.

From outer space at nighttime, Asimov says, Trantor looks like a "giant conglomeration of fire-flies, caught in mid-motion and still forever."[1] "Trantor's deserts and its fertile areas were engulfed," he says, "and made into warrens of humanity, administrative jungles, computerized elaborations, vast storehouses of food and replacement parts. Its mountain ranges were beaten down; its chasms filled in. The city's endless corridors burrowed under the continental shelves and the oceans were turned into huge underground aquacultural cisterns."[2] Canopied under a ceiling of millions of steel domes, like a colossal iceberg, nine-tenths of Trantor's social life takes place underground in climate-controlled air and light, with programmed downpours. Nobody any longer recognizes day from night, whether the sun shone or not, and after a while few care. The countryside is but a fuzzy memory of ancient hearsay; only the Imperial Palace and Trantor's Streeling University have real green space. Newcomers would tell you that the air seemed thicker in Trantor, the gravity that much greater, its sheer immensity unnerving.

Asimov gives us a brilliant vision of urbanization gone to the max, a veritable utopia-cum-dystopia. In mentioning Asimov under so suggestive a rubric as "perspective/prospective," Lefebvre already recognized in the late 1960s the seeds of Trantor in our urban midst. With Asimov, he's seemingly calling for us to open out our perspective on thinking about urban life, daring us to open it out onto the largest remit possible, to grasp the totality of capitalist urbanization wholesale and whole-scale, to live with that startling immensity, to make it our own. In so doing we might then be able to think more clearly about politics—about prospective, progressive politics under planetary urbanization.

Lefebvre wants us to know that such a modus operandi is nothing other than *transduction*, his method of launching the here and now into a future becoming, into a here tomorrow—and the day after tomorrow (as Nietzsche might have said).[3] What kind of take on present reality can open up future reality and help us glimpse it as it moves onward, forward? By the time Lefebvre had published *La révolution urbaine* (1970), he began hinting at this new reality: not a sci-fi reality but something already here, now: "The complete urbanization of society," he says, in his opener to *The Urban Revolution*.[4] He's being ironic, of course, but only slightly. Because, he adds, "This hypothesis implies a definition: 'urban society' is a society that results from a process of complete urbanization. Today, it's virtual, tomorrow it will be real."[5] The progression/ periodization is evident: we should no longer talk of cities as such, Lefebvre said in *Le droit à la ville*, urban society is more appropriate; yet in *La révolution urbaine*, he began thinking that we shouldn't even be talking of urban society but of *planetary urbanization*, of the complete urbanization of society, of something that's both here and about to come here soon. Trantor is here yet not quite here. But we can expect it any day now.

Fast-forward four decades. Asimov's extraterrestrial universe seems closer than ever to home, closer to Lefebvre's own terrestrial prognostications: planetary urbanization is creating a whole new spatial world (dis)order. For in 2006, the balance had tipped: the majority of the world's inhabitants, 3.3 billion people, lived in urban agglomerations, not rural areas. By 2030, it's set to be 4.9 billion, some 60 percent of the world's population. By then, an extra 590,000 square miles of the planet will have been urbanized, a land surface more than twice the size of Texas, spelling an additional 1.47 billion urban dwellers. If the trend continues, by 2050 75 percent of the planet Earth will be urbanized.[6] City-regions are now congealing into huge metropolitan agglomerations, like the planet's hitherto largest, the thirty-five-million Tokyo-Yokohama megalopolitan region of "Greater Tokyo" (Yokohama is officially an "incorporated city"). In China's ever-burgeoning terrestrial megaurban galaxy, expanding hinterlands around Shanghai and Beijing and in the Pearl River Delta contain urban forms of at least 40 million inhabitants.[7]

Shanghai is the planet's fastest growing megalopolis, expanding a massive 15 percent each year since 1992, boosted by $120 billion of foreign direct investment that's utterly reconfigured urban space. Half the world's cranes are reputed to be working in Shanghai's Pudong district;[8] rice paddies have been filled with modern skyscrapers and vast factories; outlying farmlands now host the world's fastest train links and the tallest hotel; and four thousand buildings with twenty or more stories have gone up since 1992, ensuring that Shanghai has twice the number of buildings as New York. With 171 cities of more than one million inhabitants, China itself since 2000 has commandeered nearly half the world's cement supplies.

As of 2011, the number of metropolises globally with over a million inhabitants reached 479 (in 1950, there was only a handful).[9] Now, there are twenty-six megacities with populations exceeding ten million people; nineteen of the largest twenty-five metropolises are found in the developing world, with 70 percent of the planet's urban dwellers. Here's the league table of the world's ten biggest metropolises:

Tokyo, Japan	34,300,000
Guangzhou, China	25,200,000
Seoul, South Korea	25,100,000
Shanghai, China	24,800,000
Delhi, India	23,300,000
Mumbai, India	23,000,000
Mexico City, Mexico	22,900,000
New York City, United States	22,000,000

São Paulo, Brazil   20,900,000
Manila, Philippines   20,300,000

In a way, though, for any political urbanist these facts and figures aren't so interesting; nor are they what's at stake, either analytically or politically. The real point is that urbanization is increasing its reach everywhere, and that this everywhere now somehow reaches into the urban process and into our lives. Nowadays, in Louis Wirth's faithful words, urbanism is "a way of life," a way of life requiring a new way of seeing and a different structure of feeling. What Wirth said in 1938 still sounds smart: "The degree to which the contemporary world may be said to be 'urban' is not fully or actually measured by the proportion of the total population living in cities. The influences which cities exert upon social life are greater than the ratio of the urban population would indicate, for the city is not only in ever larger degrees the dwelling-place and the workshop of modern man, but it is the initiating and controlling center of economic, political, and cultural life that has drawn the most remote parts of the world into its orbit and woven diverse areas, peoples, and activities into a cosmos."[10] The urban, then, is apparently shapeless and seemingly boundless and formless, riven with new contradictions and tensions in which it's hard to tell where borders reside and what's inside and what's outside.

Yet to *bound* something, to construe our field of vision as a *container*, is an inexorable human preoccupation, seemingly an inexorable human need: the need to restrict reality so we can cope, so we can comprehend. Hence the infinite array of concepts brandished to identify what this new "city" form might be: *endless city, shrinking city, 100-mile city, global city, megacity, arrival city, indistinguishable city, incorporated city*, and so forth. What's interesting about these labels is that all try to follow Lefebvre's lead and come to grips with the death of their object, or the death of the theorists' subject—the city—knowing full well that something has happened, is happening, and that it's hard to get an analytical grip on it. The city was once whole and solid, steel and concrete, there and only there. Now, "it" is slippery, and no longer an "it," not responding to those old laws of gravity. What's interesting here, too, is that every label, no matter how diverse, how insightful, how catchy, still struggles to retain the social scientific rigor of the term "city."

Lefebvre wasn't so convinced. Urban society, he'd announced in *Le droit à la ville*, "constitutes itself on the ruins of the city."[11] In *The Urban Revolution*, he reiterated the claim, bolder and in louder decibels: "The city exists only as a historical entity"; it "no longer corresponds to a social object. Sociologically, the city is a pseudo-concept."[12] For that reason, let's stop using the term "city," he urges, let's change our terminology; let's name the new object that isn't a physical object in the usual sense of the term; let's use instead the terms "urban society" or "urban fabric"; let's try to identify a new theoretical and virtual object that's in the process of becoming. The term "urban fabric" doesn't narrowly define the built environment of cities but, says Lefebvre, hinting of Louis Wirth, it indicates "all manifestations of the dominance of the city over the countryside." As such, "a vacation home, a highway, a supermarket in the countryside are all part of the urban fabric." Meanwhile, "urban society" serves a theoretical need and, as we'll see in chapters to come, frames a political ambition. It's a hypothesis that represents both a point of arrival for a bigger perspective on an existing reality and a point of departure to study a new, emergent reality.

II. Blind Fields and Ways of Seeing

Urban society outstrips our cognitive and sensory facilities; the mind boggles at the sensory overload that today's urban process places upon us. The problem is compounded if we continue to think "city," if we perceive things through a "city" lens, through the notion of "objects," "categories," and "things," perceiving them through the traditional language and concepts of industrial growth. We need to change our perspective, rethink the urban, says Lefebvre, in order to think prospectively, otherwise our epistemology will fumble in a veritable "blind field." Urbanization isn't a highly developed manifestation of industrialization, but—and this is the startling thing about Lefebvre's "urban revolution" thesis—industrialization all along has been a special sort of urbanization, flipping on its head the traditional Marxist notion of the historical development of the productive forces.

Marx and Engels never gave us an explicit "urban mode of production," Lefebvre says, but if we look closely at their oeuvre in a way they did: the city was itself a developmental force—the seat of modern industry, the division of labor, the reproduction of labor-power, and technological innovation. The rise of the industrial city wasn't only vital for the expansion of the productive forces; it was also crucial politically for an ascendant bourgeoisie asserting itself in the passage from feudalism to capitalism. Marx didn't know, could never have known, that urbanization harbors the logic of industrialization. Marx hadn't seen that industrial production implies the urbanization of society, that mastering the potentialities of industry demands a specific understanding of the urban process. Beyond a certain level of growth, urbanization creates industrial production, produces industrialization, and furnishes fertile conditions for the latter, converting industrial contradictions into contradictions of the city, eventually posing anew the urban question, converting it into the question of planetary urbanization.

I've been thinking about how to define this shift in perspective. It's maybe not so much a search for a brand new theory, as Rem Koolhaas says, but putting a new spin on an old theory (like Lefebvre's), giving it a new vocabulary, making this theory more *effective* and *affective*. The best I could come up with is to describe this shift in perspective as a move away from an *epistemology of cities* toward an *ontology of the urban*. It's no longer an issue of trying to develop a new theoretical understanding of cities under capitalism as it is about grappling with an *affective being* in a world that's increasingly urbanized. It's not a theoretical postulate out there but an ontological reality inside us, a way of seeing ourselves and our world. It's something immanent rather than extrinsic. Thus another "way of seeing,"[13] another way of perceiving urbanization in our mind's eye, is to grasp it as a complex adaptive system, as a chaotic yet determined process. As a concept, even a "virtual concept," the term "planetary" already connotes a perspectival shift and conjures up more stirring imagery, maybe even more rhetorical imagery, something seemingly extraterrestrial and futuristic. Already we are propelled into a realm in which our perceptual parameters are stretched, broadened, opened-out; somehow, four-dimensionality seems old-hat. "Planetary" suggests something more alive and growing, something more vivid than the moribund "global" or "globalization." The use of the term "planetary" really charts the final frontier, the telos of any earthly spatial fix—an economic, political, and cultural logic that hasn't been powered by globalization but is one of the key constituent ingredients of globalization, of the planetary expansion of the productive forces, of capitalism's penchant to annihilate space by time and time by space.

The inner boundedness of the traditional city and of our traditional notion of the city form was prized open by the advent of the industrial city; by capitalist industrial production shedding its geographical and temporal fetters; by the development of new modes of transport; by the invention and reinvention of new technologies, products, and infrastructure; and by sucking people in when business cycles surged, only to spit them out when markets dipped. From being once *absolute* spaces, cities became *relative* spaces, spaces relative to one another in what would, in the second half of the twentieth century, become a global hierarchy, dictated by comparative economic advantage. This historical shift from the absolute to the relative preoccupied Lefebvre in his two great books from the 1970s: *The Urban Revolution* and *The Production of Space*.[14] He had taken these circumstances as somehow revolutionary, revolutionary in the sense that Gramsci would have deemed it: as a *passive* revolution—pregnant with all things contrary, for sure, with progressive possibilities, yet counterrevolutionary nonetheless, a kind of revolution from above, one in which, as Marx said in the *Manifesto*, "the bourgeoisie had played a most revolutionary part."[15]

So when Lefebvre urges us to reframe the city as "the urban," he is urging us to abandon the standard frame, to reposition our vision and redescribe what we see as a Cubist artist might have seen it. Which is akin to an Einsteinian revolution in the spatial and human sciences, akin to when Einstein began devising his general theory of relativity, problematizing the Newtonian conception of gravity with its assumptions of absolute time and space. It was a new way of seeing our world, even if it all went beyond our immediate world, beyond our own capacity to see; Einstein's cosmology was itself the harbinger of quantum theory, for the probabilistic theories of "complementarity" and "uncertainty" pioneered in the 1920s and 1930s by Niels Bohr and Werner Heisenberg—even though Einstein had a hard time accepting that role.

Moving from the notion of *a city* toward *the urban* expressed a paradigm shift on a par with Einstein, a shift from the absolute to the relative, an affirmation of curved time and space. Capitalist gravity doesn't only occur over absolute space, over a passive surface: space and time are themselves capitalist constructs, and the mass and velocity of commodities, of capital and money shifting around the market universe, creates its own bending and warping of time and space, its own space-time dimensionality. The virtual reality of global financial markets plays havoc with isotropic planes of space and with linear conceptions of time, of present and future, confirming time's arrow, not only warping space but physically tearing it apart, too, creating a hidden speculative realm of financial quarks and neutrinos coursing forward and backward at the speed of light—and at the touch of a trader's keyboard.

III. Concrete Abstractions and Abstract Expressionism

If a city is a complex adaptive system, the change in tack from "cities" (in the plural) toward "the urban" (in the singular) marks a simplifying movement, an analytical sidestep from the concrete to the abstract. The urban, we might say, is more precisely a *concrete abstraction*, the terrain of theoretical knowledge—or, in Lefebvre's lexicon, an "illuminating virtuality" (*Urban Revolution*, 17). Thus the urban represents a theoretical object and a "possible object," a concrete abstraction similar to how Marx posits the world market as the very basis of capitalism; to be sure, we could easily transpose "urban" for "world market" without losing any clarity of Marx's meaning. In *Capital III*, Marx said, "The immanent necessity of this mode of production is to produce the world market on an ever-enlarged scale."[16] In the *Grundrisse*, the sentiment is redoubled: "The tendency to create the world market is directly given in the concept of capital itself. Every limit appears as a barrier to be overcome."[17] In *The Communist Manifesto*, the formation of the world market is more famously evoked:

> The need of a constantly expanding market for its products chases the bourgeoisie over the whole surface of the globe. It must nestle everywhere, settle everywhere, establish connections everywhere. The bourgeoisie has through its exploitation of the world market given a cosmopolitan character to production and consumption in every country. . . . In place of old wants, satisfied by the productions of the country, we find new wants, requiring for their satisfaction the products of distant lands and climes. In place of the old local and national seclusion and self-sufficiency, we have intercourse in every direction, universal interdependence of nations.[18]

In Part III of *Theories of Surplus Value*, Marx says it is "only foreign trade, the development of the market to a world market, which causes money to develop into world money and abstract labor into social labor. Abstract wealth, value, money, hence abstract labor, develop in the measure that concrete labor becomes a totality of different modes of labor embracing the world market."[19] In the sense that Marx describes things here, the world market is, like Lefebvre's "urban," an actual reality and a *concept* of reality. The world market and the urban are real enough, vital necessities for the reproduction of capitalism on an expanded scale; both are embodied in nameable people, in living agents and actual economic practices, in institutions and organizations; both are a vast web of exchange relations based around money and capital and culture; both assume the "bounded" form of the commodity-form that Marx spoke about. Yet, at the same time, both should be conceived as fluid processes circulating around the globe; both flow as nonobservable phenomena, too; both, in other words, assume the "value-form" and are apparently boundless. Though, as Marx says, the two forms are relative, the form and the function, the perceptible and the imperceptible: exclusive, yes, but equally "two inseparable moments, which belong to and mutually condition each other."[20]

There's another way we might frame "the urban," frame it in our mind's eye. It's the way, for instance, Spinoza conceives *substance* in Part I of *Ethics*; this vision has more in common with Marx than meets the eye. Substance, for Spinoza, is the very essence of nature and reality, its bedrock content, indivisible in itself and only perceivable and conceivable through its manifold *attributes*. Each attribute, says Spinoza, "expresses the reality or being of the substance."[21]

Substance is, of course, Spinoza's pantheistic theory of God, his notion that God is immanent in all reality, including ourselves; it is a theological "value-form." Thus, maybe the form of this notion holds, too, for the immanent nature of the urban, for its complex ontological tissuing, for the fabric that now clothes our daily lives. What's getting affirmed here is the urban as a single, indivisible substance whose attributes—the built environment, transportation infrastructure, population densities, topographical features, social mixes, political governance—are all the formal *expressions* of what pervades it ontologically. These attributes are mutually irreducible and really distinct. They have their own mode of *extension* (they grow, expand, concentrate, deconcentrate), and their identity of order corresponds somehow to substance. Such attributes are how the urban looks and how it can be seen and known and felt. They are, in short, its tangible, perceptual "commodity-form."

Like the giant drip canvases of Jackson Pollock, and the fractals his art is meant to represent, there's chaos to these attributes yet an underlying order to its substance, to *the* substance, to the underlying urban structure. If Cubist art captured the relativizing tendencies and contortions of an emergent urban space, the spontaneous flowing skeins and explosive nebulae of Pollock's late abstract expressionism offer pictorial representations of the formless form of the planetary urban process and its substance. It is often said of Pollock's mural-size drip paintings, especially those completed during the period 1947–1950, that they give the impression of infinite expandability, an experiential feeling of expansion and enlargement, a volatile dynamism that seems to want to break free of its own borders.[22] As Pollock himself was wont to claim, "here there's no center, no beginning, no middle or end"; entering necessitates a daring leap onto a moving train, not knowing quite where it's headed, only having a vague sense of where it's been. "Unframed space" is how Pollock's widow, artist Lee Krasner, described these paintings with their boundless kinetic energy and chaotic, dense processes of high complexity containing an almost hidden scaling order—just like contemporary planetary urbanization.

Pollock's skeins and swirls, spirals and drips are often so intense, so dense, that they engulf the whole substance of the canvas; there's no space left, little daylight between buildings and roads, no more developable canvas surface. The imagery is electrodynamic, hydraulic and energetic, and somehow quintessentially urban. What's equally significant here is how this perspective evokes what Clement Greenberg called "the crisis of the easel picture," the crisis of the classic framing—maybe the classic framing of the city. Greenberg's intent was to affirm the decentered, polyphonic picture, one that did away with an upright viewpoint and dispensed with any beginning, middle, and end. Greenberg invoked a principal ingredient: "Fatal ambiguity."[23]

Chaos and repetition cohere in free-flowing composition, mimicking the flows of capital unleashed in the deregulated world market. Flows of investment that produce space, that seemingly have the same vital, spontaneous energy of a Pollock loop, power the "secondary circuit" of capital into real estate, a circuit of investment that formerly ran parallel to the "primary circuit" of capital, to industrial production, but which now, Lefebvre (*Urban Revolution*, 159) says, has grown to be relatively more important in the overall global economy. The secondary circuit flows as fixed and usually immovable capital, like office blocks and transport infrastructure, roads and warehouses, marinas and apartment complexes, a whole built investment for production and consumption, all of which has value imprisoned in space and cannot be devalued without immanent destruction.[24]

The secondary circuit was once a "buffer" against crisis, says Lefebvre (*Urban Revolution*, 159); now, we know, it's the mainstay of a global and increasingly planetary urban economy, one of the principal sources of capital investment. Hence over the past fifteen to twenty years it has been the medium and product of a worldwide real estate boom. But the secondary circuit is a source of new instabilities and problems as well, particularly when it gets lubricated by financial (fictitious) capital and underwritten by the state. The other noteworthy aspect of the secondary circuit of urban spatial production is how it is now inextricably entwined with the so-called tertiary circuit of capital, with investment into science and technology, knowledge production and exchange, and thoughtware practices that profit from cyberspace yet flourish materially from ground space.

In the early 1970s, Lefebvre said this secondary circuit got caught up in the "consensual" politics of states' neomanagerialist bureaucrats negotiating with a new species of entrepreneurial private-sector neoliberals. (He'd recognize later how the former often congeal into the latter and then go on to control national governments around the world.) In the 1980s the neoliberal paradigm foisted themes of growth, productivity, and competitivity to the forefront of dominant political-economic ideology, running roughshod over concerns for equality, democracy, and social justice. Transnational monopoly capital began to gobble everything up, everywhere, in order to increase value-added and to accumulate capital. Capital danced to the same frantic beat that Marx sketched out in the *Manifesto*. The explosion of urban growth has consequently been a process of uneven development, of homogeneity and fragmentation. Rural places and suburban spaces have become integral moments of neoindustrial production and financial speculation, getting absorbed and reconfigured into new world-regional zones of exploitation, into megalopolitan regional systems, a phenomenon that swallowed up old-style city-forms as urbanization sheds its skin and corrodes its shell. "The oyster had opened its shell," said Jean Gottmann.[25]

Never before has the urban process been so bound up with finance capital and with the caprices of the world's financial markets. The global urbanization boom, with its seemingly insatiable flows into the secondary circuit of capital, has depended on the creation of new mechanisms to wheel and deal fictitious capital and credit money, with new deregulated devices for legalized looting and finagling, asset stripping, and absorbing surplus capital into the built environment. David Harvey neatly labels all this "accumulation by dispossession," upgrading and updating Marx's theory of "primitive accumulation," mobilizing it in a twenty-first-century neoliberal context.[26] In *Capital*, Marx said the history of primitive accumulation is always epoch-making, always acting as a lever for the capitalist class in the course of its own formation (and re-formation). The process is simple enough: "the divorcing of the producer from the means of production."[27] As written in the annals of capitalism, primitive accumulation, Marx thought (876), took many forms; though in these annals the ink still seems wet: "When great masses of men are suddenly and forcibly torn from their means of subsistence, and hurled onto the labor-market free, unprotected. The expropriation of the agricultural producer, of the peasant, from the soil is the basis of the whole process."

Yet, in our times, Harvey makes clear that primitive accumulation by dispossession signals other fresh terrains for speculation and market expansion: asset stripping through mergers and acquisitions, raiding of pension funds, biopiracy, privatization of hitherto common assets like water and other public utilities, and the general pillaging of publicly owned property. Baron Haussmann once tore into central Paris, into its old neighborhoods and poor populations, dispatching the latter to the periphery while speculating on the center; the built urban form became simultaneously a property machine and a means to divide and rule. Today, neo-Haussmannization, in a similar process that integrates financial, corporate, and state interests, tears into the globe and sequesters land through forcible slum clearance and eminent domain,[28] valorizing it while banishing former residents to the global hinterlands of postindustrial malaise.

IV. Interlude: On World Market Street

Let me change tack and tonality for a moment: In "The Spinoza of Market Street," a short story penned by another Isaac—not Asimov but Nobel Laureate Isaac Bashevis Singer—Dr. Fischelson is a sickly, withdrawn urban man. For the past thirty years, we learn, he's studied the seventeenth-century Jewish-Dutch philosopher Baruch Spinoza. He reads nothing else but *Ethics* and knows every proposition by heart, every axiom, every corollary, every note of Marx's preferred philosopher. But the truth is that the more Dr. Fischelson studies Spinoza's *Ethics* the more he finds unclear passages, puzzling sentences, and cryptic remarks. The doctor once studied philosophy in Zurich but now, shunned by the synagogue, he passes lonely hours compiling spidery annotations on the philosopher from Amsterdam, while at the same time a stomach ailment, which has plagued him for years, grows worse by day.

From his garret window, Dr. Fischelson observes the world outside—the two worlds outside: "Above him were the heavens, thickly strewn with stars . . . that infinite extension, which is, according to Spinoza, one of God's attributes. It comforts Dr. Fischelson to think that although he was only a weak, puny man, a changing mode of the absolutely infinite Substance, he was nevertheless part of the giant cosmos, made of the same matter as the celestial bodies."[29] When he tires of looking upward at the planetary scale, Dr. Fischelson drops his glance downward to "Market Street," to a planet closer to home. On a summer's evening, the street never looked so crowded:

> Thieves, prostitutes, gamblers and fences loafed in the square. The young men laughed coarsely and the girls shrieked. A peddler with a keg of lemonade on his back pierced the general din with his intermittent cries. A watermelon vendor shouted in a savage voice, and the long knife which he used for cutting the fruit dripped with the blood-like juice. Now and again the street became even more agitated. Fire engines, their heavy wheels clanging, sped by; they were drawn by sturdy black horses which had to be tightly curbed to prevent them from running wild. Next came an ambulance, its siren screaming. Then some thugs had a fight amongst themselves and the police had to be called. A passerby was robbed and ran about shouting for help. . . . Merchants continued to hawk their wares, each seeking to out-shout the others. "Gold, gold, gold," a woman who dealt in rotten oranges shrieked. "Sugar, sugar, sugar," croaked a dealer of overripe plums, "Heads, heads, heads," a boy who sold fish heads roared. (8)

Here is the half-lit bedlam Dr. Fischelson scorns. Here "the behavior of this rabble was the very antithesis of reason. These people were immersed in the vainest passions, were drunk with emotions, and, according to Spinoza, emotion was never good. Instead of the pleasure they ran after, all they succeeded in obtaining was disease and prison, shame and the suffering that resulted from ignorance. Even the cats which loitered on the roofs here seemed more savage and passionate than those in other parts of town" (9).

But then, just as he's at his sickest, Dr. Fischelson meets Dobbe, a dark spinster, a bagel seller with a broken nose and mustache above her upper lip; she'd never had any luck with men. She lives in the adjoining attic room and one day discovers Dr. Fischelson's door ajar. She knocks yet receives no reply. So she enters only to find "the old heretic" lying on his bed fully clothed, his face as yellow as wax. At first she thinks he's dead. But he stirs, comes round, and Dobbe, overcoming her fear, begins to cook and comfort this isolated man. Soon they fall for each other, marry, and make love on their wedding night. All the doctor's ills and neuroses suddenly disappear; powers long dormant awaken in him. And putting away for good his worn copy of *Ethics*, Dr. Fischelson "closed his eyelids and allowed the breeze to cool the sweat on his forehead and stir the hair of his beard. He breathed deeply of the midnight air, supported his shaky hands on the windowsill and murmured, 'Divine Spinoza, forgive me. I have become a fool'" (24).

Singer's tale, set in the Warsaw ghetto before Hitler's arrival, is one of the nicest things anybody ever wrote about Spinoza. It is also one of the most florid descriptions of a burgeoning metropolis that could be anywhere in today's developing world. In tossing away his copy of *Ethics*, in marrying Dobbe, in having sex with her, Dr. Fischelson finally starts to *become* more Spinozian. He not only came to life but also began to participate in *common* life, empathizing with another person, embracing her in joy and love. In getting Spinoza wrong, Singer's Dr. Fischelson actually says something more interesting about Spinoza. Outside his window, he looks down on the bedlam of Market Street, looks down on it literally and metaphysically, on its brutal comings and goings, on its cries and cackles, on the adventures and misadventures of its common rabble.

Now this rabble is nothing else than the toiling, disorderly throng, the Lazarus-layered urban masses engaged in the ordinary wheeling and dealing of daily life. (Sarkozy describes their French counterparts as *racaille*: "scum" of the earth.) Yet perhaps it's not too difficult, with a little imagination, to see how this self-same rabble somehow constitutes—has to constitute—a latent political constituency, a normative ideal, even the decisive political subject in any twenty-first-century social struggle. This rabble is the Joycean Here Comes Everybody (HCE), since its reach has gone truly global. It is epic in its proportions and millionfold in the scale of its prospective rank and file—a quantity that one day might express itself qualitatively. One day it might assert its own numbers and transcend its motley nature to reason itself into a singular soul, affirming its own associative ties as it fights for liberation and collective joy.

Dr. Fischelson never imagined how this rabble down below could ever be cut from the same cloth as the planetary heavens he admired so much up above; he never imagined how Market Street might also belong to the same cosmic force of infinite thought. But it does.[30] What's more, if the rabble is an empirical category yearning to assert its "normative letters" as an ought, as an HCE, then the context of its coming together, its common space, would presumably resemble Dr. Fischelson's Market Street as well as market streets the world over. Perhaps, then, we should rename this context as *world market street*, highlighting its global plurality and how this street is now every street, the sum of all the world's streets, because it somehow internalizes the highs and lows of all the world's commerce and brings Marx's classic notion of the world market into the fray of the potential drama. World market street functions as something abstract yet also as something "terribly real" (Althusser's words), terribly concrete, providing knowledge of a reality whose existence it reveals, a reality that is at once territorial and deterritorial, both place-bound and placeless.

World market street, in short, is a topographical abstraction, designating a street full of disparate people—real, concrete people. Yet it's also an abstract process circulating and flowing with international value and capital. World market street depicts a specific topography much as Althusser suggests Marx "topographically" uses *infrastructure* and *superstructure* to demarcate economic relations from political and ideological "instances" in a social formation.[31] "A topography," Althusser says, "represents in a definite space the respective sites occupied by several realities."[32] So by combining into a single topography, into a definite space, world market street tries to visualize all those streets where the world market—abstract wealth, value, money, and abstract labor—brings itself concretely to bear. Maybe it's there, looking out from world market street, from Dr. Fischelson's metaphysical garret, where we have another way of seeing, another perspective and cognitive map for perceiving urbanization, for seeing a single urban substance; and it's there, along world market street, immanent in its substance, where we can embrace a radically monist ontological alternative to urban life—and find a prospective staging for radical planetary politics.[33]

V. Lost Cities

What the world market does to urban society, and how urbanization is itself driving the world market, is the subject of one of Lefebvre's last essays, "*Quand la ville se perd dans une métamorphose planétaire*," first published in *Le monde diplomatique* in 1989.[34] The title says it all; an atypically downbeat Lefebvre is on show, two years before his death, dying like his cherished traditional city: "when the city loses its way," he writes, when it goes astray, "in a planetary metamorphosis." One can no longer write as whimsically and gaily about the city, Lefebvre laments, nor with the same lyricism that Apollinaire once wrote about Paris. Now, the situation is more sobering, more depressing, and somehow the octogenarian author of *Le droit à la ville* mirrors this depressing state of affairs. The more the city grows, develops, extends itself, and spreads its tentacles everywhere, he says, the more social relations get degraded and the more sociability is torn apart at the seams.

As this city extends, Lefebvre says, as it urbanizes hitherto unurbanized worlds, and as it urbanizes rural worlds, strange things equally happen to labor markets: they, too, seem to get obliterated. Traditional forms of work, secure forms of salaried and decent-paying jobs, seem to melt into the air as fast as "urban forms" settle everywhere and establish connections everywhere. People the world over migrate to the city looking for work only to discover there's no more work—at least no more dignified "formal" work that pays a living wage. Once, they came for steady jobs, such as factory jobs, but those industries have now gone belly-up or cleared out to someplace cheaper or somewhere even more exploitable and expendable. Cities have lost their manufacturing bases and, says Lefebvre, in consequence have lost their "popularly" active productive centers.

Each year millions of peasants and smallholders across the globe are thrown off their rural land by big agribusiness or corporate export farming, by the "rational" dynamics of the neoliberal world market. These people lose the means to feed themselves as well as the means to make a little money.[35] So they come to an alien habitat they can little afford or understand, a habitat that is frequently neither meaningfully urban nor exclusively rural but rather a blurring of both realities. It's a new reality the result of a push-pull effect, a vicious dialectic of dispossession, sucking people into the city while spitting others out of the gentrifying center, forcing poor urban old-timers and vulnerable newcomers to embrace each other out on the periphery, out on assorted zones of social marginalization, out on the global banlieue—left to fend for themselves on *world market street*.

All this has now begotten a "specific dialectic," Lefebvre suggests (16), a paradox in which "centers and peripheries oppose one another." Yet the fault lines and frontiers between the two worlds aren't defined by some straightforward urban–rural divide, nor necessarily by anything North–South; rather centers and peripheries are *immanent* within the accumulation of capital itself, *immanent* within its "secondary circuit of capital." Profitable locations get pillaged as secondary circuit flows become torrential, just as other sectors and places are asphyxiated through disinvestment. Therein centrality creates its own periphery, crisis-ridden on both flanks. The two worlds—center and periphery—exist side-by-side, everywhere, cordoned off from one other, everywhere. The "menace," Lefebvre says, is that this amorphous monster we call "the urban" becomes a planetary metamorphosis totally out of control. Urban society is born of industrialization, a force that shattered the internal intimacy of the traditional city and that gave rise to the giant industrial city Frederick Engels documented. But it has now superseded itself, been killed off by its own progeny. Industrialization has, in a word, negated itself, bitten off its own tail, advanced quantitatively to such a point that qualitatively it has bequeathed something new, something pathological, something economically and politically *necessary*: planetary urbanization.

Citizen and city-dweller have been dissociated; what has historically been a core ideal, a core unity of modern political life has, Lefebvre says, perhaps for the first time, perhaps forever, been wrenched apart, prized open. City-dwellers now apparently live with a terrible intimacy, a tragic intimacy of proximity without sociability, of presence without representation, of meeting without real encounter. The tragedy of the city-dweller is a tragedy of having hoped excessively, and of seemingly having these hopes serially dashed. Lefebvre's tonality throughout this essay is Céline-like in its journey to the end of the night. Yet he can't quite resist a few Whitmanesque flourishes, throwing out one final thought about what a new democratic vista might look like: it will surely necessitate a reformulation of the notion of *citizenship*, he says, one in which urban-dweller and citizen somehow embrace one another again, but in a new way. Indeed, "the right to the city," he concludes (17), now "implies nothing less than a new revolutionary conception of citizenship."

Frustratingly, though typically, Lefebvre never tells us what he means by such a loaded term as "revolutionary citizenship." Yet this is an opportunity for us, an invitation to make our own voyage, to develop our own content in our own age. In a while, I will try to work through what I think Lefebvre meant by revolutionary citizenship and what he might have said had he still been around today. For the time being, though, I will leave the theme dangling: before we can get that far we first need to consider that other part of Lefebvre's revolutionary equation: the right to the city.

CHAPTER TWO

Here Comes Everybody

Problematizing the Right to the City

Mass amateurization is a result of the radical spread of expressive capabilities.
Clay Shirky

I. HCE and RTTC

It's in James Joyce's dazzlingly inventive masterpiece, *Finnegans Wake*, published on the brink of World War II, where the acronym "HCE" first enters the scene, coined after the book's antihero, a certain Humphrey Chimpden Earwicker, barkeep and man of the world. Throughout *Finnegans Wake*, Joyce puns and plays with H. C. Earwicker, whose dreaming mind becomes the psychological space in which the *Wake*'s drama unfolds. If *Ulysses*'s Leopold Bloom is an Every(day)man, then old Earwicker, old HCE, is an Every(night)man, a universal dreaming figure. Thus the other epithet Joyce gives Humphrey, the other use of the acronym HCE: *Here Comes Everybody*, the "normative letters," Joyce says, of a "manyfeast munificent," a sort of Jungian archetypal image of our collective, desiring unconscious, reliving in a single night's sleep the whole of human history.[1] The dreamer is "more mob than man," jokes Joyce,[2] "an imposing everybody he always indeed looked, constantly the same as and equal to himself and magnificently well worthy of any and all such universalization."[3]

For a while I dreamed of calling this book *Here Comes Everybody*, this urban book, because today those normative letters, this HCE, seem to capture what life on planet Earth actually is: urban life, planet urban. A few years back, however, Clay Shirky, a freelance writer and sometime communications professor at New York University, beat me to it. He penned a book bearing those exact same normative letters—*Here Comes Everybody*—bearing an intriguing subtitle, *The Power of Organizing without Organizations*.[4] I'd gravitated toward this book, jealously, with eager expectations of high-spirited Joycean inflections, of Joycean influences, of Joycean puns and artistry, and of Joycean desire. In fact, there's none to be had: it's as if Earwicker never existed, had never had his great fall. Instead, *Here Comes Everybody* is an artless book, a superficial book in many ways, *un*-Joycean in its lack of existential depth about human life; and yet, ironically, or maybe not so ironically, in its very superficiality it makes a pretty convincing case for the new forms of sociability our digital age begets. Perhaps the lack of content is Shirky's major point, his major strength: that what we have now *is* a banal world of virtual flows and forms without any content, a deterritorialized world where territoriality doesn't matter anymore, where everybody *really is* getting together on Facebook and Twitter; and it's there, through new digital media, where our collective instinctual behavior is now getting expressed, where our *real* future becoming resides.

Shirky's book quickly became a bestselling user guide for the new social media movement; and its thesis applies as much to the corporate sector as the revolutionary sector, to business organization as well as grassroots organization. In this latter respect, we're not too far removed from John Holloway's autonomous Marxist chant from 2002: *to change the world without taking power*, to organize without organizations. Shirky's great appeal, and doubtless part of the book's success, is his optimism, his inclusive *everybody*, his popularism and pluralism. Social media, he reckons, have the potential to empower everybody; they can *de*professionalize certain select sectors of the creative professions (like journalism and photojournalism); engender creative, collaborative work for lots of "ordinary," nonspecialist people; and they can coordinate unprecedented mass activism and mobilization. As Shirky writes, now "we have groups that operate with a birthday party's informality and a multinational's scope" (48).

Shirky's ideas are hip and contagious, especially when framed around such suggestive and provocative rubrics as: "Cooperation as Infrastructure"; "Ordinary Tools, Extraordinary Effects"; "The Global Talent Pool"; "Rapid and Simple Group Formation"; "A Possible Future for Collective Action"; "Revolution and Coevolution." Shirky's optimism spills over into the world of social protest: "Why is so much collective action focused on protest," he asks, "with its emphasis on relatively short-term and negative goals? One possible explanation is that it is simply easier to destroy than to create; getting things started in a group takes a lot more energy than trying to stop them. That explanation is hard to support, though, given the fecundity of other kinds of social media. Once you know what to look for, evidence of group creativity is everywhere."[5] Collective action, says Shirky, is perhaps more focused on protesting *against* something than affirming a cause because the latter is simply harder to do; it is harder to build a politics based on sharing and collaboration and then use it positively to create. As a result, Shirky thinks "that collective action requires a much higher commitment to the group and the group's shared goals than things like sharing of pictures or even collaborative creation of software" (312).

In the pages of the *New Yorker* magazine, Malcolm Gladwell endorses this latter belief while taking Shirky's central thesis to task. Gladwell is surprisingly radical in his gritty offline bent. He thinks that new social media let the faint-hearted unite within the homely confines of their own four walls. Online activism, Gladwell says, even as a form of protest, of grumbling about things one doesn't like, is gutless at heart and inspires only "weak-tie" radicalism. It can't provide what social change really needs: people risking life and limb, as in the 1960s lunch counter sit-ins in Woolworth's, which kick-started the African American Civil Rights Movement. What mattered most there, according to Gladwell, was the *physicality* of bodies, bodies being present in space, the "strong-tie" connections that bonded people to a cause and to each other.

Shirky considers online activism an upgrade from the past. "But is it simply a form of organizing weak-tie connections," Gladwell asks, "that give us access to information over the strong-tie connections that help us persevere in the face of danger? It shifts our energies from organizations that promote strategic and disciplined activity toward those which promote resilience and adaptability. It makes it easier for activists to express themselves, and harder for that expression to have any effect." In high-risk activism, what seems crucial is your personal commitment to a movement, your personal contacts, your "critical friends" who gather, who show up in physical form somewhere, and who get the shit beaten out of them by the cops if you make wrong (or right!) decisions. "The kind of activism associated with social media," Gladwell says, "isn't like this at all. Twitter is a way of following people you may have never met. Facebook is a tool for efficiently managing your acquaintances. . . . This is in many ways a wonderful thing. . . . But weak ties seldom lead to high-risk activism. . . . In other words, Facebook activism succeeds not by motivating people to make a real sacrifice but by motivating them to do things that people do when they are not motivated enough to make a real sacrifice. We are a long way from the lunch counters of Greensboro."[6] As such, for Gladwell, the revolution will never be tweeted.

In one sense, Shirky and Gladwell are both right. In another sense, they're both wrong—wrong because perhaps neither thesis is incommensurate with the other, and each thesis is insufficient in itself. Isn't it possible, then, to conceive of activism today as at once weak-tie and high-risk, both online and offline, deterritorialized and reterritorialized, invariably at the same time? Dialectical, in other words. Indeed, wouldn't the Joycean dream space, the normative space of HCE, locate itself somewhere in-between, somewhere that's both and neither, somehow spaced-out and spaced-in, every day and every night, a flow as well as a thing, taking place here as well as there? (Gladwell might have forgotten that in many countries like Iran and China even weak-tie online activism is a risky business, enough to get you arrested and tortured by the authorities. It, too, requires lots of courage.)

Maybe another way of conceiving online and offline activism, and of Shirky's and Gladwell's online and offline modes of thought, is how Marx conceives of the circulation of capital in his introduction to the *Grundrisse*: as a series of interrelated movements, of dialectical shifts of fixity and flow, of production and distribution, of consumption and exchange. Only instead of capital in motion, what's getting plotted now is the circulation of *revolt*, necessarily on a planetary scale. In other words, activism happens someplace, is produced someplace, materializes itself offline, consummates itself somewhere. But it circulates elsewhere; moves virtually, online; and transforms itself emotionally, modifying itself continuously in its overall dialectical groove. "The conclusion we reach," says Marx, "isn't that production, distribution, exchange and consumption are identical, but that they all form the members of a totality, distinctions within a unity."[7] Each supplies the other with its objects, Marx insists; each begets its other. The circulation of immaterial revolt is, in this light, a factor of production in concrete subversion.

Framing the debate thus likewise raises questions about the city itself: Would a book about Here Comes Everybody now necessarily have to be a book about the city? Would the city constitute the "strong-tie" space in which an offline HCE expresses itself? If so, are its normative letters embodied in RTTC, in the *right to the city* movement? Is HCE really another way of reframing RTTC, which is to say its tautological reconstitution? Or, conversely, if we take Shirky's thesis to heart rather than to task, if we really run with it, is there still any role for the city at all? Wouldn't the principal dialectical fault-line lie between a virtual and a terrestrial activism? Isn't what counts that you're online, in tune, there in spirit—and, occasionally, just occasionally, there, somewhere, in kind? But where, we might ask, is this *somewhere*?

When "the right to the city" (RTTC) was voiced as a radical "cry and demand" in the late 1960s, its principal theorist was of course Henri Lefebvre. Lefebvre was the first scholar not only to conceptualize this democratic right but also to do so within Marxism, affirming it when the majority of people on Earth were then rural dwellers. But he saw things coming, saw certain things becoming. Fifty years on, though, how does RTTC fare now that Lefebvre's urban revolution has extended its borders and corroded almost all residues of agrarian life? Lefebvre's fabled urban revolution has largely consummated itself;

but has it equally consumed itself, devouring the city itself, rendering a rethink of the whole question of a right to the city, a rethink in light of the paradox of digital media and planetary urbanization?

II. RTTC Then: A Brief History of a Concept

Lefebvre's thesis, first expressed in the mid-1960s, could be distilled into the following proposition: Without a center there can't be any urbanity; what was taken away must be politically reclaimed. The right to the city was the right to reclaim centrality, the right to the city as a use value, the right to reinvigorate both urban life and Marxist politics. (For Lefebvre the two went hand-in-hand.) Such was the leitmotiv of a series of books he penned, in rapid-fire succession, on the city and urban politics in the latter half of that tumultuous decade. The first was a historical book, *La proclamation de la Commune*, from 1965, a text that got Lefebvre into trouble with Guy Debord and the Situationists because the latter accused him of plagiarism. The Situationists had drafted their very own "Theses on the Commune" in 1962, fourteen of them, in which they'd made pretty much the same points as Lefebvre: The 1871 Commune was the biggest festival of the nineteenth century; it was essentially leaderless; and it was "the only realization of a truly revolutionary urbanism to date."[8]

Lefebvre, like the Situationists, was interested in the idea of *style*, the Communards' revolutionary style. Out of this interest he sketched what he called "the theory of the event": What constitutes a revolutionary event; what are its objective and subjective moments; what was unique and general to events; and how can we interpret such an event historically and geographically, politically and sociologically? This is what Lefebvre tried to do with the Commune, on the basis of archival work on Communard diaries and historical documents, carried out at Milan's Feltrinelli Library. With *La proclamation de la Commune*, Lefebvre suggested that Marxist revolutionary strategy would have a city basis, not a factory basis; it would have a spontaneous, anarchistic moment, too, taking the form of an urban social movement, involving petty bourgeois elements and artisans as well as the "traditional" working class. With this book, which still warrants English translation, it isn't clear whether Lefebvre was excavating the past or foreseeing the future present (May 1968).

On the run up to 1968, Lefebvre wrote *Le droit à la ville* with high hopes that his thinking on the city might enter the collective consciousness of *soixante-huitards*. To a certain extent it did: When one thinks of the student street protests, one instinctively thinks of Lefebvre's clarion call, "the right to the city." But Lefebvre's May 1968 book was actually *The Explosion* [*l'irruption*] (1968), written (or dictated) as cars were still smoldering in central Paris and when students were still on the streets.[9] The dialogue dramatically lives out a lot of the thesis on the right to the city, even down to being ignored by the French Communist Party. *The Explosion* in question was really *The Eruption*, a better title, because that indicates something erupting like a volcano, not exploding like a bomb. A bomb implies something random, something purely stochastic where and when it explodes, whereas a volcano has a certain determinacy, a certain predictability, a certain causality. So, too, with May 1968 as an urban uprising. Lefebvre uses his theory of event taken from his Paris Commune book to look again at what was unique and general in events, at what was old and new, structural and superstructural, urgent and needed.

In all these books, and in *The Urban Revolution* (1970) and *La pensée marxiste et la ville* (1972) that followed in the "post-1968 decade," Lefebvre likens suburbanization and "New Town" expansion to a "de-urbanized" kind of urbanization. It was an explicit class warfare, he insisted, a denial of working-class urbanity, whose rank-and-file in France found themselves decanted and banished to the burgeoning peripheral *banlieues*, to new high-rise housing estates. At the same time, the rich bourgeois and assorted well-heeled conquered the center, whose playground it henceforth became, dancing to the tune of rentier and financial capital, to real estate speculation, and to "historic" preservation and gentrification. "I have the feeling," Lefebvre mused back in the late 1960s, "that the center is becoming 'museumified' and managerial. Not politically, but financially managerial. The metamorphosis of the city and the urban continue."[10]

The practice seemed a lot more appropriate to continental Europe than to North America, of course, where rich and middle-class people, especially white middle-class people, had done precisely the opposite, long ago fleeing the center in favor of the periphery. In much U.S. urbanism, the right to the city, the right to centrality, is precisely what many urban dwellers already have. Needless to say, it's a right not worth very much, given that those with power and wealth had long suburbanized themselves, leaving to the dispossessed the task of reassembling the motley shards of downtown centrality. To be fair, Lefebvre's real point still stands solid: in both instances an *anti-urban* trump card has been played. "The suburbs are urban," Lefebvre says, "within a dissociated morphology"; they constitute "the empire of separation and scission between elements of what had been created as unity and simultaneity"; the old center, meanwhile, "remains in a state of dispersed and alienated actuality."[11]

The city, for Lefebvre, is "an exquisite *œuvre* of praxis and civilization."[12] This makes "it" very different from any other product, from any other commodity like, say, a car. "This *œuvre*," Lefebvre said, "is use value and the product is exchange value." But the eminent use of the city, that is, of its streets and squares, buildings and monuments, is "*la fête* (which consumes unproductively, without any other advantage than pleasure and prestige)" (66). And this unproductive pleasure should be a free-for-all, not a perk for the superprivileged. To be sure, throughout history cities have been seats of commerce, places where goods and services got peddled, where spaces were animated by trade and rendered cosmopolitan by markets. Medieval merchants, Lefebvre says, "acted to promote exchange and generalize it, extending the domain of exchange values; yet for them the city was much more than an exchange value" (101). Indeed, it's only a relatively recent phenomenon that cities *themselves* have become exchange values, lucre in situ, jostling with other exchange values (cities) nearby, competing with their neighbors to hustle some action—a new office tower here, a new mall there, rich *flâneurs* downtown, affluent residents uptown.

Industrialization commodified the city, set in motion the decentering of the city, created cleavages at work and in everyday life: "Expelled from the city," Lefebvre writes, "the proletariat will lose its sense of *œuvre*. Dispensable from their peripheral enclaves for dispersed enterprises, the proletariat lets its own conscious creative capacity dim. Urban consciousness vanishes" (77). "Only now," reckoned Lefebvre in the 1960s, with his own emphases, "are we beginning to grasp the *specificity* of the city," a product of society and of social relations yet a special feature within those relations (100). Urbanization *reacts back* on society, for better or for worse, and has run ahead of industrialization itself. It's only now, Lefebvre adds, again using his own emphases, that the "foremost theoretical problem can be formulated": "For the *working class*, victim of segregation and expelled from the traditional city, deprived of a present and possible urban life, a practical problem poses itself, a *political* one, even if it hasn't been posed politically, and even if until now the housing question . . . has masked the problematic of the city and the *urban*" (100).

The latter allusion is to Frederick Engels's famous pamphlet *The Housing Question* (1872), in which Marx's faithful collaborator denounces those petty-bourgeois reformists who wanted to resolve squalid worker housing conditions without resolving the squalid social relations underwriting them. Although Lefebvre concurs with Engels's analysis and critique, as well as with his *political* reasoning, he cannot, circa the late twentieth century, quite adhere to Engels's practical solution:

> The giant metropolis will disappear. It should disappear. Engels possessed this idea
> in his youth and never let it go. In *The Housing Question*, he'd already anticipated,

"supposing the abolition of the capitalist mode of production," an equal as possible repatriation of the population over the entire land. His solution to the urban question precludes the big modern city. Engels doesn't seem to wonder if this dispersion of the city throughout the surrounding countryside, under the form of little communities, doesn't risk dissolving "urbanity" itself, of ruralizing urban reality.[13]

"There can't be any return to the traditional city," Lefebvre insists, notwithstanding his affection for his native Medieval Navarrenx or his admiration for Engels, just as there can't be any "headlong flight toward a colossal and shapeless megalopolis" (148). What we must do, he says, is "reach out and steer ourselves toward a new humanism, a new praxis, toward another human being, somebody of urban society" (150). This new humanism will be founded on a new right, the right to an oeuvre, *the right to the city*, which will emerge "like a cry and demand," like a militant call-to-arms. This isn't any pseudo-right, Lefebvre assures us, no simple visiting right; it isn't a tourist trip down memory lane, gawking at a gentrified old town; nor is it enjoying for the day a city from which you've been displaced. This right "can only be formulated," he says (158), "as a transformed and renewed right to urban life," a right to renewed centrality. There can be no city without centrality, no urbanity, he believes, without a dynamic core—a vibrant, open public forum, full of lived moments and encounters, disengaged from exchange value. "It doesn't matter," he says, "whether the urban fabric encroaches on the countryside nor what survives of peasant life, so long as the 'urban,' place of encounter, priority of use value, inscription in space of a time promoted to the rank of a supreme resource amongst all resources, finds its morphological base, its practical-material realization" (158).

III. RTTC Now: A Brief Reality of a Concept

Lefebvre's propositions today, forty years on, raise as many questions as they provide answers. The right to the city is a powerful and seductive battle cry; it has been mobilized by many groups across the globe, forged fruitful alliances, and prompted courageous activism. But is it now a battle cry that perhaps shouts in the wrong field of battle, even bawls the wrong refrain, limiting itself by running the wrong ticket? (Lefebvre's language of the proletariat or working class, meanwhile, also sounds rather quaint.) Recently, urban theorist and planner Peter Marcuse joked that the only word he doesn't have a problem with in "The Right to the City" is "to." "*The right*" and "*the city*" struck him as singularly problematic, as shibboleths the Left might want to reconsider, might even want to reformulate.[14] "A genuine right to the city," says Marcuse, "requires the abolition of the rule of private finance, and thus with it the rule of private capital, over the economy, and indeed over the world economy as a whole," and straightway we are propelled onto a much broader political terrain than the city itself. The right to the city is a right, Marcuse reckons, that means "a lot more than the right to Times Square."[15]

The right in question isn't a right for everybody but rather one that must pivot on two axes, on two sections of society, those excluded from the plenty all around them, and those discriminated against; in short, the exploited and the oppressed, the deprived and the discontented. They are the vanguard, as it were, the huge swaths of the world's population in contemporary times, the Here Comes Everybody. In a real sense, it is not the city that releases people from the daily round of oppression and exploitation but democracy, a democratic society in which people have the right to create one's own life, wherever one finds oneself. Plainly, getting that far, finding a democracy expressive of peoples' rights, is a right that, en route, will engender social conflict. Pursuing the right to the city will necessitate and necessarily involve struggle and conflict. The goal cannot be achieved by any consensus, technocratic fix, or compromise of interests nor by co-optation or reappropriation. "Between equal rights," Marx famously said in *Capital*, "force decides." It cannot be anything other than a politically effective confrontation.[16]

One thing that's evident from the rights battle nowadays is how it also motivates the Right as well as the Left. If anything, the Right has won the rights fight because it has converted its own rights into a legal force, a tactical right that has become a watchword for conservative rule. In the United Kingdom, for example, the Tory government is quick to give back to people their rights to self-management, to self-empowerment, because this means the state can desist from coughing up for public services. Self-empowerment thereby has become tantamount to self-subsidization and self-exploitation, mollified under the rubric of "community/social enterprise" and the voluntary "third sector." In a Public Services White Paper (July 2011), Prime Minister David Cameron advocates the need to "loosen the grip of state control," calling for the opening up of most public services to competition, to enable a "general right to choose."[17] "The human element should be in the driving seat," the White Paper says, "not politicians or bureaucrats." "Community rights" are bestowed onto urban communities up and down the United Kingdom; though as Bob Colenutt suggests, "they are not what they seem." What they signal, what they presage, is continuing local austerity programs mixed with intensified privatization at the national and global scales. It is, in short, neoliberalism without tears, a political and financial bonanza for the Right.

Thus rights can be positive and negative depending on how you swing or on how you frame them politically: they are empty signifiers that need filling with content; and once you fill them their implications can put even the most well-meaning rights demander on the defensive. Thus even the idea of filling rights with content seems a politically bankrupt ploy. Mark Tushnet helps illuminate why: "Once one identifies what counts as a right in a specific setting, it invariably turns out that the right is unstable; significant but relatively small changes in the social setting can make it difficult to sustain the claim that a right remains implicated." As such, "rights-talk" is "so open and indeterminate that opposing parties can use the same language to express their positions."[18]

A noteworthy example of what Tushnet means occurred in March 2010 at the United Nations–organized World Urban Forum in Rio de Janeiro, where both the UN and the World Bank incorporated "the right to the city" in their charter to address global urban poverty. On the other side of the street in Rio, on the "Left" side, at the Urban Social Forum, a people's popular alternative was simultaneously being staged, a direct response to the bigwig gathering that activists saw as an urban equivalent to Davos's World Economic Forum. Activists at the Urban Social Forum were appalled by the ruling class's reappropriation of a hallowed grassroots ideal, of *its* right not *theirs*. David Harvey, who spoke at both events, said when he'd declared that "the concept of the right to the city cannot work within a capitalist system," fellow panelists at the World Urban Forum fell embarrassingly silent.[19] Maybe it's unsurprising that Harvey's comment should turn off the mainstream. But maybe what's more interesting is what this might mean for leftists: Does it imply that the right to the city is a right that can only be expressed in a postcapitalist reality? Is the city the *medium* or the *product* of revolutionary assault, the *means* or the *outcome*? The language, again, is indeterminate and unstable, and it arguably offers little political leverage.

The question of "the city" is just as tricky as the rights question. Maybe we can express the conundrum as follows: The urban process is now global because it is energized by finance capital; ergo democratization has to be global. However, at the same time, according to right to the city theorists like Lefebvre, and to a certain extent Harvey, we have to separate out the city and give it some political specificity, some political priority in contemporary struggles against neoliberalism, and even some priority with respect to a Marxist politics. So, on one hand, the city needs to be considered globally because urbanization is global, masterminded by transnational finance capital. On the other hand, in this global struggle the city somehow holds the key, though only if it is "considered in the broadest sense of the term," at its broadest territorial scale. (The revolution "has to be urban," says Harvey, "or nothing at all."[20]) The specificity of the city seems to be that there's no longer any specificity; the right to the city is a global struggle that needs to be grounded in the urban. Perhaps it's just me, but isn't this logic somehow tautological? Aren't we left going around in circles?

One problem is analytical confusion, the bundling together of "city" and "urban" without any conceptual delineation, let alone political identification. The latter, related problem here emerges when we (correctly) identify the dominant role finance capital plays in global neoliberalism but then, in the same breath, voice some looser political invocation that "the city" (and confusingly "the urban") must now be the principal site for the implementation of this right. The shift from one to the other doesn't quite stack up, analytically or politically; in fact, it strikes as a theoretical and political non sequitur.

In *The Urban Revolution*, Lefebvre says generalized urbanization reconstitutes the city at a higher level, that "the urban" supersedes "the city" and that the latter contains the seed form without being able to bring the former into flower. The Lefebvrian urban revolution—at least the "good guy" revolution from the bottom up—is precisely to make the urban flourish from its city basis. It's true that Lefebvre invariably adds confusion: he opens up the playing field onto an urban plane only to close it back down again when demanding "the right to the city." The city is a historical entity, he says, a pseudo-concept, a ruined concept. Yet, for all that, he still wants to hold on to this *city* right, despite himself. In *The Urban Question* (1977), Manuel Castells says that here Lefebvre "destroys any causal relation between the form (the city) and human creation (the urban)," because after prioritizing content (the urban), he suddenly flips back to affirm the security of form (the city).[21] It's as if, like Einstein, Lefebvre couldn't quite live with the implications of his own reckoning, with his own brilliant *correctness*. Castells was less smitten. His grumbles with his former teacher are perhaps more compelling now than they were in the mid-1970s, compelling because they reveal what was wrong yet right in Lefebvre; they also reveal how Castells oddly ended up endorsing a line that tallies with his old *maître*.

Castells reckons that Lefebvre peddles an *ideological* thesis; Castells likes neither the reification of the city nor that of urban society. In shifting the ballast toward "the urban," what we have here, says Castells, is "something very close to Louis Wirth's thesis concerning the way social relations are produced. It is density, the warmth of concentration that, by increasing action and communication, encourage at one and the same time a free flowering, the unexpected, pleasure, sociability and desire. In order to be able to justify this mechanism of sociability, Lefebvre must advance a mechanistic hypothesis that is quite unjustifiable: the hypothesis according to which '*social relations are revealed in the negation of distance.*' And that is what the essence of the urban is in the last resort."[22]

Castells himself bundles together city and urban, viewing each as ideologically obfuscating for any Marxist politics struggling within late capitalist reality. From Castells's standpoint, the idea of "the city" and "the urban" as discrete objects of analysis, let alone political demands, makes no theoretical sense. One could argue that it never made any theoretical sense, that treating in isolation the effects of urbanization—of according relative theoretical priority to a process and product so intimately bound up with the dynamics of global capitalism, with its system of production, exchange, distribution, and consumption—was and still is absurd. These days, a lot of urban intellectuals gleefully hail the death of rurality, even the death of nature itself: with ubiquitous urbanization there's no longer anything that really constitutes "pure" countryside as the former has devoured the latter. They are doubtless right; I am sympathetic to this vision. But if that's the case, the logic has certain implications: if urban society is everywhere, then perhaps it's simultaneously nowhere, at least nowhere that merits particular analytical definition. This is the nub of Castells's counterargument. Why not, then, just drop "the urban" and stick simply with "society"? Isn't "the urban" a chaotic conception, an inadequate idea (as Spinoza might have said)? Perhaps it means that to go in search of the urban today is to go "*in search of a lost object*," especially when one goes in search of it with new social media.

The latter, italicized phrase was written forty years ago by Castells. Whatever way you look at it, Castells says, "the term 'urban' is irrelevant."[23] What can we possibly mean by "the city," he wonders, and by this process we term "the urban process"? Is it the agglomeration, the urban region we're talking about? If so, how to distinguish between "urban" and "regional," and why make the distinction anyway? And which aspects are to be studied? "Social classes? Housing satisfaction? The symbolic attraction of historical buildings? Transport? Air pollution? Neighborhood social participation? Voting in local elections? Residential mobility? Industrial location? Neighborhood renewal?" (55–56). As Castells says, the list is theoretically endless, and extremely disparate; and there's nothing here that's exclusively "urban" either.

But then one could beg to differ, pointing out that surely it's the spatial setting, that "space" somehow matters. True enough. Still, if the spatial setting of social and political life is now entirely "urban," and if this urban is equally "global," then the subject matter loses its specificity: it becomes limitless. Something urban, say, "urban society" or even "urban sociology," now becomes general "society" and "sociology." How could it be otherwise? How could we deny that the fundamental features of "urban society" aren't the direct consequence of the capitalist mode of production, of industrialization and postindustrialization; that urban contradictions are now social contradictions gone global? But again, one might counter that surely there's something we could conceivably describe as "urban culture"? Somehow, this doesn't go either: urban culture, like urban society, is, Castells says, equally redundant; worse, it's *ideological,* ideological in the sense that Althusser conceives ideology: an *imaginary distortion,* "not a system of real relations that governs the existence of individuals."[24]

In *The Urban Question,* Castells claims that urban culture isn't a concept or a theory but, "strictly speaking, a myth" (83). "It recounts," he says, "ideologically, the history of the human species. Consequently, the writings of 'urban society' which are based directly on this myth, provide keywords of an ideology of modernity, assimilated, in an ethnocentric way, to the social forms of liberal capitalism." The idea of a definable "urban culture," Castells thinks, reverts to the cultural and ecological-functionalist approaches of Louis Wirth, and of Robert Park and his Chicago School, all of whom stress the *dimension* of the city. Urbanism is its very own "way of life"; social contradictions, as such, get displaced into specifically urban contradictions. It's the spatial structure, not the capitalist social structure, that apparently sucks. This, for Castells, is an imaginary representation of the urban world behind which a real reality resides.

Alas, urban culture as ideology isn't just restricted to academic tradition or to "official urbanism" (planners, architects, technocrats, etc.); "it penetrates the thoughts of those who set out from a critical reflection on the social forms of urbanization" (86). There's even a Marxist version of this ideology of urban society, espoused by Lefebvre himself. For Lefebvre, urban society has superseded industrial society; industrialization is subordinate to urbanization, the mode of production to the mode of urbanism. Thus the revolution must now be urban as well. But isn't this, Castells wonders, just a left-wing rehash of Wirth's thesis of "urbanism as a way of life," whereby sheer density and concentration in the city counts most of all, is the means through which social relations are produced and revolutionized? Hasn't Lefebvre reversed Marx's materialist problematic? Isn't this "an urbanistic theorization of the Marxist problematic" rather than "a Marxist analysis of the urban phenomenon" (86–87)? Under these circumstances, the city gets projected, detrimentally, onto the whole terrain of capitalist society, to the degree that the former, rather than serving as an expression of the latter, now shapes it. What we're left with is a curious form of Marxist spatial fetishism, a theoretical reification of both the city and the urban; in the bargain, the city, in both theory and politics, now functions not as the dependent but as the independent variable.

To be sure, even if we accept the "city" as a specific terrain for political struggle, prioritizing it over a struggle that is first and foremost over social relations, one might ask: What would the right to the city actually resemble? Arguably, the Paris Commune is no longer so instructive, either theoretically or pragmatically, as the great festival of people reclaiming the center of the city, tearing down those statues of the dead bourgeois generations, abolishing rents and property speculation for a while, letting artisans control their own labor process as Proudhon willed. But how to deal with the central banks and all those flows of capital and commodities? (Remember, even a spectacular act of city dismantling—the downing of New York's World Trade Center—barely stopped world trading for a day.)

What's more, if we look at twentieth-century revolutionary history, it's equally clear that wresting control over cities has often been the icing on the revolutionary cake. By then, the social movement had already been built, the bonds already forged; taking control of the city announced the culmination of victory, the storming of the Winter Palace, the demolition of the Berlin Wall, the last battle in a dogged war of position, the social movement's final, joyous fling; highlighting how, in many ways, the revolutionary juices of modern times haven't had their source in the city at all but have flowed *from* the countryside onto the city's streets.[25]

It's almost as Régis Debray said in *Revolution in the Revolution* (1967): the city has been the "empty head," largely impotent, deaf to the plight of those who feel accumulation by dispossession the most; it's the rural hinterlands, mountain jungles, and abandoned *banlieues* that constitute the "armed fist" of rebellion. "The city, for the guerrilla movement," wrote Debray, "was a symbol, *the purpose of which was to create the conditions* for a coup d'état in the capital."[26] Mao, Che, Castro, and Ortega (in Nicaragua) all knew this, and with Subcomandante Marcos they'd doubtless concur: the city doesn't so much radicalize as *neutralize* popular elements. The city, in this reading, isn't so much a Lefebvrian dialectical oeuvre as a Sartrean *practico-inert*, the prison-house of past actions, the formless form of a passive totality, of inert bricks and mortar that gnaw away, that inhibit active praxis. The practico-inert, says Sartre in *Critique of Dialectical Reason*, opposes active activity because its antidialectic announces that dead labor dominates over living labor, that praxis has been absorbed into an objective alien form, into the city itself.[27] And while in *La métaphilosophie* (1965) Lefebvre was critical of Sartre's formulation of the urban as practico-inert, the latter understanding nonetheless explains the relative conformity of urban populations today, the majority of whom are former peasants and people with rural roots, a millionfold mass such as never existed before—a flow of dynamic people who soon become vagrants or unemployed, subemployed, and multiemployed attendants, trapped in shantytowns, cut off from the past yet somehow excluded from the future, too.

The dialectician Lefebvre often said the urbanization of the countryside is also ruralization of the city, that planetary urbanization means a strange collision and collusion of city and rural worlds, a strange amalgam of entangled loyalties, and a strange existential schizophrenia for those trapped within. In a sense, this same dialectic and dichotomy forms the basis of John Berger's novel *Lilac and Flag* (1990), his "old wives' tale of the city," a fictionalized rendering of the city-countryside problematic but one that arguably reveals for us a few facts. Berger's narrator, an aged peasant woman who remains in the village after everybody has left, is leery of the city. For her, when push comes to shove, there are really only two types of people: peasants and those who feed off peasants. Her tale is of Zsuzsa and Sucus, a.k.a. Lilac and Flag, two lovers who are trying to tread their slippery way through the spectral metropolis of Troy, a paradigmatic megacity of expressways and concrete blocks, of money values and deceit, of immense freedom and brutal imprisonment.

Sucus lives with his mother and father on the fourteenth floor of an anonymous high-rise on the periphery. Clement, Sucus's papa, came from the village as a teenager and worked all his life opening oysters. One day Clement has a freak accident when his TV catches fire: he gets badly burned and slips away in a hospital. Clement has always wondered whether his son could find a job. "There are no jobs," Sucus tells papa on his deathbed, "except the ones we invent. No jobs. No jobs." "Go back to the village, that's what I'd like to do," says Clement to his son. "See the mountains for the last time."[28] Half the men in the ward, he says, remember either their village or their mothers; that's all they think about. Sucus's generation, though, doesn't know the village, so they can never go back anywhere; and yet this generation can't quite find itself in the alien city either, even in the city in which it was born. Sucus's generation can go neither backward nor forward: it has nostalgia for neither the past nor the future. Meantime, they're not prepared to take the same shit their parents did. Their expectations are different. But their prospects are nonexistent.

Sucus once sold coffee outside the local prison, but somebody, in an organized heist, stole his flask. Then he gets a job as a laborer on a building site. Yet he punches the hard-ass foreman and is sacked. In fact, all Sucus has in life are two things: his wits and his woman, Zsuzsa. But Zsuzsa has even less going for her and lives way out in a makeshift blue shack at Rat Hill, one of Troy's many shanties. Her brother, Naisi, has a submachine gun and is hip in his smooth leather boots, yet he gets in deep with neighborhood toughies who sell drugs and is later gunned down by the cops. ("We're born outside the law," Naisi says, "and whatever we do, we break it.") Zsuzsa is a happy-go-lucky drifter, a sexy flirt who lives day-to-day and hand-to-mouth. She can't read words but knows how to read signs in the street and also on peoples' faces. She calls her lover Sucus "Flag" and wants him to call her "Lilac," after a song.

Together, Lilac and Flag pilfer passports from an overnight train, a first-class sleeper at the so-called Budapest Station. Against all odds, they consummate their union and spend the booty on a passionate night in an old-money hotel that saw better days a century ago. Yet somehow, among all the drama, we sense that menace lies ahead for at least one of them, that the great white death-ship moored nearby at Troy's dockside awaits new passengers; and in this heavenly floating palace lifeboats aren't necessary because now everyone is out of danger.

From firsthand lived experience, Lilac and Flag know our metropolises are run by corrupt politicians and crooked police, by shyster real estate corporations and financial institutions whose corruption is both blatant and legalized. They know the rules of the urban game are rigged against them. Their tragedy is a tragedy of arriving too late (or perhaps too early?). When their parents came there were still steady jobs, such as factory work, to be had. But those industries went bust or cleared out long ago. Berger knows better than anyone how millions of peasants and smallholders across the globe are each year thrown off their rural land by big agribusiness and corporate export farming; so, as "seventh" men and women, they move to the city in search of work that's increasingly disappearing, migrating to an alien habitat they can little afford or understand.

Their sons and daughters understand this habitat better, well enough to know that now there are no decent jobs left, only insecure, underpaid work and overworked workers everywhere in the city's informal layers: busboys and valet parkers, waiters and barmen, cleaners and security guards, builders and buskers, hawkers and hustlers. Berger's Sucus, like his millionfold namesakes the world over, loitering on world market street, is a latent political subject waiting in the wings, perhaps even hoping against hope. Yet he's waiting for something closer to home, something trivial—something he can touch and smell and feel—and for something larger than life, something that's also world-historical. He's waiting, that is, for a praxis that can somehow conjoin both realms at once, square the lived with the historical, meld two sides of a praxis, as Lefebvre frequently said, "that go badly together."[29]

IV. From RTTC to the Politics of the Encounter?

If the right to the city won't do, what else might? Are other ways to frame the debate, other more politically fruitful alternatives, more empowering for a radical politics of today? If a concept didn't fit or somehow didn't work, Lefebvre insists we should always ditch that concept, abandon it, or give it up to the enemy. For Lefebvre, the whole political utility of a concept isn't that it should correspond with reality but that it enables us *to experiment with reality*, that it helps us to glimpse another reality—a virtual reality that's there, somewhere, waiting to be born inside us, between us. Maybe the idea of the encounter can spawn a different way of conceiving the urbanization of the world and of straddling the dialectic between the lived and the world-historical. The notion of encounter is a tale of how people come together as human beings, of why collectivities are formed and how solidarity takes hold and takes shape, and also how intersectional politics shapes up *urbanly*. The encounter is like a twinkling, radiant cosmic constellation, an expression of a plurality of participants who conjoin within an open form (and forum), within a dynamic structured coherence, within a configuration that makes itself rather than simply lies there, preexisting, in a passive state.

Suffice it to say here that the recent tumult in Tunisia, Egypt, Greece, and Spain, as well as that of the Occupy movement, expresses itself as a dramatic politics of the encounter. In each case, whether in Tunis or Cairo, in Madrid or Athens, in New York or London, while encounters unfold on capital city streets, the stake itself isn't about the city per se; rather, it's about *democracy*, about democracy in times of capitalist crisis, about something simpler and vaster than city politics as we once knew it. It's also something more, as I'll suggest later, than just class struggle. A lot of the activism and organizing was done deterritorially, through Facebook and Twitter, and was essentially leaderless, punctuating a series of radical moments, Lefebvrian moments that intersected and overlapped. People quite simply encountered one another by virtue of an affinity taking hold, just as Shirky's *Here Comes Everybody* envisaged. Of course, stuff had been gurgling within the bowels of society: undercurrents, clandestine organization, politicking, subversion, and growing dissatisfaction; but when things explode, when they really erupt, as they did, when the proverbial shit hits the fan, it's invariably by surprise.

One of the catchiest slogans for young Spaniards who mobilized across their recession-ravaged land was: "no jobs, no houses, no pension, no fear." (Michael Douglas had Gordon Gekko voice much the same sentiment to young Ivy-leaguers in *Wall Street 2*: "You're the NINJA generation," he goaded at a lecture.

"No Income, No Jobs and No Assets. . . . So what you're gonna do about it?")
Many in Spain are new kids on the block, new protesters, with little to lose and
everything to gain. Yet what they want is more than their city. They're politically naive but have wised up fast, coming of age together. They are disgusted
with unions, who do nothing to represent their interests, and disillusioned with
both of Spain's main parties, who are corrupt and unresponsive. Consequently,
they've acted en masse. Protests bloomed over Twitter and Facebook, triggered
by WikiLeaks documents exposing government officials' less than forthright
behavior; meanwhile, the latter's attempt to shut down previously legal websites
through antipiracy laws riled this new social media generation.

People here encounter one another because of certain situations, because of
certain collisions in time and space, because of certain attributes. People discover "interpellated" group commonality because bodies and minds take hold
in a space that is at once territorial and deterritorial, in a time that isn't clock or
calendar time but eternal time. One could even say that this coming together of
bodies and minds, this common action, is a process that involves subjectivity
yet is itself without any subject. But the process will, has to, unfold and take hold
somewhere, somewhere *urban* in its broadest sense. So, yes, we need to rethink
"the urban" at its widest and deepest sociospatial manifestation, just as Lefebvre
and Harvey urge; as an abstract category, for sure, yet as a category also with
definition and content, as something concrete and socially and geographically
inclusive, as a *new form of centrality and citizenship*. Somehow, we're back to
where we were at the end of the previous chapter. But we're not quite going
round in circles, because we've advanced our understanding of how we must
now frame this centrality and citizenship. We need to build upon Lefebvre's
insights and shortcomings; we need to take onboard Castells's critique. We need
to focus on planetary urbanization as a process that's begotten skyscrapers as
well as unpaved streets, highways and backroads, bywaters and marginal zones
that feel the wrath of the world market—its absence as well as its presence. The
urban nowadays is loaded with weeds as well as wealth, with undergrowth as
well as overgrowth; it's a vast space where the fight for the transformation of the
world will now take place. Yet the urban isn't a point fixed in absolute space. It's
no longer a fixation on a center, no longer really any point at all, but a space of
and for encounters: a space of and for a citizenship that might intervene in the
current, rather dubious, neoliberal hegemony.

CHAPTER THREE

The Urban Consolidates

Centrality and Citizenship

Like many named places . . . it was less an identifiable city than a grouping of concepts. . . . She looked down a slope, needing to squint in the sunlight, onto a vast sprawl. . . . The ordered swirl of houses and streets, from this high angle, sprang at her now with the same unexpected, astonishing clarity as the circuit card had. Though she knew less about radios than about Southern Californians, there were to both outward patterns a hieroglyphic sense of concealed meaning, of an intent to communicate.

Thomas Pynchon

Social relations are revealed in the negation of distance.

Henri Lefebvre

I. Abstract-Expressive Urbanization

The city in history established itself from the cradle of absolute space, developed as an internal force that needed to expand and push outward in order to augment its power. The city in history has modified and been modified by successive modes of production, by advances in social and technical relations of production. Under capitalism, the city became the center of gravity; a whole industrial mode of production pivoted on it. After a while, if we can believe Lefebvre, as the city developed under this industrial mode of production, it actually began to transform that industrial mode of production, even became its own mode of production. And yet, for all this, the city under capitalism could never transform its capitalist basis. How could it? If we thought otherwise, we'd fall back onto the silliest fetishism; Castells's objection about an "urban revolution"—with "urban" rather than "revolution" the independent variable—would hold firm. Such modification without transformation meant, for the city, only one dialectical outcome: *implosion-eruption*. An internal scattering over time, a breaking up and caving in, a progressive earthquake-like spatial rendering,

a ripping open of the traditional city form. At the same time, a sudden eruption has occurred and red-hot magma has been spewed over vast distances;
a kaleidoscope of congealed lava has solidified in its wake, in a form still
unfamiliar to us.

This implosion-eruption created a city–urban dialectic; from an identifiable city to a circuit-board patterning with a hieroglyphic sense of concealed
meaning. Pynchon's heroine, Oedipa Maas, from *The Crying of Lot 49*, puts this
shift perfectly. Now we are left wallowing in relativity, searching for clarity, still
not quite believing that God plays dice, that the real estate market is our new
casino, that our future resides in financial futures and options. Paradoxically, it's
tempting to say that capital now needs fixity more than ordinary people: capital
produces the urban as a conceived space and we are left to inhabit it as lived
space. Of course, we produce it too: we are all workers, as Herbert Muschamp
liked to insist, producing our own factory merely by walking down the street.
That was how he summarized Lefebvre's *The Production of Space*: human beings
collectively make spaces just by encountering other human beings.

Capital's dilemma, though, is the problem of the $M–C–M'(M'=M+\Delta M)$ circuit that Marx identified. Money circulates, generating more money and capital.
It goes into one end of the process yearning to come out of the other larger
than before—as money plus an increment, as capital. Yet to do so some mediation is needed. Money and capital can't quite accumulate ex nihilo, not quite;
money has to touch earth somewhere, metamorphose into a commodity form,
if only to dispossess an existent commodity form. It needs to do so in order to
accumulate capital on an expanded scale and to recommence the process anew.
Capital, Marx says in the *Grundrisse* (548), "travels through different phases of
circulation not as it does in the mind, where one concept turns into the next at
the speed of thought, in no time, but rather as situations which are separate in
time. It must spend some time as a cocoon before it can take off as a butterfly."

Here the city—or is that the City?—becomes the necessary "bearer" of that
moment of circulation, a safe haven, a cocoon from which capital can launch
its circulation globally. Capital creates formlessness, yet formlessness unnerves
it as a social force, as a ruling class intent on business. It needs the reassurance
of absoluteness, in all senses of the term. If God does play dice, that is patently
bad for market confidence. Thus capital worries little about its inexorable urge
to create spaces of relativity, such as chaotic spaces of the world market; yet it
has a hard time living with it, even with a competitive relativity and insecurity
among its own, within its citadel. This is why the stakes of the city (City) have
changed in our age of planetary urbanization: rather than keeping people inside
the citadel, people must now be kept out. So the walls go up, the barricaded

zones, the barbed wire fences. In our global monetary system, zones of absolute security proliferate as control stations that now resemble wartime bunkers.
Market universes may be somehow extraterrestrial and high-tech; yet medieval
fiefdoms seem to prop up that system on the ground. Capital now needs solidity
and security more than we, the people, do. They're on the defensive, interior-
izing themselves through fear, which is justifiable because they have a lot to
lose, much more than we do. It isn't so much their desire for centrality as their
ruthless quest for *centralization*.

Hence the dialectical possibility for real people today: contrary to the rheto-
ric that capital commands space and people only have place as their battleground, have only some subordinate locale rather than a larger planetary stake,
it's perhaps the other way around. Rather than populate "the city," we, as a collectivity, are compelled, often willy-nilly, to inhabit urban space. We are relative
whether we like it or not. Planetary urban society is now inside us, each time
we switch on a TV set, listen to the radio, go online, enter a Twitter stream,
SMS someone. Our horizons have opened up. Meanwhile, those of capital's, as a
class, now need fire-walling and need to be closed down.[1]

The revolution will certainly be urban, but it's a very special notion of "urban" and "revolution" that's now at stake. It's actually to agree with Castells:
the urban is nothing in itself, nothing outside dynamic social relations, nothing outside of a coming together of people. The urban isn't the passive surface
over which people encounter other people, nor over which capital simply circulates: the sheer proximity of people to other people, the sheer simultaneity
of activities, of events and chance meetings, *is the very definition of urban society itself*. In encountering one another, people produce space—relative urban
space. They become urban people, Lefebvre says: "polyvalent, poly-sensorial,
capable of complex and transparent relationships with the 'world.'"[2] They become "people of the world," Baudelaire might have said, of the "whole world."[3]

In *The Urban Revolution*, Lefebvre uses a beautiful turn of phrase: "the urban
consolidates" [*l'urbain rassemble*"], he says.[4] The urban becomes urban because
it creates its own definition, because, as a complex web of social relations, hanging together somehow, it engenders and expresses a specific kind of sociability.
The urban is a bringer together and a transformer of everything in that coming
together: capital and goods, people and information, activity and conflict, confrontation and cooperation. The urban concentrates things, intensifies, creates
simultaneity and difference, creates difference where no awareness of difference
existed; and ditto, what was once distinct and isolated becomes conscious of its
own universality in that particularity. This is why Marx endorses its coming,
the becoming of urbanization. *The urban consolidates*: it is both particle and

wave, flow and thing; its own random uncertainty principle that prevails in everyday life.

Therein Lefebvre's other great expression, the one Castells hated, speaks volumes: "social relations are revealed in the negation of distance."[5] Not only is this a brilliant definition of what urban society is today, and how any revolution might come about; it also mimics to a T Manuel Castells's celebrated thesis that late capitalism operates predominantly as a "space of flows," as a "network society." Everything he negatively attributed to his elder in *The Urban Question* is now something Castells himself practices; although instead of the "urban" it is "the network" that is decisive. Instead of space being the quasi-independent variable, as he once condemned Lefebvre for positing, for Castells technology is now the quasi-independent variable, the driver not the driven; what was once urban space for one is now the space of technology for the other. And yet, the brilliance of the two men is that, together, unwittingly, in their push–pull complementarity, they founded a superstring theory of space, a holistic theory of the dynamics of planetary urban space in the era of digital media—if only we lace them up with one another.

Urban society is characterized, perhaps above all else, by this network society, this abstract-expressive *space of flows*. Castells's description of the concept he's patented over recent years describes perfectly the way we must reconfigure the becoming of Lefebvre's urban society:

> The space of flows refers to the technological and organizational possibility of practicing simultaneity without contiguity. It also refers to the possibility of asynchronous interaction in chosen time, at a distance. . . . However, the space of flows is not placeless. It is made of nodes and networks; that is, of places connected by electronically powered communication networks through which flows of information that ensure the time-sharing of practices processed in such a space circulate and interact. While in the space of places, based on contiguity of practice, meaning, function, and locality are closely inter-related, in the space of flows places receive their meaning and function from their nodal role in the specific networks to which they belong. Thus, the space of flows is not the same for financial activities as for science, for media networks as for political power networks . . . the space of the network society is made up of an articulation between three elements: the places where activities (and people enacting them) are located; the material communication networks linking these activities; and the content and geometry of the flows of information that perform the activities in terms of function and meaning. This is the space of flows.[6]

This is equally the space of urban society. The space of flows expresses itself *urbanly* through the idea of fabric or tissue. Flows are the capillaries and arteries of blood and energy that nourish this vital urban tissue, that keep its cells alive, or that sometimes leave them partly dead; that simultaneously provide overnutrition and undernutrition, that enable cells to pulsate and squirm, to flicker and flare up, depending on which part of the tissue we're talking about and where it's situated vis-à-vis the rest of the urban's inorganic body. Such an understanding lets us see the urban's complex circuit card, its networked tissue, its mosaic and fractal form, stitched together with pieces of delicate fabric. Outside of human woof and weft, the urban creates nothing, is nothing. The urban serves no purpose and has no reality outside of a human reality, outside of exchange, outside of union, outside of human proximity and human concentration, outside of human encounter. "The signs of the urban," Lefebvre says in *The Urban Revolution* (118), "are signs of assembly: the things that promote assembly (the street and its surface, stone, asphalt, sidewalks) and the requirements for assembly (seats, lights)." The urban is, he says,

> pure form: a place of encounter, assembly, simultaneity. This form has no specific content, but is a center of attraction and life. It is an abstraction, but unlike a metaphysical entity, the urban is a concrete abstraction, associated with practice. Living creatures, the products of industry, technology and wealth, works of culture, ways of living, situations, the modulations and ruptures of the everyday—the urban accumulates all content. But it is more than and different from accumulation. Its contents (things, objects, people, situations) are mutually exclusive because they are diverse, but inclusive because they are brought together and imply their mutual presence. The urban is both form and receptacle, void and plenitude, superobject and nonobject, superconsciousnesses and the totality of consciousness. (118–119)

Few, perhaps, have so beautifully defined something so indefinable.

II. Urban Uncertainty Principle: The Dialectics of Centrality

Given all this, the manner in which Lefebvre conceived centrality in *The Right to the City* now strikes as both inappropriate and wrong, both analytically and politically. In the 1970s he seemed to sense this himself. He began to nudge along the debate about centrality in *The Urban Revolution*, and then took it a little further again in *The Production of Space*, published four years on. While writing the former book, Lefebvre had already started to envisage in his imagination the latter book; he'd already envisaged the *need* for this latter book on space. But what kind of book? A curious footnote—Lefebvre was never a big footnoter—to the important "Urban Form" chapter of *The Urban*

Revolution offers clues.[7] There, Lefebvre notes, "form unifies three aspects of the city. The 'right to the city' becomes the right to centrality, the right to not be excluded from urban form, if only with respect to the decisions and actions of power."

The allusion is hasty and done flippantly. But Lefebvre tries to cover his back; he tells us "these topics will be discussed in further detail in my *Théorie de l'espace urbain*." This "Theory of Urban Space," of course, eventually materialized as *The Production of Space*. Mysteriously, "the urban" had now dropped out of the equation. Why? Perhaps because a title like *The Production of Urban Space* would have been a tautology, adding another redundant word "urban"—redundant because it is already *implicit* in any definition of space, not only in the text but in the world. Indeed, even as early as the 1970s, around the time of the 1973 oil crisis, on the eve of fiscal crisis of the state, the production of space was, de facto, the production of urban space; any theory of the spatial production could only ever henceforth be a theory of global-urban spatial production. And yet, as ever with Lefebvre, that footnote leaves us wondering, necessitates we work a bit to figure out its intent. "The right to the city," he says, "becomes the right to centrality." But what is this right to centrality? "The right not to be excluded from urban form," Lefebvre rejoins. The problem here is that the right to the city and the right not to be excluded from urban form are theoretical gestalts that don't add up to a single political image; they're irreconcilable. Between *The Right to the City* and *The Urban Revolution*, "the city" had morphed into "the urban." The absolute form of the city had, in the bargain, become relatively formless. Thereafter the formless urban morphed simply into "space." What was once absolute now became relative; what once had a definable form now became relatively formless, became planetary, was everywhere, was space *tout court*. What had gone analytically was both absoluteness and form. So, too, in politics, apparently. Lefebvre had decentered his own concept of the city, only to recenter it as "the urban," which has a different understanding of centrality and center. The right not to be excluded from the urban *does not* equate to the right to the city, despite what Lefebvre says: radical analysis and politics cannot, and should not, hold on to both ideals at once. One has to go to move forward, to embrace the possibility of urban society. If one loses the right to the city, or voluntarily gives up this right, if one desists from thinking in terms of solid "city," as an absolute, then one gains renewed capacity to forge a politics based on something else, something more open-ended and dynamic; riskier, perhaps, because it lacks a clear basis and definitional space. Yet this risky, open-ended politics is more apt for our age of formless urbanization and more attuned to a political landscape in which less contiguous modes of communication are subversive tools for organizing new kinds of centrality and *horizontal* concentration.

In *The Production of Space*, Lefebvre makes an interesting comparison between Marx's *Capital* (volume 1) and his *Grundrisse* notebooks, preferring the latter because of its analytical openness and formlessness and its prospective politics. In *Capital*, says Lefebvre, Marx concerns himself with exposition rather than content; he clings to a strict formal structuring, to a logical rigor of argument, which impoverishes, Lefebvre says, because of its reductionism and its rigid and closed nature. "Whereas *Capital* stresses a homogenizing rationality founded on the quasi-'pure' form . . . the *Grundrisse* insists at all levels on difference." Less rigorous, Lefebvre admits of the *Grundrisse*, "less emphasis on logical consistency, and hence a less elaborate formalization and axiomatization"; but this "leaves the door open to more concrete themes, especially in connection with dialectical relations."[8] *Capital* moves inward, inside a bounded frame; the *Grundrisse* pushes outward, toward the periphery, annihilates space by time, and time by space, like the process of urbanization itself, like a new notion of centrality.

What, then, might centrality constitute in this vast, networked urban society, in this abstract-expressive space of flows? To begin with, centrality can no longer be about being at the center of things. We must give up the ghost of this line of thinking: the search for centrality as a journey to the center of the Earth is a fruitless quest, a mission seeking a nonexistent holy grail. We must reposition ourselves elsewhere, in a new space, one without an absolute center, not geographically located in bounded space. Instead, centrality should be thought of as a locus of actions that attract and repel, that structure and organize a social space, that define the urban. Centrality isn't the way Lefebvre defined it in the 1960s, as an absolute center of a city that needs taking back, like the Communards reclaiming central Paris; urban politics can't invoke that model anymore. In *The Production of Space*, Lefebvre hints as much, even if he never says so straight up. Instead, centrality is something that is the cell form of the urban, its atomic structuring, its sine qua non. Centrality calls out for content, for people and acts, for situations and practical relationships. It implies simultaneity, a simultaneity of everything that comes together in a social act at a point or around that point, and at a certain time. To that degree, centrality is movable, always relative, never fixed, and always in a state of constant mobilization and negotiation; sometimes it decenters itself.

To say "urban space" is, accordingly, to say center and centrality in a counterintuitive voice, to say that "it doesn't matter whether centrality is actual or merely possible, saturated, broken up or under fire, for we are speaking here of a *dialectical centrality*."[9] The production of centrality resembles a spider's web, a collective of spiders, the sum of their bodies and spaces, of how they make their webs, how they are attached to them, dependent on them. The production of centrality is akin to how a spider spins its web as an extension of its body, with its symmetric and asymmetric structuring, the silky strands that are woven, secreted; this web is at once the spider's terrain and a tool of its actions, its own social network.

Centrality, Lefebvre says, "is a gathering-together and meeting of whatever coexists in a given space. What does coexist in this way? Everything that can be named and enumerated. Centrality is therefore a *form*, empty in itself but calling for contents—for objects, natural or artificial beings, things, products and works, signs and symbols, people, acts, situations, practical relationships."[10] As a form, centrality implies a form of simultaneity, of networks cohering, hanging together, a weblike conjoining somewhere: "the simultaneity of 'everything' that is susceptible of coming together—and thus of accumulating—in a social act, at a point or around a point," a point where accumulated energies must eventually erupt.

Centrality must blow *centralization* asunder. Centrality shouldn't be conflated with centralization. The latter fulfills a "totalizing" mission of control and domination, a striving to concentrate wealth and knowledge, information and power; the former must give birth to a new democratic logic and strategy, to a new capacity for concentration mediated by information, communication, and concentration both near and far, contiguous and virtual, through the negation of distance and a reaching out to distance. Centrality must fill in the pores of urban space, fill them in with people, with people assembled, encountering one another, communicating with one another, acting with one another. A human flow.

Centrality is where people encounter one another as the nemesis of centralization. Yet any centrality, once established, is destined—as is true for lots of occupations and assemblies of people—to suffer dispersal, to dissolve or to implode from efforts of saturation, attrition, and outside aggression. (The latter may be labeled more pithily: *eviction*.) The basis of centrality can never, should never, become fixed, but it might be in a constant state of mobilization, of regrouping and reconcentration, of centering and recentering itself, of cohering here and juxtaposing itself there—a spatial play of repetition and difference. At that point, around that point, centrality expresses itself as an encounter between *citizens*. Citizenship, much like centrality, *reveals itself through the negation of distance and through the reaching out to distance*. It's the point of convergence of both, a dialectic that is both a *perception* and a *horizon*, a structure of feeling as well as a way of seeing—seeing oneself and one's planet. Its singularity around the point at which it occurs, if it occurs, will be so powerful and clear-cut that it will be self-sufficient; no border patrols can ever prevent its passage.

III. Spiritual Citizenship of the Universe

Lefebvre's declaration that the right to the city implies nothing less than a new revolutionary concept of citizenship, mentioned in chapter 1, thus doesn't hold water. Revolutionary citizenship has to imply something else than the right to the city, which is too inward in its political expressiveness. Citizenship must be conceived as something *urban*, as something territorial, yet one in which territoriality is narrower and broader than both "city" and "nationality." A citizen of the block, of the neighborhood, becomes a citizen of the world, a universal citizen rooted in place, encountering fellow citizens across the corridor and at the other end of the planet.[11] Urbanization, ironically, makes this sense of belonging possible, makes it both broader and narrower, even as it sometimes rips up the foundation of one's own dwelling space, dwelling in a narrow sense. (In a way, this is what Marx meant in the *Manifesto* when he lobbied for a cosmopolitan "world literature," for a moment when "intellectual creations of individual nations become common property.") This kind of citizenship is one in which *perception* replaces passport and *horizon* becomes almost as important as habitat. This perception is simultaneously in place and in space, offline somewhere local and online somewhere planetary, somewhere virtual. If we want to call this perception a newly formulated cognitive map in our heads, we can. What is important in this mapping is that it maps the totality, that it works when people see these two realms coming together, when perception (as a structure of feeling) and horizon (as a way of seeing) conjoin and somehow meet one another, encounter one another, suddenly give rise to a singular political awareness and to a potential political activity. Suddenly, the paint drips, the canvas take shape; suddenly, we recognize that we are in the frame, that we are the painter, the painter of modern life, the spiritual citizen of the universe.

There are no passports for spiritual citizens of the urban universe, no passports for those who know they *live* somewhere yet *feel* they belong everywhere. Or who want to feel it. This conjoining of knowing and feeling is what engenders a sense of empathy whose nom de plume might really be citizenship itself. In today's urban realm, this citizenship is more likely to be based on *affinity* rather than any notion of class. In the *Communist Manifesto*, Marx was brilliant at charting the developmental forces of the mode of production, its historical and geographical expansion, and its need to urbanize itself—to create industrial cities, move mountains, dig canals, connect everywhere, nestle everywhere—to do all of that because of its inexorable urge, because it, as a mode of production, had to. All of this had a unifying effect, due to the (often) unintended outcome of a drive to forge a world market, to manufacture a world in which soon manufacture would become outmoded, would pull the rug from beneath itself, would bite off its own tail, killing the goose that lays the golden egg. Within this depiction, Marx welcomed urbanization because it would create a physical and emotional proximity of workers, workers piled on top of one another, beside each other. Cosmopolitanism would thus equate to a kind of sharing, an awareness of common lived experience. It would create a form of collective-consciousness, Marx said, class-consciousness, wherein people would rise up, become aware, "with sober senses," of "their real conditions of life."[12]

Analytically, Marx was dead right in his capitalist narrative, save for one thing: his proposed ending. The idea of the working class as the ultimate nemesis of bourgeois society is no longer politically performative in Marx's story, and it will no longer be the principal stuff that unites one person with another within some kind of revolutionary citizenship. If the working class remains an object of cultural curiosity, it can, at the same time, no longer be regarded as a political subject. What gels people together nowadays is something more and something less than class, something both more complex and simpler, something that doesn't only emerge from the workplace but from a dwelling space—this time "dwelling" in its broadest sense. It isn't something necessarily about living space as about *the totality of political and economic space in which one now belongs*. Once, people went out into the world and discovered it, often through the world of work; now the world comes to people and discovers us, sometimes whether we like it or not. Nowadays, if people identify with other people it is because of something else shared, because of something that cements us together and bonds us across frontiers and barriers. I'm not sure the world of work is where this bonding takes place for a lot of people. Is it, then, an urban-consciousness rather than a class-consciousness that bonds? Yes and no. It is affinity that bonds, and the urban is the site though which this affinity takes place: a staging, to be sure, but not a passive staging when the curtain goes up and the play actually commences. The urban somehow helps affinity grow and helps it become aware of itself, aware that other affinities exist in the world, that affinities can encounter one another and become aware of one another in a social network connected by a certain tissuing, by a spider's webbing, by a planetary webbing.

In the 1970s, around the time of Lefebvre's *The Production of Space*, Murray Bookchin's *Post-Scarcity Anarchism* argued that the affinity group "could easily be regarded as a new type of extended family, in which kinship ties are replaced by deeply empathetic human relationships—relationships nourished by common revolutionary ideas and practice." These groups, says Bookchin, "proliferate on a molecular level and have their own 'Brownian movement.'"[13] Affinity groups don't assume the role of a vanguard, Bookchin reckons, but function as *catalysts* within a popular movement. They provide initiative and consciousness, not leadership and dictatorship. They offer sensitive appreciation of solidarity within everyday behavior. There is no bureaucratic fiat from a distant party committee room but a looser, autonomous hanging together of participants, adaptive to changing political and social circumstances. In affinity group encounters, "class" perhaps evokes something meaningful only in the context of *class-conscious* ruling elite. Those who don't rule, the bulk of us, are an assorted and fragmented layering of disparate peoples who are neither conscious of class nor motivated to act in the name of any class. Nonetheless, these people, which is to say "us," *are* often motivated by a desire to act against a ruling class, to take action against an undemocratic system that this class so evidently props up. We who encounter one another, who find affinity with one another, aren't so much class-conscious as *collectively conscious of an enemy*, collectively conscious of a desire to do something about that enemy, and collectively conscious about wanting no truck with that enemy's game.

This is a different tack to Marx's in the *Communist Manifesto*. There, Marx spoke of the "modern working class," a group, Marshall Berman points out, "that has always been afflicted with a case of mistaken identity." "Many of Marx's readers," Berman says, "have always thought that 'working class' meant only men in boots—in factories, in industry, with blue collars, with calloused hands, lean and hungry. These readers then note the changing nature of the workforce: increasingly white-collar, working in human services . . . and they infer the Death of the Subject, and conclude that the working class is disappearing and all hopes for it are doomed. Marx did not think the working class was shrinking: in all industrial countries it was already, or in the process of becoming, 'the immense majority.'"[14] The basis for Marx's political arithmetic is a logic that's rather simple: the modern working class "is a class of laborers who live only so long as they find work, and who find work only so long as their labor increases capital. These workers, who must sell themselves piecemeal, are commodities, like every other article of commerce, and are constantly exposed to all the vicissitudes of competition and the fluctuations of the market." The crucial factor isn't working in a factory, or with your hands; neither is it necessarily anything to do with being poor. Rather, the crucial reality is, Berman says (11), a "need to sell your labor in order to live, to carve up your personality for sale, to look at yourself in the mirror and think, 'Now what have I got that I can sell?'"

One of the great virtues of this definition of the working class is its *inclusiveness*, its flexibility. By this reckoning, when we do the sums, when we tote things up, it seems that this working class isn't just you and me, it's practically everybody else, practically *here comes everybody*. It's a definition that hinges on our relationship to the means of production and to the global system of capital accumulation. Almost all of us have to carve ourselves up, look at ourselves in the mirror, Berman suggests, and ask ourselves how much we're worth. Still, what seems a great conceptual virtue is also its major drawback, its potential failing. If the working class is now pretty much everybody, everywhere, then, like the city itself, it is at the same time pretty much nowhere, now bursting its seams as something formless. And if the working class is now everybody, its definition serves no analytical or political function anymore; it no longer has any identifiable specificity within itself or any kind of object yearning to be a subject. In other words, the concept serves no strategic purpose, has no organizing pull, because we are no longer sure around what basis it will organize itself. The working class is thus a kind of *lumpenconcept*, setting itself free from its object like Marx's industrial reserve army: it is too loose a notion, too flabby an understanding, to reveal anything meaningful to us, other than we all need to find work to live. This is hardly news.

If anything, what's equally evident is that for millions of the world's population, they know they'll never find work again or even find work for the first time—"No work, no work, no work," said Berger's Sucus. Instead, they have to invent it for themselves, find the means to bend the rules, to work the system for themselves.[15] Others actively disaffiliate themselves from any laboring public as we once knew it; in so doing they create another life form for themselves and for their families and enter the ever-swelling ranks of a constituency André Gorz provocatively labels a "non-class."[16] The latent political muscle that Marx accorded to the working class hasn't disappeared, Gorz says:

> Instead, it has been displaced and has acquired a more radical form in a new social arena. . . . It has the added advantage over Marx's working class of being immediately conscious of itself; its existence is at once indissolubly subjective and objective, collective and individual. This non-class encompasses all those who have been expelled from production by the abolition of work, or whose capacities are under-employed as a result of the industrialization (in this case, the automation and computerization) of intellectual work. It includes all the supernumeraries of present-day social production, who are potentially or actually unemployed, whether permanently or temporar-

ily, partially or completely. It results from the decomposition of the old society based upon the dignity, value, social utility and desirability of work.[17]

Berman himself counters, claiming, "Marx understands that many people in this working class don't know their address. . . . They may not discover who they are, and where they belong, until they are laid-off or fired—or outsourced, or deskilled, or downsized. And other workers, lacking credentials, not dressed so nicely, may not get the fact that many who push them around are really in their class, despite their pretensions, share their vulnerability. How can this reality be put across to people who don't get it, or can't bear it? The complexity of these ideas helped create a new vocation, central to modern society: the *organizer*."[18]

But here again, this idea seems conceived from a past age, from a golden age of labor organizing, a lament from an age when organizing was a *professional* occupation—like a photojournalist, like a newspaper book critic. Is this still the case today? Doesn't organization somehow organize itself, especially when it really matters? A major strength of Shirky's *Here Comes Everybody* is precisely this "do-it-yourself-with others" spirit, this idea that grassroots organizing no longer needs any mediator, no Leninist intellectual to reveal "with sober senses, one's real conditions of life," one's *true* class status. A lot of people already know this. And even if they don't know it, they can still manage to organize themselves—or actually get organized without even consciously knowing it. People create group commonality because of a taking hold of bodies and minds in space, face-to-face through "strong-tie" offline activism but also through online "weak-tie" association. The two flanks strengthen one another, glue the notion of affinity, and give a new dimension to the idea of a group taking hold, of group consummation: *speed*, the speed at which crowds assemble, the speed at which demos take place, the speed at which people of different groups and ages today encounter each other, organize one another.

The emergent Here Comes Everybody, glimmers of which we've recently witnessed in the Occupy movement, is expressive of an affinity politics, of associative ties latent within everyday life. In lots of instances, affinity groups aren't so much concerned with seizing power as having people regain control over their own lives. That's the crux of a desire to be citizens again: to regain control over one's life and to do so in some kind of participatory democracy, one in which we're able to collectively call the shots and somehow able to express ourselves. What bonds one affinity group to another, what compels an affinity group encounter to "take hold"? *Common notions*, we might say, using the term in the Spinozian sense. Affinity group unity won't likely be founded on some simple class-consciousness, nor even on any particular place-consciousness (like a right to the city); instead, it will be founded on notions that Spinoza says are *common* to us when we piece together a certain way of seeing our lives vis-à-vis others' lives, or when we see ourselves in relationship with other people along the same horizon; our circumstances are really their circumstances. We share those circumstances; it is *our* common circumstance of life on earth; our "I" becomes equally a "non-I," an every "I," an every*body*.

VI. The Global "Family of Eyes"

Murray Bookchin's ideas about affinity still retain considerable analytical force, but his vision of citizenship and idea that rampant urbanization is destroying cherished citification seem backward-looking and politically *passé*. His own accusation that ossified classical Marxism draws its inspiration from the past comes back to haunt Bookchin himself. Bookchin says affinity groups are always rooted in the popular movement, which seems bang-on; however, he says that *localism* grounds affinity groups, that affinity is gelled by face-to-face interaction, by the power of localized autonomy. This was said pre-Internet and pre–digital media. Bookchin's common notions of affinity consequently strikes as nostalgic; and his quest for a common citizenship sounds a lot like a search for lost time and space, for the romanticism of *authentic* encounter, when authenticity meant unmediated encounter, unmediated social relations, being present and only present, a presence without absence. Bookchin couldn't have seen how, one day—our day—absence and presence would actually go together, form a powerful unity of expression, and voice a program here as well as there, simultaneously as wave and particle. Ironically, nostalgia itself is a way not to be present in the present: because rather than yearning for an absent future, one immanent within the present, nostalgia yearns for an absent past that's long gone.

"We have lost sight," says Bookchin in *From Urbanization to Cities*, "of the historic source and principal arena of any authentic politics—the city. We not only confuse urbanization with citification, but we have literally dropped the city out of the history of ideas—both in terms of the way it explains the present human condition and the systems of public governance it creates."[19] Bookchin's lament is a return to cities, to citification, in the face of pathological urbanization; urbanization, he says, is somehow *against* cities. The process has devoured the product, and Bookchin wants that old product *back*. Moreover, this product, if refound, if reclaimed, can even act as a buttress against the process, can keep it at bay, dam its inexorable tide—if only the walls of the citadel are tall and thick enough, and if only they can be reconstructed at some larger, regional scale. Bookchin's penchant is Hellenic: Aristotle's polis is the free city, the Paris Commune, a confederation of neighborhood assemblies, stretched out regionally, revolving around an agora, a vibrant civic center. There, weekly participatory meetings would debate planning and administrative issues, do so without unwieldy bureaucracies, "in a consciously amateur system of governance." All of which would be "face-to-face democracy of the most radical kind."[20]

"A consciously amateur system of governance" is intriguing; but to frame it around an entity called "the city" seems altogether wrong. To expect futuristic modes of life to be face-to-face and nothing but is ludicrous in the extreme, more utopian than any Asimovian science fiction. Back in the mid-1980s, Bookchin didn't use the term "resilience" à la mode of certain urban planning and architectural circles today; but his program nonetheless strikes as such. Roger Keil, a geographer and urbanist from Toronto, recently critiqued resilience and what he says there seems equally true against Bookchin: "This use of resilience implies the emphasis on regionally defined socio-spatial relations as the basis for resilience against the uprooting and de-centering effects of larger scale processes of restructuring and change. Yet, instead of building defensive bulwarks against globalization and its implied disturbances, resilience must be about sustaining open and creative relationships of humans amongst one another."[21] Bookchin's desire is to keep centrality at the absolute center, to *confine* the polis to a village-like milieu, to affirm closure and enclosure. Yet this is to shy away from the trials and tribulations of planetary urbanization. It is to voice political ambition without any real political ambition, without any real engagement with the new reality before us, *within* the new political landscape opening up around us, quite literally, which is stretching our horizons laterally and letting us grow worldwide. Why close it down? Why look backward? Why break the big down into little bits?

Bookchin pits the urbanization of sprawl against the compactness of the polis. But, as Keil notes, "the reality of today's urban world offers a more differentiated landscape than the one suggested in the typical, caricatured, and widely used dichotomy of sprawl and compactness," of urbanization versus citification:

> The everyday lives we live in this complex landscape straddle the sustainable and the unsustainable all the time. What and who my communities are during one day and how they need to be sustained changes continuously. In order to find my way through the maze of relationships, I need to start where I am and not in an

imaginary place that is either reviled (like sprawl) or celebrated (like the compact city). . . . Ultimately, life in the expanding urban fringe is now the reality in which strategies of sustainability are being negotiated. If we are moving away from the condemnation of sprawl and accepting its reality as a discursive plane on which negotiation over our future will have to take place, we are forced to [think and] act differently.[22]

For Bookchin, the urban megalopolis isn't human-scale, nor is it a controllable or viable form of city life. Perhaps the loaded words here aren't "controllable" or "viable" at all, but "city life"? It is this term that needs reframing: life is city-based, and the city should be an unmediated life-form, place-bound. Reconciling personal life with city life around *only* locality is to truncate individuality, is to abandon the complexities and possibilities of nonplace technological and social life, is to delimit the broad and wide-ranging social networks people can and do actually have each and every day. Manuel Castells has offered his own, surprisingly anarchistic vision of a network society, a corrective to and "rehashing" (#) of Bookchin's: "Technology turns out to be anarchism's ally more so than Marxism's. Instead of large factories and gigantic bureaucracies (socialism's material base), the economy increasingly operates through networks (the material foundation of organizational autonomy). And instead of the nation-state controlling territory, we have city-states managing the interchange between territories. All this is based on the internet, mobile phones, satellites, and informational networks that allow local-global communication and transport at a planetary scale."[23] Global whole or urban-local part? Isn't the former now just the indivisible extension of the latter, its substance?

Just as there was an empowering irony to Parisian nineteenth-century Haussmannization, so, too, is there empowering irony to global neo-Haussmannization in our day. Haussmann's urbanization tore out the heart of old medieval Paris and reinvented the concept of center, of a downtown of bright lights and conspicuous consumption. Center and periphery would change forever. An erstwhile pesky proletariat took to the shovels, manned the building sites, and stopped making trouble. Soon they found themselves dispatched to a rapidly expanding *banlieue*, to the new suburbs mushrooming in the distance, banished from the center they created through their own act of labor. In one sense, Paris gained as an independent work of art, as an aesthetic experience admired to this day by every tourist and visitor. Yet, in another, it lost something as a living democratic organism, as a site of generalized liberty. Hence Haussmann not only patented what we'd now call "gentrification," with its commodification of space. He also pioneered an urban practice, bankrolled by the state, in cahoots with a financial and rentier elite: divide-and-rule gerrymandering through urbanization itself, gutting the city according to a rational economic and political plan. The logic of the city would never be the same again.

Writ large were contradictions. These contradictions would become urban contradictions—nineteenth-century contradictions that have since intensified and diversified into twenty-first-century global-urban contradictions. In *All That Is Solid Melts into Air*, Marshall Berman took Baudelaire under his wing to highlight how Haussmann's infamous *boulevards* prized open a modern form of urban publicity. "The new Parisian boulevard," Berman says, "was the most spectacular innovation of the nineteenth-century, and the decisive breakthrough in the modernization of the traditional city."[24] The boulevards, of course, wreaked devastating destruction, smashed through whole neighborhoods that had lived and evolved, tightly knitted, for centuries. Now, though, for the first time in history, these broad and long boulevards had opened up the whole city to its inhabitants. "Now," writes Berman (151), "after centuries of life as a cluster of isolated cells, Paris was becoming a unified physical and human space."

For Berman, Baudelaire's *Paris Spleen* poem, "The Eyes of the Poor," vividly shows what this new kind of extroverted urbanization can do to private bodies in public space (and to public bodies in private space). Two young lovers sit near the window of a dazzling new café, lining one of Haussmann's newly minted boulevards. They dreamily look at each other. They're inside, sharing one another's company, admiring one another, yet they're able to survey through the window the gaiety outside, the street activity, the delightful bustle of *la nouvelle vie parisienne*. After a while, a ragged homeless family passes by. Enamored by the café's garish opulence, they stop. They peer in; the kids press their noses against the gleaming windowpane, admiring the decor and people inside. "How beautiful it is!" Baudelaire has his ragpickers explain. "How beautiful it is!" But they know it's not for them, not for their type. Yet their fascination, Berman says (149), "carries no hostile undertones; their vision of the gulf between the two worlds is sorrowful, not militant, not resentful but resigned." (Collective resentment would culminate a decade or so later.) The male lover is touched by "this family of eyes" outside; he feels a strange kinship with them, a strange affinity, despite the social distance. But his lover is unmoved; she wants the patron to shoo them away, to move them on, somewhere else, anywhere so long as it's out of *her* sight. "These people with their great saucer eyes," Baudelaire has her declaim, "are unbearable!" At that moment the two lovers love each other a little less.

Haussmann's urban reality is romantic and magical; private joys sprung from wide-open public spaces. One can henceforth be private in the crowd, alone yet amid people; one can be inside while outside, outside while inside. There are walls *and* there is transparency. There is social closure *and* physical openness. There is public invisibility *and* private visibility. Berman says that Baudelaire's "Eyes of the Poor" poem evokes a "primal scene," a primal scene "that reveals some of the deepest ironies and contradictions" of modern capitalist urbanization (149–150). It's the "and" that expresses the duplicity; the coexistence between apparently contradictory realities isn't a "but" but an "and." They go together, inextricably. For Berman, the setting that now "makes all urban humanity a great extended 'family of eyes' also brings forth the discarded stepchildren of that family. The physical and social transformations that drove the poor out of sight now bring them back directly into everyone's line of vision. Haussmann, in tearing down the old medieval slums, inadvertently broke down the self-enclosed and hermetically sealed world of traditional urban poverty. The boulevards, blasting great holes through the poorest neighborhoods, enable the poor to walk through the holes and out of their ravaged neighborhoods, to discover for the first time what the rest of their city and the rest of life are like."[25] They are but one step away from asserting themselves as citizens, citizens of a wider universe, citizens expressing adequate ideas about all kinds of common notions they're now capable of developing.

Haussmannization and its neo-Haussmannization counterpart share a historical and geographical lineage. But the primal scene of its progeny needs updating and upgrading; now it involves superstructural software as well as infrastructural hardware. Those boulevards still flow with people and traffic, even if the boulevard is now reincarnated in the highway, and that highway is more often at a standstill, gridlocked and log-jammed at every hour. The significant change is how today's Grands Boulevards flow with energy and finance, with information and communication; they are frequently fiber-optic and digitalized, ripping through cyberspace as well as physical space. Neo-Haussmannization is now a global-urban strategy that has peripheralized millions of people everywhere; Baron Haussmann's spade work pales alongside it. Neo-Haussmannization has peripheralized so many people, in fact, that it makes no sense anymore to talk about these peoples being peripheral. As cities have exploded into megacities, and as urban centers—even in the poorest countries—have gotten decentered, gotten glitzy and internationalized, "Bonapartism" projects its urban tradition onto twenty-first-century planetary space. The "family of eyes" has gone global. Those "great saucer eyes" are media eyes, all seeing, and, with the Internet and WikiLeaks, often all-knowing too. People can now see the global elite along this planetary information and communication boulevard, see them through the windowpanes of postmodern global-urban life; people can see them and their own reflections as though they were an immense reservoir of electrical energy. We might even say that a global family of eyes now truly *encounters* itself as a family, as an emerging citizenry, as an affinity group that yearns to repossess what has been dispossessed. Their big saucer eyes now look on with indignation, in the public realm, doing so with animosity as well as awe. Now, there's not so much a world to win as a whole world to occupy. A whole world that's really people's own backyard.

CHAPTER FOUR

The Politics of the Encounter

Everything is formed out of connections, densities, shocks, encounters, concurrences, and motions.
Lucretius

What matters about this conception is less the elaboration of laws, hence of an essence, than the aleatory character of the "taking-hold" of the encounter, which gives rise to an accomplished fact whose laws it is possible to state.
Louis Althusser

You can pull up the flowers, but you can't stop the spring.
Rebecca Solnit

I. Taking Hold by Surprise

Some of the best and profoundest lines ever written about "the encounter" are Louis Althusser's, done in the 1980s, during the final, troubled decade of his life. At first blush, these "later writings" seem to be a direct refutation of his earlier, famous (and infamous) structural Marxism of the 1960s, brilliantly voiced in texts like *For Marx* and *Reading Capital*; they seem to express Althusser's own epistemological break, with a hyperdialectical Marxism getting replaced by a more metaphysical, nondialectical one. Now, "overdetermination" translates into a strange, chancy, almost-divine undercurrent that haunts both conscious and unconscious processes of life and politics. But Althusser would likely beg to differ: In those great early books, he'd doubtless contest, a nonteleological Marxism was consistently affirmed, a social theory and philosophy that saw Spinoza rather than Hegel as the true precursor of Marx; already here was a Marxism not so much about fixed laws as laws of *tendencies*, a Marxism not about essences but about possibilities that *depend*, that have neither definitive beginnings nor ends; things happen contingently, stuff comes together, collides and colludes by surprise, doing so because of a readiness to interlock.

Althusser would be quick to acknowledge, too, how the "encounter" features in "untold passages" in Marx, in his mature oeuvre—in the first volume of *Capital*'s "Working Day" chapter and in the "theory of the transition" from feudalism to capitalism, best articulated in "The Secret of Primitive Accumulation." Marx, says Althusser, "explains that the capitalist mode of production arose from the '*encounter*' between 'the owners of money' and 'proletarians stripped of everything but their labor-power.'" "It so happens that this encounter took place, 'took hold,' which means that it did not come undone as soon as it came about, but *lasted*."[1] History takes hold because of encounters between immanent objective forces—resultant of past, contingent encounters that somehow lasted—*and* a subjective reality that is even more uncertain and unpredictable. Actions come without guarantees; potential outcomes can never be foreseen in advance. It is at particular moments or conjunctures when and where forces connect; when and where they come into collusion and collision with one another; when and where they take shape, take hold, take off, transmogrify into something historically and geographically *new*. Such is the mark of the non-teleology of the process, the brilliant and slippery logic of Althusser's "aleatory materialism." No speculative philosophy this; it has nothing to do with an "idealism of freedom" since it is deeply, ontologically, materialist: materialism's repressed tradition, in fact, a hint of the existence of human freedom in the world of necessity, of possibility buried within the plane of immanence.

If anything has changed from the 1960s, it is perhaps that these "later writings" wax much more lyrically and poetically. Althusser is a lot more figurative and allegorical than he ever was; he shows rather than explicitly tells, gives us form without any content, contingency without contextuality. There is no better illustration of Althusser's poetry than his beautiful beginning, the opening lines to "The Underground Current of the Materialism of the Encounter," destined a book but only materializing as nineteen-odd pages of longhand script. "It is raining," says Althusser, on another dreary Parisian day. "Let this book therefore be, before all else, a book about ordinary rain."[2] But this ordinary rain is equally a profound rain, the rain of Lucretius's atoms falling parallel to one another, the rain of the parallelism of Spinoza's infinite attributes, the rain that reveals the whole history of philosophy, of the universe, of life on Earth. Ordinary, wonderful rain, raining down, providential and antiprovidential rain. The rain of life pitter-patters down into the "void" of prehistory, before the beginning of time and space. Steadily it falls, raining atoms—"the dance of atoms," Lucretius calls it in *The Nature of Things* (circa 50 B.C.).

Everything falls, atoms in parallel with one another. They fall, unconnected from one another, blind to one another, restricted from one another. They fall,

fall until *they swerve*; something intervenes, something contingent breaks the parallelism, an "infinitesimal swerve," Althusser says, the "*clinamen*," so small that it is hardly noticeable.[3] And yet, it alters the whole course of history, creates time and space, because in an almost negligible way the swerve induces the encounter. One atom of the rain encounters other atoms; vertically falling rain criss-crosses with other drops of falling rain; they connect and rain into one another, strike one another, encounter one another, pile up with one another. Suddenly, somehow, there's an agglomeration of raindrops, of rain atoms, and a chain reaction is unleashed: the birth of something new, a new interconnection, a new reality due to the swerve. Atoms rain as bodies falling through "empty space," Lucretius says, "straight down, under their own weight, at a random time and place, / *They swerve a little*. Just enough of a swerve for you to call / It a change of course."[4] From this, Althusser qualifies, "it is clear that the encounter creates nothing of the reality of the world, which is nothing but agglomerated atoms, but *that it confers their reality upon the atoms themselves*, which, without swerve and encounter, would be nothing but agglomerated *abstract* elements, lacking all consistency and existence. So much so that we can say that the *atoms' very existence is due to nothing but the swerve and the encounter* prior to which they led only a phantom existence."[5]

The encounter is thereby "the accomplishment of the fact," a pure effect of contingency. Before the accomplishment of this fact, Althusser ironizes, "there is only the *non-accomplishment of the fact*, a non-world of *unreal* existence." The thesis, meanwhile, expresses the primacy of positivity over negativity, of Spinoza over Hegel, of a dialectical reason of sorts. But it is one that negates itself, negates all teleology of End; it's a process that has no divine master plan nor even a subject as such, only a collectivity of comings together, of sheer *co-presences* defining their own singular object, the becoming-objective of the world, the creation of objectivity itself. Althusser's Parisian rain thus moistens the world and whets (wets) the appetite of history, structuring its outcome, structuring its structure. His words, like my own here, are abstract, the concepts metaphysical; but it is perhaps not hard to glimpse, as we'll soon glimpse, how the encounter of the natural order contains the germ of the maturation of the encounter of the political and urban order.

What is encountered are elements that have an *affinity* and *complementarity*; those elements that encounter one another express a readiness to collide-interlock, taking hold like water becoming ice, like mayonnaise emulsifying, like milk curdling. Things take hold, are taken hold (*sur-prise* in French), by *surprise*. "Every encounter is aleatory," says Althusser, "not in its origins (nothing ever guarantees an encounter), but in its effects. In other words, every encounter might not have taken place, although it did take place."[6] The world of history gels at certain felicitous moments; ordinary rain becomes supernatural rain, rain that dampens everyday life, rain that encounters sunshine, takes hold radiantly, takes us in and sometimes over the rainbow. "This is what strikes everyone so forcefully during great commencements, during turns of history, whether individual or of the world, when the dice are, as it were, thrown back on the table unexpectedly, or the cards are dealt out again without warning, or the elements are unloosened in the fit of madness that frees them up for new, surprising ways of taking hold."[7]

II. Encountering the Urban, Urban Encounters

Atoms rain ordinary urban rain, elements that have encountered one another because of the swerve, induced by encounters created by prior swerves, those that created, and go on creating, new densities of connections and "combinations" (Marx's words), ripe for further swerves. The *clinamen* strikes, rains rain so hard on the old order, on the old city, that the swerve has created a new world urban order, the plane of immanence for new encounters, for a newer aleatory materialism of bodies encountering other bodies in public. Things here encounter each other *within and through urban space*; the urban confers the reality of the encounter, of the political encounter, and of the possibility for more encounters.

At the beginning of *The Urban Revolution*, Lefebvre plots his own encounter theory of transition—transition not from feudalism to capitalism, nor even from capitalism to socialism, but the passage from the city to urban society. (True enough, the passage from capitalism to socialism is, for Lefebvre, *implicit* and *incubated* in this city-urban shift.) He illustrates the city-urban movement in a little diagram (15), even if in reality the transition from city form to urban society was never linear, never a simple rupture from one reign to another; instead, it was a combination of elements that over time and through space became ready and ripe to encounter one another, elements such as market expansion and penetration, market crises, technological change, demographic growth, political and social struggle, violence and disorder, all culminating at a particular point to create something quantitatively and qualitatively new and different. They combined and took hold in the city to create a swerve that gave birth to urban society, much the same way as Althusser and Balibar chart the transition from feudalism to capitalism: as contingent encounters of diverse and often disparate elements encountering each other. The urban was born in the succession from agrarian society to the industrial city, from one encountering the other, from the latter transforming into urban society. There are, Lefebvre explains, "no 'ruptures' as contemporary epistemology understands the term." There are only "simultaneities, interactions, or inequalities of development through which these moments (these 'contingents') can coexist."[8]

So within the urban, within its plane of capitalist immanence, we encounter an assembly of objects, an assembly of people and activity, a virtual object that creates a real and prospective site for sustained and newer, superimposed encounters, for fresh combining and assembly, for a gathering of essential elements of social practice. The urban becomes the site as well as the nemesis of the encounter, its positive, unifying capacity as well as its negative charge, its demonic power of separation and dissociation with disintegrated and lonely, rather than loaded, crowds. One part of the urban is where social unification and social integration encounter one another, and they do so with a positive, dynamic energy, with a creative lifeblood of attraction and incorporation; rain falls until the swerve makes the atoms assemble and reassemble into forms that enable us to collectively see and act. Yet another part of the urban contains negative energy, in the form of repulsion, a minus charge generating a dialectical force field in which centers forever oppose peripheries and vertical rain falls forever vertically, without ever swerving, without ever breaking the eternal void. Atoms fall separately and are separated.

For good reason are *separation* and *segregation* social realities that Lefebvre hates. They're the enemy of urbanization, he says, "the enemy of assemblies and encounters," profoundly anti-urban impulses, enemies of what his own potted definition of "the urban" is: assembly in space, encounters in space, a dense and differential social space. Separation "breaks the unifying power of urban form."[9] But the contradictory form of the urban is, of course, that it is essentially formless because urbanization tends to break any limits that try to circumscribe its own form. It's like trying to know, with certainty, both the movement and the position of a subatomic particle, both its wave and particle characteristics—the paradox between process and product, between movement and outcome, between urbanization and the urban, how it rains, when it might swerve. Still, we know that there is a form of sorts to the urban—even if that form is empty in itself, a void: it is always *relative* form, floating form, contingent and uncertain form, only becoming real, only beginning to define itself ontologically when the urban is filled by a certain notion of proximity, by people and activity, by events coming together in this proximity, through the swerve, through the creation of concentration and simultaneity, density and intensity. The urban, we might say, is the place of the drama resultant from the encounter *and* the site where we encounter the drama of the encounter itself. The urban has order and disorder encounter one another; the urban both enables and thwarts, promotes encounters and abolishes encounters. Nowadays, it is the product and place of online and offline encounters, the social network in which these two realities swerve into one another. Can segregation, the enemy of the encounter, arrest the movement toward democracy? "Can revolutionary upheaval," Lefebvre asks, "break the boundaries of urban reality?" "Sometimes," he says, "it can."[10]

III. Occupation as Encounter

We have seen recently how the boundaries, if not broken, at least have been tested; encounters have dramatized the streets of our current planetary urban order, profiting, as it were, from this planetary order, enlarging even this planetary order. Our perspective and our prospective have been stretched, opened out after so many decades of closure. We've glimpsed a little of the *clinamen*, the swerve, effect on our streets. We've seen encounters unfold in the "heart" of "the city," yet the stakes of organization and protest aren't about the city per se; rather, they are something about democracy, something vaster and simpler than the city as we once knew it, an ensemble of bodies, hastened together by digital media. One instance of a politics of radical encounter began on September 17, 2011, when a handful of dogged activists ventured to the center of America's financial universe, justifiably griping about growing income inequality and the stranglehold of big money and big corporations over U.S. democracy. The turnout was small and its impact initially disappointing. But within a month, amazingly, a social movement was taking hold and gathering strength and numbers; over the following two months, they'd be joined by thousands of supporters, who put up tents and built a makeshift library, field hospital, canteen, and department of sanitation. Suddenly, too, the protest captured the popular imagination, not only of ordinary Americans but also of ordinary, disaffected people worldwide. The Occupy Wall Street movement was born.

Encamped in Lower Manhattan's Zuccotti Park, thousands of demonstrators began organizing their spontaneity themselves, without either organizations or leaders. Mobilizing favorable public opinion, soon an online global "conversation" grew at the same time as offline street protests, inspired by "Arab Spring" uprisings in Tunisia and Egypt, took place across the planet. These events happened not only in New York but also in Los Angeles, Oakland, Boston, Phoenix, Madrid, Rome, Stockholm, Lisbon, Sarajevo, Tel Aviv, Hong Kong, Berlin, Athens, Vancouver, and Sydney (the list is in no way exhaustive). In London, in mid-October 2011, two thousand people assembled in front of St. Paul's Cathedral and were addressed by WikiLeaks founder Julian Assange. Demonstrators likewise decided to stay put in tents, well over a hundred of them, and began constructing an alternative radical lifeworld for themselves (#OCCUPY LSX), with an information center, library, meeting space, canteen, and a group of tents patched together where people met, spoke, and debated strategy and ideas—the so-called Tent City University. Occupiers duly threatened the City of London as well as the Church of England (St. Paul's Canon Chancellor, Giles Fraser, a sympathizer of the activism, quit when church bigwigs announced it wanted to oust occupiers on "health and safety" grounds). "The current system is unsustainable," ran Occupy LSX's Initial Statement. "It is undemocratic and unjust. We need alternatives; this is where we work towards them." Celebratory intellectuals like David Harvey and Manuel Castells passed through, offering encouragement and solidarity, inspiring huge crowds when they spoke, and, in turn, getting inspired by huge crowds when they spoke. This was impassioned soapbox oratory at its best, a genuine dialogue of the discontent and disaffected.

Demonstrators everywhere have shown to the world that masses of people—old and young alike—share the same sense of frustration and rage. Participants simultaneously acted and reacted, have been both affected and affecting; joy and celebration, tenderness and abandon, online and offline activism all have found structuring and definition. "The beauty of this formula," went an Occupy Wall Street statement, "and what makes this novel tactic exciting, is its pragmatic simplicity. We talk to each other in various physical gatherings and through virtual people's assemblies . . . we zero in on what awakens the imagination and, if achieved, would propel us toward the radical democracy of the future."

With the emergence of this global movement, at last, there's something leftists can write home about, something to celebrate, salute, support. Everybody can henceforth don the "occupier mask" themselves, join in, grin that mischievous and devilish Guy Fawkes grin and affirm our own phantom-faced defiance of big money and big business. Enough is enough: "V" is for Vengeance. And, along the way, *Indignados* discovered their own numbers: "We-are-the-99-Percent!" Demonstrators adopted the Guy Fawkes mask to conceal their faces and remain anonymous on the street, in front of the cops. But behind the mask, behind the disguise, behind that anonymity, demonstrators have discovered and expressed their true identities.

The idea for the mask came from the flamboyant revolutionary hero of David Lloyd and Alan Moore's graphic novel *V for Vendetta*, set in a futuristic dystopian Britain. The chivalrous, avenging masked adventurer, himself inspired by Edmond Dantès (a.k.a. the Count of Monte Cristo), later made it to Hollywood, in a 2006 film directed by James McTeigue, starring Natalie Portman and Hugo Weaving. In its wake, the mask, patented by Warner Brothers, became readily available in comic book shops everywhere, at 10 bucks a pop: "The mask. The masquerade. . . . Almost white this mask, with something of a debonair and Harlequin look, the cheeks a little rouged, the lower lip a little pink, the eyes a little more than slits that seemed to smile at times, at other times to squint, yet always having something of the vulpine. The ebony-painted goatee, the inky-black mustachios forever curling upward at the ends. The smile forever fixed."[11] "The truth is," V told every TV watcher in futuristic London, "there is something very wrong with this country, isn't there." He was there to remind the world "that fairness, justice, and freedom are more than words. They are *perspectives*." "People should not be afraid of their government," he went on. "Governments should be afraid of their people."[12]

The July 2011 issue of *Adbusters*, the Vancouver-based anarchist magazine, ran a poster of a little ballerina atop the Charging Wall Street Bull. Below it, there was a Twitter hashtag, backgrounded by gas-masked insurgents breaking through a fog of tear gas, and the following caption: "WHAT IS OUR DEMAND? #OCCUPYWALLSTREET. SEPTEMBER 17TH. BRING TENT." September 17th is the birthday of the mother of Kalle Lasn, *Adbusters'* sixty-nine-year-old editor, a day worth celebrating. "The left had been chattering on about revolution for a long time," said Lasn, "but we've basically been howling to the moon. And then, all of a sudden, a bunch of young people in Egypt using social media were able to mobilize not just 500 or 5,000 people, but 50,000 people. They inspired us with their courage and with their techniques." "America needs its own Tahrir," thought Lasn.[13] If you tweet it, they'll come, experience from the Arab Spring suggested. And come they did, all over the street, and all over the world. It was an announcement full of the same menace, the same gravity, and the same sense of ominous vengeance as V's hijacked air-call to take down the Houses of Parliament on November 5, picking up the pieces from where the other Guy Fawkes left off centuries earlier.

It sort of began in December 2010, the *clinamen*, ushering in the encounter, taking hold, swerving, by *surprise*, just a little. The vertical rain of autocratic rule had been soaking Tunisia for years. Dictatorship gripped and brutalized common citizens like the twenty-six-year-old street vendor Mohamed Bouazizi from Sidi Bouzid, a nondescript town 125 miles south of Tunis. For years police routinely harassed Bouazizi, fining him, confiscating the wares he peddled from his cart, making him jump through bureaucratic hoops. On December 17, a female cop confiscated his balance scale and apparently slapped him about. He marched to the municipal HQ; but, as ever, his complaint was fobbed off. Outside the building's gates, Bouazizi set himself ablaze; paint thinner and a match did the trick. His flaming body was the trigger for mass mobilization, unfolding in the capital Tunis. By January 2011 a mass uprising was in the offing. Word quickly went out over the Internet and on Facebook and You Tube. Soon protests spread across to Egypt, to Mubarak's fraudulent and corrupt government, where twenty-eight-year-old Khaled Said, accused of hacking a drug-dealing police officer's cellphone, was arrested and beaten to death in a cell. Another swerve. Over Facebook boomed the cry, "We are all Khaled Said." A "day of rage" took place on January 25, 2011, in Tahrir Square, whose eventual scope and scale amazed everybody. Muslim Brothers, Christians, and feminists all clasped hands; Tahrir Square was unofficially occupied by the people. Mubarak would be forced to step down.

By late spring, the offensive had spilled over to Europe, in a strange, contingent, unrelated/related chain-reaction, upping the ante from political dictatorship to economic dictatorship. The rains were still raining but they were also swerving now, a lot. On May 15, 2011 several hundred thousand people piled into Madrid's central square, Puerta del Sol, including the unemployed, subemployed, and smart young people whose prospects for ever working looked grim. The lack of opportunities, austerity fears, and frustrations with what politicians were doing (and not doing) in a meltdown economy made people mad as hell, indeed, *outraged*: *Los Indignados*. Encounters were going viral. Ten days on again, the contagion spread to Greece, amid its Eurozone crisis and devastating structural adjustment programs to please European central bankers; encampments multiplied in Syntagma Square, in the shadow of Parliament. Protests turned violent. In the second week of demos, half-a-million Greeks flocked into the nation's principal urban space. "Yes, we can!" went their collective chant.

When September 17, 2011 finally came around, demonstrators gathered by the Charging Bull at Bowling Green, a few blocks south of Wall Street. The initial plan had been to hold a "General Assembly" at Chase Manhattan Plaza. But the plaza had been fenced off by the police the previous night. A snap decision called for a different tactic. Option two: head for Zuccotti Park, a couple of blocks further north, up Broadway. The small, obscure park, barely a couple of acres, was formerly known as "Liberty Plaza," and its nominal as well as de facto reclamation wasn't lost on occupiers. Since 2006 the park had been privately owned by Brookfield Office Properties, fronted by a certain John Zuccotti. In a quirky legal technicality, the fact that the park was privately owned meant it had no explicit closing hours (like Central Park and Union Square), so protesters couldn't be legally evicted, not immediately anyway. All New York officials were able to nail occupiers for was noise menace, especially using amplified sound without a permit. To circumvent this, "the people's microphone" came into its own, avoiding bullhorn amplification and instead relying on word of mouth—quite literally—to spread the message. Everyone within earshot simply repeated what was passed on, repeating where and when things were happening in the park.

With these events, Zuccotti Park began to define its own concept of urban centrality, shaping the trajectory, the swerving, of Manhattan and world radical politics. Its centrality wasn't the way Lefebvre once defined centrality in *The Right to the City*, as an absolute center of a city that was being taken back, like the Communards reclaiming central Paris, with a hammer blow to a specific site and then barricading that reclaimed site defensively. Instead, it's not so much occupying a center as creating a *node*, a node that represents a fusion of people and the overlapping of encounters, a critical force inside that diffuses and radiates outward—rain that creates its own tidal wave. Thus centrality at Zuccotti Park represented the culmination of encounters, a new capacity for concentration, a tipping point, mediated by social media, which helped marginality center itself and helped it do so *horizontally*. After a short while, sister occupations appeared all over America, all over the world, in big and small urban areas, in and through urban space everywhere, assembling crowds, calling General Assemblies, combining action with ideas, or rather action with more than ideas: action with *perspectives*, whose meme has become #OCCUPY EVERYWHERE. The encounter had prompted a movement, and this movement remains in motion to this day. Swerving rain. Rain awaiting the next monsoon season.

IV. Here Comes Everybuddy

Occupation as encounter, encounter as occupation, isn't a Hippie thing; it isn't like 1968. It would be a mistake to draw too many historical parallels other than the observation that both movements drummed drums and sang joyous songs. Forget 1968: what we've had since September 2011 is something radically new and different, something fresher, more futuristic, and complexly electric rather than simply acoustic. The greatest difference forty-odd years on is *social media*: that changes everything; all bets are now off and, indeed, all bets are very much now on. Social media changes the *tactics*, the *tempo*, and the *terrain* of any activism—the three Ts. There's very little here that resembles the student and antiwar movement of the 1960s. True, the protagonists are likewise young and invariably educated, sometimes supereducated; almost everywhere, from the Middle East to the Midwest, protesters are disproportionately young people who hail from the privileged rungs of society. And yet, for these privileged college-educated kids, an upending economy shows no signs of letting them benefit from any rosy capitalistic future. There are few spoils to anticipate in their thirties. Privileges have run dry, except for the 1 percent. For all the antiwar fervor from the 1960s, none of the young then ever doubted their rights to help themselves to the whole consumerist bit; a degree would assure a job, a good job, later on. Not anymore. Today's young activists form a loose coterie of "youth-interrupted," the careerless, prospectless, assetless generation—the NINJA generation.

Tent-pitching tweeters tend to be in their twenties, still servicing college loans, and they are prompted to act by a sense of betrayal. They're sobering up fast, knowing they can no longer have any expectations, that the reality of the *now* merits no expectations. As *New York Times* columnist James Carroll explained, the phenomenon is planetary, spawning a burgeoning set of multilingual neologisms to describe this social positionality and downward mobility. In Japan, says Carroll, comes "freeters," still freeloading off their parents; in the United Kingdom, there's the "neets," meaning "not in education, employment, or training." In Spain, they are called "ni-ni," neither workers nor students; in Germany, we have "nesthockers," or nest-squatters; in Italy, "bamboccioni," grown-up babies. All remain in post-studentdom, neither student nor adult, a state of suspended "waithood."[14] But their protests suggest they're not willing to continue to wait. They've been pushed over the edge: whatever they were waiting for is no more worth the wait.

What they've voiced is a broadly anticapitalist agenda expressing indignation with the system; they indict reckless financial speculation, unaccountable bankers, corporate tax dodging, and corporate welfare. They see nothing worthwhile in traditional party political machines, either, and are almost as leery of crony unionism. Scant attention is paid to old ideological battle lines, to bawling the same old demands in the same old "vertical" manner. Participants gel because of affinity, because of a common identification, because they share and want to express common notions about themselves and about the world. Meanwhile, the gelling takes hold quasi-anarchically. Decisions are made by consensus, within the General Assembly, facilitated through debate and discussion, not via domination. Organization spreads out like a tentacle, like an amorphous web, delicately structured yet robust enough to resist, because this structure is often elusive and difficult to pin down; its power base isn't hierarchical and thus isn't easily identifiable for any enemy. It doesn't rise upward but spreads outward. It absorbs rather than gets smashed. It is pliable rather than cast in stone; it can't be toppled. And if the movement's flowers can be ripped up, its spring won't stop flowing, won't stop raining.

Social media are central for helping all this come into play, for helping the swerving, for helping transform a virtual presence into a physical presence (and vice versa). These social media are key tactical tools. Henceforth, organizations self-organize, affinity networks are hypernetworked. Within every occupation, protesters aren't so much concerned with seizing power, nor are they conscious of belonging to any class. All want to disengage from the market "rationality" of neoliberalism; all want to confront a small minority of the world's population that commandeers global finance and global governance. Citizens in the encounter comprise disparate groups of people who have an uncanny knack of engineering "smart spontaneity," of creating encounters in the heat of the moment and in the heat of the movement. Like bourgeois production they arrange rendezvous *just-in-time*. Twitter and Facebook, mobile phones and sms messaging, Blackberry BBM texting, have all collapsed space and diminished the time of organizing, of rounding up troops or shifting them elsewhere, of supplying reinforcements when and where needed, of dodging heavy police presences. Spontaneous street assembly can be managed and orchestrated as well as media staged. A newly forming, looser alliance of concerned citizens, spanning the globe and dialoguing across borders and barriers, all find a collective lingua franca in an activism that invariably comes home to roost in bites as well as bytes.

In *Here Comes Everybody*, Clay Shirky rightly points out how social media enable groups to punch above their weight, how they mobilize the few while having the significant impact of the many. At the same time, anonymous minorities discover they're not so anonymous and alone as they once thought; others who are like them are out there, too, are everywhere in fact. They are actually an emergent majority, one in the making, one making itself; if not a "Here Comes Everybody" then certainly a "*Here Comes Everybuddy.*" The pun is Joyce's, from *Finnegans Wake*, giving the nod to Facebook addicts everywhere, to the millions upon millions who now cohere as a sort of "mega-underground."[15] What is significant about this mega-underground is that its virtual reality has revealed itself in actual material reality, on the ground somewhere, in the formation of face-to-face groups and crowds of occupiers. Bill Wasik, one of *Wired* magazine's senior editors, recently said this mega-underground comprises "groups of people for whom the rise of Facebook and Twitter has laid bare the disconnect between their real scale and puny extent to which the dominant culture recognizes them. For these groups, suddenly coalescing into a crowd feels like stepping out from the shadows, like forcing society to respect the numbers that they now know themselves to command." "What's really revolutionary about all these gatherings," continues Wasik— "what remains both dangerous and magnificent about them—is the way they represent a disconnected group getting connected, a mega-underground casting off its invisibility to embody itself, formidably, in physical space."[16]

V. Encountering Space, Spaces of Encounter

Such gatherings in physical space, in public space—in forcing space to be public again—shouldn't, however, be confused with a sense of place, with a grounding in the *city*. The tactics of this movement, as well as the tempo of its dynamics, its ebbing and flowing, its crowd coalescence, its just-in-time activism, *create* a new terrain of struggle that is different from the streets of Paris in the 1960s, different from the campus revolts, different from the barricade-building of old. Just as it is silly to think that revolutions are realized online, it is almost as silly to underplay how the strong-tie and weak-tie politics nourish each other; together, they create a new time and space of protest. The temporal aspect is perhaps obvious; the spatial maybe not. Indeed, this new space is a space neither rooted in place nor circulating in space, but rather it is one inseparable combination of the two, an insuperable unity that we might describe as *urban*: an abstraction becoming concrete, the concrete becoming abstract. This unity is simultaneously urban and post-urban, an urban politics that somehow breaks the boundaries of the urban itself, of urbanism going beyond itself. Another way of putting it is to say that the urban is a concept and a reality that is there but no longer present under its own name, no longer visible as its own reality; neither content nor form but rather something *immanent* in the occupation itself. The occupation, in short, expresses *the practice of urban immanence*.

Squares like Tahrir in Cairo or Zuccotti Park in Manhattan are urban public spaces not for reason of their pure concrete physicality but because they are meeting places between virtual and physical worlds, between online and offline conversations, between online and offline encounters. That is why they are public: because they enable public discourses and public conversations to talk to each other, to meet each other, quite literally. They are public not because they are simply there, in the open, in a city center, but because these spaces are made public by people encountering one another in them. We can rename them *spaces of encounter*, spaces in which social absence and social presence attain a *visible* structuration and political coherence. The efficacy of these spaces for any global movement is defined by what is going on both inside and outside, by the here and the there, by what is taking place in them and how this taking place is greeted outside them, by the rest of the world, how it inspires the rest of the world, how it communicates with the rest of the world, how it *becomes* the rest of the world. The relationship can only ever be reciprocal, a dialectic of inside and outside, of here and there, of absence and presence.

The occupation dramatizes the necessarily *expansive* nature of the revolt against capitalism, drawing the outside within itself while enlarging its own sphere of activity, propelling it onto the outside. The all-encompassing dynamic of globalization and planetary urbanization means that the particular can be amplified, magnified, and multiplied as something general. From this standpoint, the question of geography is now tantamount to the question of teleportation, of being here and there at once, or almost at once, of absences as much as presences, of particles and waves expressing their dynamic complementarity. As such, the stake of protest is not strictly the city nor even the urban; yet perhaps, just perhaps, it is something about contemporary planetary *urban society* that enables these protests to be made, that permits and engenders such a definition of protest, a definition in which people collectively can now publicly express themselves, encounter one another and talk to one another, as citizens in front of the whole wide world.

An occupation's centrality, to repeat, doesn't come from its inert physical presence in a central location; occupations have actively staked out centrality. They have *made* those central locations. That's precisely why they can never be evicted, even when they get evicted. You can't evict a revolution. A revolution is a process; a revolution is a *perspective*, which constantly moves on and changes its purview, its ways of seeing and structure of feeling. Its perceptions and horizons are just beginning to be felt and seen, just beginning to encounter each other, reveal themselves to one another, everywhere. Perhaps one of the buzzwords we can glean from Occupy politics is *expression*, that these groups encounter one another to express themselves, to express their affinities and dissatisfactions, their nonverbal desires. These encounters are expressing political ambitions before the means to realize them have been created or invented. One of the things that strikes here is how this *Here Comes Everybuddy* expresses a hitherto unknown and unacknowledged mode of solidarity latent within everyday life, a new form of empathetic human relationship—of *common notions* based on *adequate ideas*.

In his great book on Spinoza, Deleuze claims that every adequate idea is an idea that is *expressive*, expressive of our "active affections." Active affections, says Deleuze, are necessarily joyful, necessarily active, necessarily expressive of an activity that overcomes sadness and passivity. "So if our power of action increases to the point that we come into its full possession," writes Deleuze, "our subsequent affections will necessarily be active joys."[17] Joyful passions lead us closer to the ability to activate our own power, to express our *conatus*, our power to do, to strive and to achieve something in that striving. Deleuze thinks that a central motif of Spinoza's intuitive reason is "the effort to organize encounters in such a way that we are affected by a maximum of joyful passions." Joyful passions occur only because they base themselves on "adequate ideas," and all adequate ideas emerge through notions we understand as agreeing with our body and our mind, with our collective bodies and minds; there is a necessary complementarity between bodily feeling and conceptual understanding. These notions are somehow general to us, common to us, hence *common notions*, the brilliant discovery of Spinoza's *Ethics*, the key item therein. A common notion is something that bonds us biologically and mentally, corporeally as well as cognitively, a bit like the recognition of the 99 percent. This is the recognition that, when all is stripped away (like lonely King Lear on the heath feeling the existential chill), life is no more than this—that in the end, when all is seemingly lost, all is never quite lost because we have one another. We can still express a common understanding, have common ground, hold common notions; we are still able to sleep with one another, body next to body, bodies huddled in tents next to one another, bodies in agreement, bodies sharing naked life. (The other 1 percent, consisting of those who flee the tents, who dress fancily, is still in denial.) Once we enter into the realm of common notions, Deleuze says, we enter into "the domain of *expression*: these notions are our first adequate ideas, they draw us out of the world of inadequate signs,"[18] those we recognize now as a life lived as folly, the inadequate life lived by the dominant few.

The common notions that bond occupants, that have sustained occupiers, that flag out and express collective affinity, that express the reasoned-imagination of young people today, seem to me to be something more than Marxist class-consciousness, something deeper; not expressive of a right or even of any demand but of a looser common desire to live differently, to live together in a system that does things differently, operates differently, produces differently, and, perhaps above all, is controlled differently. What we've seen unfold here is more akin to Spinoza's "second kind of knowledge," to a knowledge organized around the identification of common *relationships*, knowledge that has moved on from a confused, everyday common sense—from a knowledge, as Gramsci told us, that is laden with chaotic, fuzzy conceptions about how we live. Spinoza's second kind of knowledge is more like Gramscian "good sense," a commonality on its way to discovering life's essence.

This is a commonality that isn't afraid of technology; it is one that embraces the future, that still sees a future. In a way, participants know *they are the future*.

It's true, of course, that their common notions express an implicit Marxist voice in that they deny the current logic (and illogic) of capital—of capital accumulation on an expanded scale, of accumulation by dispossession, of a capitalism that bears little similarity to the classic, mild-mannered Smithian market system, with its morally virtuous, well-intending invisible hand. This current system functions on little else apart from brute finagling and rampant corruption, and its only virtue lies in its ability to create monopolies intent on buying off venal politicians (or elevating venal businessmen to politician-hood; even nicer work if you can get it!). It is a system, everybuddy knows, based on asset stripping and commons plundering, on raiding the public coffers through privatization, on corporate fraud, on awarding gigantic bonuses to serial-failure businessmen and bankers, on rolling the dice on the stock market and running off as fast as one can with the booty. It is also a system that has shown little or no commitment to investing in living labor in actual production. And when all collapses, as it inevitably does, antisocialist free-marketeers come running to the state, cap in hand.

Common notions in Spinoza's second-level knowledge "find in the imagination the very conditions of their formation," says Deleuze. The application of these common notions implies "a strange harmony between reason and the imagination," Deleuze says, "between the laws of reason and those of imagination."[19] In this grand scheme of things, imagination develops images of a reality out of which feelings emerge, feelings that somehow get transformed into ideas about feeling, and these ideas absorb feeling and imagination into a clear-sighted, clear-headed concept. Hence it becomes an adequate idea because it attaches itself to a common notion, a reasonable notion, a notion in which imagination and reason encounter one another. The unity emboldens itself to be expressed actively, in action, in an implicitly expressed twenty-first-century urban politics—its debut form in fact.

This is the specter that now looms large, that has now exited the shadows to enter the limelight; no more does it sit behind its PC, tweeting alone. A mega-underground is reshaping the overground, haunting it globally, remaking the very fabric of the urban reality that Lefebvre hinted at forty years ago. The force of this mega-underground still remains latent; it has yet to exert its capacity power, its full numerical capability; it still doesn't punch at its true weight, with all its muscle. It's perhaps that which unnerves the powers-that-be so much, or at least it *should* unnerve them: that latent capability, that contingent possibility that people might still encounter other people, lots of them, millions and millions of them, to form dissenting crowds in urban public space.[20] The urban consolidates, creates, and is created by difference; the urban lets particularity and difference identify its own universality, encounter its own universality, create universal citizens who go on to make the urban public realm and who play out their own common notions in public. There, we arrive at another way of defining the contemporary urban scene: *it lets adequate ideas become common notions in public*, doing so because the urban makes a public and provides a public with a forum for its own collective expression. It realizes virtuality, and it makes virtuality virtually real. It is a mode of expression that owes a lot to new technology, and thus the relationship between a politics of the encounter and urban space is deeply wound up with technology, with new digital media, with the sort of "network society" that Castells had brought to the forefront of our political-economic culture. The network society is an urban society, something virtually urban, as Lefebvre might say, an expression of urban virtuality.

Without mentioning the urban directly, this is also what Derrida seemed to be getting at in "Virtual Reality in Politics," from his "ghostly" reading of Marx in the mid-1990s, which also, incidentally, answers critics of the Occupy movement who grumble that there's no explicit demands or no coherent, practical (i.e., effective and actual) program voiced. "If we have been insisting so much . . . on the logic of the ghost," says Derrida, awkwardly yet profoundly, "it is because it points toward a thinking of the event that necessarily exceeds a binary logic, the logic that distinguishes or opposes *effectivity or actuality* (either present, empirical, living—or not) and *ideality* (regulating or absolute non-presence). This logic of effectivity or actuality seems to be of a limited pertinence. The limit, to be sure, is not new. . . . But it seems to be demonstrated today better than ever by the fantastic, ghostly, 'synthetic,' 'prosthetic,' virtual happenings in the scientific domain and thus the domain of the techno-media and thus the public or political domain. It is also made more manifest by what inscribes the speed of virtuality irreducible to the opposition of the act and the potential in the space of the event, in the event-ness of the event."[21]

The dialectical (and Faustian) link between technology ("techno-media" in Derrida's terminology) and the urban isn't lost on Lefebvre. In one of his long-forgotten books, *La pensée marxiste et la ville* (1972), the thesis he expounds is precisely how one implicates the other, how the development of science and the application of technology (read: new digital media and automated work) is both a cause and an effect of the urban. Technology signals the knell of the city, he says, boldly and loudly, perhaps a little provocatively, since, in part, it is predicated on overcoming the limits of the city itself; it thereby enables the urban to come into existence, to expand its *planetary* domain. Put a little differently, industrial capitalism was city-based; immaterial, cognitive capitalism is preeminently *urban*. The end of work is tantamount to the end of the city and vice versa.[22] The assertion "end of," needless to say, is rhetorical, given what we are dealing with here is a reality without foreseeable "ends," without definitive breaks and clear demarcations. What we have, instead, are transformed forms, a transitional gelling of encounters between the past, present, and future, a taking hold, to the degree that the end of work merely signals a new basis for the activity of work, one done in a post-postwork culture, in an urban-based, planetary social formation.

Lefebvre points out how Marx himself explored these tendencies presciently in the *Grundrisse*. A society of nonwork can only ever be, Lefebvre says, following Marx, an urban society; it's a society that has "overcome" the separation between the country and the city and that valorizes itself through the "general intellect." This is a society, says Marx, in which technology "suspends" labor from "the immediate form," so that dead labor valorizes living labor (and not the other way around). It spells job cuts, deindustrialization, layoffs, downsizing, and unemployment—the whole bit of contemporary work (and postwork) relations we recognize in our midst, *the contextual reality for mega-underground occupational activism*. All of which means, bluntly, the end of any expectation that working people have any rights to dignified work and a living wage, to cushy salaried employment, to a job for life; all expectations of a paternal capitalism are illusory and delusional. When "labor-time ceases to be a measure of wealth and value," Marx says, then and only then will a new era experience its birth-pangs.[23] In the *Grundrisse* (cf. 699–712), Marx, Lefebvre thinks, projects the immanent possibilities in a planet transformed into a vast form of fixed capital, immanent possibilities in a world in which the only labor that now really counts is no longer the labor of hardware but of thoughtware, of immaterial labor, of cognitive no-collar capitalism.

Lefebvre, like Marx, regales the prospect. He says so in *La pensée marxiste et la ville* because he thinks Marx regaled the prospect, too: a thoroughly urbanized society inevitably ends work as we know it and overcomes the old divisions of labor in both their social and detailed forms. Marx's tack in the *Grundrisse* is that of an optimist, rubbing his hands gleefully at the sight of "this foundation getting blown sky-high" (706), seeing a world that "suspends" labor and that revolves around "dead labor," the production of social life under the control of the "general intellect," as pregnant with its contrary, as a "moving contradiction." How so? Because it reduces the time of "necessary labor," Marx says (708). Here we have all the instruments available, all the wherewithal for creating "the means of social disposable time," for the "reducing of labor time for the whole society to a diminishing minimum," and for "freeing everyone's time for their own development." "Is this utopianism, science-fiction?" Lefebvre wonders.[24] Maybe. Maybe we're back to Asimov. We'll see later, quite soon.

At any rate, there are immanent dangers. Of course there are immanent dangers. So long as urbanization continues its long march in its current guise, society will, Lefebvre says, continue to fall between a "double dependence"— between *technocracy* and *bureaucracy*. This double dependence might thwart Marx's optimism about the collective accumulated powers of intellectual labor in urban society; rather than offering liberation, the application of science simply becomes another source of value-added, of business-as-usual crises and breakdown, of exploitation and misery (especially self-exploitation of the masses under the guise of self-employment); it becomes, in other words, another ingredient in the complete and *undemocratic* urbanization of world.

CHAPTER FIVE

The Planetary Urbanization of Nonwork

The world market is a space in which everyone has once been a productive laborer, and in which labor has everywhere begun to price itself out of the system.

Fredric Jameson

Implicit in all these definitions is the assumption that the human conglomerate being dealt with is sufficiently large . . . and a further assumption is that the human conglomerate be itself unaware of psychohistoric analysis in order that its reactions be truly random.

Isaac Asimov

I. Postwork and Urban Society

In 1968, in *The Right to the City*, Lefebvre said that the right to the city was a "cry and demand" for city life. Two years on, in *The Urban Revolution*, he said we should no longer think about cities but about "urban society." Then two years on again, in *La pensée marxiste et la ville*, he's back not only using the term "city" but also using it with a new twist, making the claim we've just heard: that the development of science and the application of new technology signal the knell of the city because they're both predicated on the need to supersede the city. Information technology and automated work enable the urban to come into existence, Lefebvre says, and they enable the urban to expand its planetary domain. Thus, as soon as the urban begins its planetary long march, what we have is a resultant "postemployment" society coupled with more planetary urbanization and more industrial contradictions that are now somehow global-urban contradictions.

The industrial city had to give way to the urban, and this urban society is forever a society marked by relations we could describe as "postwork," or at least "post-salaried work." This seems to be Lefebvre's point, as he tosses ideas out—he loved the "bubbling and fermenting of ideas," he told us in *La somme et le reste*—only to leave it up to us to sort and figure these ideas out, to bottle them up in all their effervescence and volatility. Curiously, what Lefebvre says about the city–urban dialectic in *La pensée marxiste et la ville* chimes with what Fredric Jameson said recently in *Representing Capital* about Marx's manufacture–modern industry dialectic: that the passage from the former to the latter necessarily results in the formation of unemployment. Unemployment isn't so much a symptom of systemic crisis or depression as the "normal" functioning order of the system, something endemic in its everyday operations. As Jameson writes, "Unemployment is structurally inseparable from the dynamic of accumulation and expansion which constitutes the very nature of capitalism as such."[1] For many people around the world this means that they've literally "dropped out of history," they're now "officially" dispensable on the world market, and they're "officially" dispensable in capitalist urban society. We might paraphrase Jameson to express Lefebvre's own thesis: *Unemployment is structurally inseparable from the dynamic of urbanization and its expansion on a planetary scale, which constitutes the very nature of capitalism as such.* The claim is again cavalier; we need to explore it in more detail in what follows. We need to bottle it up both analytically and politically: We need to brew our own moonshine from Lefebvrian hops.

One initial difficulty in examining a work like *La pensée marxiste et la ville* is why Lefebvre should want to revert to the "city" after dissing it in *The Urban Revolution*. Urban society, he said in that latter text, is built upon the ruins of the city, and the city exists only as a "historical entity." Therein lies a little clue: it appears Lefebvre wants to write a historical text, a book about ideas of the city, of how the city has been conceptualized within Marx and Engels's analyses of the capitalist mode of production. Marx and Engels never gave us an explicit "urban mode of production," Lefebvre says in *Pensée*, but if we look closely in their oeuvre, in a way they did: the city was itself a developmental force, the seat of modern industry, the division of labor, the reproduction of labor power, and technological innovation. The rise of the industrial city wasn't only vital for the expansion of the productive forces but crucial *politically* for an ascendant bourgeoisie asserting itself in the passage from feudalism to capitalism.

The other thing that's perhaps noteworthy about why Lefebvre should then want to write a text about a body of thought (*la pensée marxiste*) and the city (*la ville*) was the relative dominance of Althusser's thought. In his opening "*Avertissement*," Lefebvre warns readers what this book is and isn't; it isn't, he says, a "*symptômale*" reading of Marx and Engels. The word "*symptômale*" is put in inverted commas because it's a term Althusser made infamous in his "Reading" of Marx's *Capital*—in his *symptomatic* reading of *Capital*. Lefebvre, on the other hand, says this is no symptomatic reading but a "thematic" reading. He always disliked Althusser's Marxist formalism, stripping bare of content Marx's method and epistemology. Thus a "thematic" reading is a reading that beds itself down specifically in *content*, which is to say, in the city; "the urban problematic within the theoretical framework of historical materialism."² What he is hinting at here is something David Harvey would, around the same time, call "historical-geographical materialism," inserting space and urbanization into Marx and Engels's theory of history. To a certain extent, one gets the impression that *La pensée marxiste et la ville* figures for Lefebvre the same way the *Grundrisse* figured for Marx: as a work of self-clarification, as a notebook for working through one's theoretical relationship with the subject matter, which in this case is the city–urban dialectic within Marxism.

A key text for Lefebvre is Marx and Engels's *German Ideology* in which the city is center stage rather than mere background. Taking leave from Marx and Engels, Lefebvre shows how the closed system of antiquity, with its feudal city as absolute space, became relativized with the industrial revolution. The industrial revolution, for Lefebvre—repeating what he said in *The Right to the City* and in *The Urban Revolution*—was really an urban revolution, and with the rise of the city came a corresponding rise of the modern state and modern property relations based on finance and speculation, all of which would fuel the further expansion of the city. Lefebvre gives us a great historical overview, with a grand historical sweep, but "the subject of history" here, he says, "is incontestably the city."³

"The greatest division of material and mental labor," say Marx and Engels in *The German Ideology*, "is the separation of town and country." "The antagonism between the town and country begins with the transition from barbarism to civilization, from tribe to state, from locality to nation, and runs through the whole history of civilization to the present day," ours included.⁴ In *The German Ideology*, Marx and Engels trot through the history of the division of labor, including its countryside and town basis, its entrenchment under "the rise of manufacturing," the development of the state and property relations, and the "forms of intercourse" that took hold within this process of continuous movement and change within the "all-embracing collisions" of history—collisions of various classes, collisions of consciousness, collisions of ideas, collisions of political conflict. Throughout, "the abolition of the antagonism between the town and the countryside is one of the first conditions of communal life, a condition which," Marx and Engels insist, "depends on a mass of material premises and which cannot be fulfilled by mere will."⁵ Huge flows of people flooding into emergent industrial cities—the "rabble," Dr. Marx calls them, like Singer's

Dr. Fischelson—are at first devoid of power, disunited, detached and desperate, entering as "individuals strange to one another" (70). Yet after a while, and after a few pages further on, Marx and Engels are able to posit Communism somewhere in the midst, somewhere there as a "form of intercourse," "overturning the basis of all earlier relations of production and intercourse." Communism will, they seem to suggest, be urban-based or it won't be. "Isn't it evident," Lefebvre asks, "that the city is at once place, instrument and *théâtre dramatique* of a gigantic transformation?"[6] Isn't it equally evident, he says, how Marx and Engels, "no more and no less," announce "*the end of the city*, amongst other ends."[7]

II. The Urbanization of the "General Intellect"

One of the most fascinating parts of *La pensée marxiste et la ville* comes in the final ten pages of Chapter 2. There, Lefebvre wrestles with Marx and Engels's *German Ideology* and with the utopian pages of the *Grundrisse*. But first he must move through Engels himself, show how, from Engels's industrial city, emerges "urban society." Engels's *Condition of the Working Class in England* (1845) spoke at length of cities as places of worker "agglomeration," of spaces where a "reserve army of laborers" are piled up on top of one another, and how "the capitalist order engenders an urban chaos." The laboring masses, Engels noted, lived in specifically demarcated areas of "great cities," in overcrowded hovels where they got ripped off in reproduction, at home, just as they got ripped off at the point of industrial production, at work. The concentration of populations like this, of course, directly accompanied the concentration and exponential accumulation of capital; the two went hand-in-hand, alongside the advance of technology and the spatial and temporal development of modes of production. But the question that preoccupied Engels then, as it did thirty years later in *The Housing Question*, was: How could you really resolve the ghettoization of workers' housing *without* resolving the problem of the capitalist mode of production itself?

But the twist here, the utopian twist for Lefebvre, comes from the "*fin du travail*," from the "end of work" (121): "What a paradox," he says, "for those who have discovered the importance of work and who assume the role of the theoretician of the working class." "And yet, we know it already, that automation of production permits us to envisage the end of productive work. Theoretical and practical possibility? Incontestably . . . Utopia certainly, but a *concrete* utopia" (121–122). "The socialization of the productive forces, the elimination of barriers, perturbations, waste, permits," Lefebvre says, "henceforth the reduction of work time and the transformation of work." The phrase could have easily come from André Gorz, who, though unacknowledged by Lefebvre, was writing about work and Marxism in the same vein as Lefebvre wrote about the city and Marxism.[8] Yet Lefebvre is more playful with the idea that the end of work correlates positively with growing urbanization, more playful with both its perils and its possibilities.[9] What transpires in "urban society" is a "service" economy, he says, as well as a gradual dominance of finance over industrial capital. He spots the germ of all this early on in capitalism's urban development and assesses whether these circumstances will really expand or gradually undermine the mode of production itself. Lefebvre insists that a service economy does produce surplus value rather than simply realize it, and that an urban constituency as an agent of revolutionary change behooves something more than "the working class." If anything, it bids its farewell.

Gorz and Lefebvre tacitly concur that Marx's *Grundrisse* is a source of extraordinary intellectual and political sustenance. Maybe Engels had never read Marx's *Grundrisse* notebooks; the latter, after all, had kept them under wraps for his own entertainment in gloomy London winter nights, circa 1857–1858. Had Marx's "general" read these notebooks, he would have likely endorsed Marx's view that the generalization of automated production, of postindustrial "immaterial" labor—which Marx there theorized—would see off capitalism in the long term. The rise of the so-called general intellect didn't symbolize the end of history and capitalism's ultimate victory but its very opposite, the beginnings of its systemic demise. Therein lies the promise of urban society, of planetary urbanization. "Capital thus works towards its own dissolution as the form dominating production," is how Marx put it.[10]

In the *Grundrisse*, Marx says the possibility to release ourselves from work comes about when living labor has materialized itself in machines, when "the technological application of science" conditions the entire productive character of capital. When the world of work is dominated by machines, when we become appendages to machines, to new technology, to informational digitized technology—when technology "suspends" human beings from "the immediate form" of work and when dead labor valorizes living labor—then and seemingly only then are we on the brink of something new and possible. "To the degree that large industry develops," Marx says, "the creation of real wealth comes to depend less on labor time and on the amount of labor employed than on the power of the agencies set in motion during labor-time, whose 'powerful effectiveness' is itself in turn out of all proportion to the direct labor time spent on their production, but depends rather on the general state of science and on the progress of technology, or the application of science to production."[11]

The degree to which human ingenuity, human imagination, scientific know-how, and the vital powers of the human brain and hand have become objectified in fixed capital—in capital that apparently rules over us—is the degree to which urban society defines our lives. At this point, Marx says, "labor time ceases and *must cease* to be a measure of value, and hence exchange value must cease to be the measure of use value. The surplus labor of the masses has ceased to be the condition for the development of general wealth."[12] And "with that," he says, "production based on exchange value breaks down, and the direct material production process is stripped of the form of penury and antithesis."[13] In the *Grundrisse*, Marx, the dialectician, seems to think up his own negation: he seems to problematize his own law of value, the theory of value he'd formulated in *Capital*, positing it as being unhinged with the growth of immaterial labor. High-tech, profit-laden, scientific, knowledge-based activities assume their own, apparently free-floating value dynamics within the overall economy, little of which can be stocked, quantified, formalized, or objectified.

There's perhaps, then, little reason to doubt Gorz's words on the matter: "By furnishing services, immaterial labor has become the hegemonic form of work; material labor is displaced to the periphery of the production process, or is summarily externalized. Although it remains indispensable and even dominant from a quantitative standpoint, material labor has become a 'subaltern moment' of the process. The heart of value creation is now immaterial labor."[14] As other writers like David Harvey have convincingly shown, expansion and capital accumulation over the past couple of decades has also had a marked penchant for dispossession; it has shown zilch commitment to investing in living labor in actual production. To believe that labor-time is the source of profit nowadays is an absurdity. Profit these days has little to do with companies mass-producing products at lower prices than their competitors. And it has little to do with them necessarily exploiting workers absolutely, prevalent as this still is.[15] Invariably, it's more to do with monopolization, with destroying competition within a given field and, as Žižek says, with *privatizing* the general intellect, with reappropriating and cashing in on scientific expertise.[16] And from this comes a profit in the form of rent, gleaned from such privatization of specialist knowledge. That is the surplus value: its yardstick isn't the temporal application of labor. The enormous growth in wealth and the rise in productivity in high-tech industries consequently means more and more redundant workers. Their services, their living labor, and their physical presence on the job are rendered defunct and are no longer required: living labor is a species en route to extinction. Instead, there's automation, computer-aided production, computer-aided design, robotics, and a coterie of human appendages; only a relatively small number of salaried jobs exist for the knowledge-based few. For the masses, Marx described their circumstances thus: "Labor no longer appears so much to be included with the production process; rather, the human being comes to relate more as watchman and regulator to the production process itself. . . . He steps to the side of the production process instead of being its chief actor. In this transformation, it is neither the direct human labor he himself performs [that counts], nor the time during which he works, but rather the appropriation of his own general productive power."[17]

Those rendered superfluous, suspended from the immediate process of production, aren't, however, just factory workers and industrial minions. They include *all* categories of workers—white-collar, blue-collar, and no-collar—and in developed as well as developing countries. Is it a blessing or curse to be freed from the relative privilege of salaried exploitation and/or from actual workplace exploitation? No more bosses; no more blue Mondays; no more watching the clock and living for weekends, dreaming of early retirement. Marx plainly saw this as both bad and good news. He sees a world that suspends labor, that revolves around "dead labor," around the production of social life under the control of the general intellect, as pregnant with its contrary, as a "moving contradiction." On the one hand, a privileged minority prospers through specialist knowledge, on the other, there's a huge number of people who are left bereft of a job and a future and who have little recourse other than their own ingenuity, their own practical spirit of self-innovation (therein resides the potential good news). Yet, for them, a reduction in the time of "necessary" salaried labor doesn't free up more disposable time for their own "self-development"; it frequently spells endless hustle in a sector that was once called "informal." And there it's not so much intellectual knowledge that counts, that helps survival, as "vernacular knowledge," learned on the street, the hard way, graduating in the university of life, which is another way we can construe the general intellect. Once again the question: "Free" working time—blessing or curse? Likely both, because both *depend*: a millionfold relative surplus population that's a crucial facet of urban life everywhere; a millionfold relative surplus population that's equally a latent political constituency in the process of making itself, a Here Comes Everybody, a 99 percent breaking down the gates of the city, remaking it as the urban realm.

III. The Flea Market in the Free Market

In 2009 the Organisation for Economic Co-operation and Development (OECD) suggested half of the world's working population, around 1.8 billion people, engage in employment somehow self-made and irregular, usually undocumented and always self-reliant.[18] These activities generate a staggering net worth of $10 trillion, earnings bettered only by the U.S. economy (with its $14 trillion). (Even the industrial might and surging factory labor force in China pales quantitatively alongside the numbers of self-reliant toilers; and the security of Chinese workers may yet be short-lived once it is really tested against the vicissitudes of the world market.) In today's highly dynamic global economy, the math is simple: as productivity grows its "official" rank and file workforce shrinks; as this "official" workforce shrinks, an even more dynamic, quasi-spontaneous system of self-employment prevails, a cut-and-paste economy whose ranks are swelling as we speak. And its self-generating rate of job creation puts any government to shame; no Walmart or Microsoft, no multinational or supra-international can compete. By 2020 the OECD reckons that two-thirds of workers of the world will be employed in this planetary system now generically known as "*Système D*."[19]

"Système D" is the slang term used in the French Caribbean and Africa for so-called *débrouillards* (from *débrouiller*: to sort out, to manage, to figure out), those resourceful peddlers and hustlers, hawkers and street vendors who figure out their lives for themselves, who pit their will and exercise their wits at street markets and unlicensed bazaars around the globe. Here self-reliance means self-reproduction and survival, and, for a few others, it announces "defiance." "Système D" has come to replace what everybody used to call the "informal" sector, with its connotations of clandestinity, of shady underworld wheeling and dealing that takes place off the map of respectable economic gain—frequently taken as a problem and brake for a poor nation's rocky road toward "development." But, suggests Robert Neuwirth, an almost-resident expert on Système D, a lot of people erroneously see the system as "a kind of bastard ward of the state—a zone that is kept around because it ensures that people will have the minimum income required to survive, and thus will not revolt against the existing order."[20] Système D is so widespread—so tied to the "formal sector," so First World as well as Third (and Second) World, so crucial as an earner for most nations, and so underground as to be positively above ground—that Neuwirth takes it all differently. Système D is not only a respectable and honest form of employment for billions of people, he says, it can also be scaled up, and it is spreading its low-tech basis everywhere, providing jobs and bringing commerce and entrepreneurialism to neighborhoods that are off the standard economic and political radar. To take it as *only* self-reproduction, as self-exploitation, Neuwirth argues, as *only* letting governments of the world off their neoliberal hook, is an absurd denial of human ingenuity and willpower.

Thus, from Los Angeles to Lagos, Guangzhou to Guadalupe, Accra to Akron, from Maxwell Street in Chicago to Rua 25 de Março in São Paulo, from Canal

Street to Clignancourt, a hyperkinetic, DIY, open-air economy flourishes, repairing, recycling, and selling, creating an urban space somewhere in-between yet in-between everywhere. Improvised yet organized in its improvisation, it's an economy populated by workers without any specific nation, "strikingly independent, yet deeply enmeshed in the legal world." Sometimes Système D even provides public services, like transportation and refuse collection (as in parts of Mexico City).[21] "It involves small-scale entrepreneurs but links them to global trading circuits. It is the economic way of the global majority, guided not by corporations or politicians or economists, but by ordinary citizens."[22]

Mike Davis isn't mentioned by name, but we might read all this as Neuwirth's rejoinder to *Planet of Slums*, with its dystopian denunciation of the "illusion of self-help." Davis pretty much dismisses everything Neuwirth affirms; self-help is really petty-bourgeois claptrap, says Davis, an International Monetary Fund and World Bank ruse, an excuse for the withdrawal of the public sector from its obligations toward citizens. You now have the "right" to be a self-managed entrepreneur; you now have the "right to the city," Davis implies, though not to a city "made of glass and steel as envisioned by earlier generations of urbanists" but to one "largely constructed out of crude brick, straw, recycled plastic, cement blocks and scrap wood. Instead of soaring toward heaven, much of the twenty-first-century urban world squats in squalor, surrounded by pollution, excrement and decay."[23]

All of this, for Davis, is counterrevolutionary, not countervailing; Système D merchants shape up as the veritable inert sack of potatoes that Marx, in *The Eighteenth Brumaire*, ascribed to the French peasantry of his day, to *Lumpenproletarian* vagabonds and mountebanks, pickpockets and tricksters, tinkers and beggars, knife-grinders and porters—"in short the whole indefinite, disintegrated mass, thrown hither and thither" onto the world market. But Neuwirth sees it otherwise, making a spirited defense of a demographic constituency that today asserts itself as an economic constituency; and, perhaps one day quite soon, might equally assert itself as a Fanonesque revolutionary constituency. One day, in other words, political power might catch up with global demographics; a latent, lagging political force, a Here Comes Everybody, waits in the wings on world market street, waits to see itself as a global family of eyes. "So here we are in this goddamned Troy without jobs," Sucus tells his father Clement in Berger's *Lilac and Flag*, an old wives' tale of the megacity. "That's history, son," says Clement. "I don't know. It's not history," his son says. "It's a kind of waiting." "There aren't regular jobs anymore. They've gone. There's no way."[24]

In "advanced" countries like the United States, Système D continues to gain ground, "boosted by economic refugees—not foreigners but people pushed out of the legal economy after the downturn of 2008 and 2009."[25] Yet a

"post–salaried work" society needs to be kept in check politically; How to pre-
serve the stability and legitimacy of a system of work without workers, ensuring
that workers (and ex-workers) remain consumers and somehow "embrace" the
world of immaterial labor? How to resist the legitimacy of that system? (The
Occupy movement has begun to express clues, if not offering a few tentative
answers.) Therein reside the threats, the threats that the desire for free time, the
yearning to work less (a yearning much of the active workforce now seems to
share in both the United States and Europe), is not thrown back in people's faces
or used as a pretext for the neoliberal state to disengage. As Mike Davis spells
out for the Majority World, these types of threats may also be used to promote
"self-help" strategies as self-reproduction, as self-exploitation, as a form of social control: "we are all entrepreneurs!" The other threat is that joblessness, insecurity around work, part-time jobs, McJobs, temporary contracts, and piece-
work tasks, performed casually and for little pay, translate into a never-ending,
highly flexible pool of workers that enterprises can tap and turn away at the
whim of their business cycles. Here the menace of Marx's "industrial reserve
army" looms: precariousness becomes the watchword for the "relative surplus
population" of our day, for the contingent worker progressively produced by the
immaterial valorization of capital.[26]

This relative surplus population boils down to the huge mass of underem-
ployed and subemployed workers likely to be part-time, on-call, self-employed,
on temporary contracts or workfare recruits or interns—who all succeed in
making the official unemployment statistics look less dire than they actually
are. These people are absorbed into an ever-expanding "personal services industry," rendered even more ruthless and competitive by the burgeoning of
temporary help agencies and contracting firms that coordinate the distribution
of contingent labor-power whose supply and demand dances to the behest of
outsourcing, cost-cutting companies. Temp agencies enable formerly displaced
workers to assume new careers that require them to quite literally float between
jobs. And not only have the numbers of people temping grown enormously
over past decades; the temporary help business is itself a booming industry.

Yet among these threats reside certain possibilities, even revolutionary potentialities. Maybe crises might be blessings rather than calamities? Maybe in
times of crises, like the crisis that appears to be lasting forever nowadays, we
can relearn how to do without work or really learn how to work the system for
ourselves. In the United States, twentysomething NINJAS are learning how to
reevaluate their "career" choices, together with the whole notion of career itself;
they're intelligent enough to know that they might not have anything deemed to
be a "career" anymore. Since joblessness has lost a lot of its stigma in America,

given there are so many people jobless, being in and out of work is no longer seen simply as a personal failing, and it may even be the cue to getting politically active. In fact, there are twentysomethings almost everywhere, especially young men, often young men of color, who live in specific neighborhoods with specific postal codes and who know they'll never work a salaried job. They know they can never count on either a pension or the "right to work."

Maybe, during crises, we can hatch alternative programs for survival, other methods through which we cannot so much "earn a living" as live a living. Maybe we can self-downsize, or even refrain from work itself, and at the same time address the paradox of work that goes back at least to Max Weber. Work is revered in our culture, yet at the same time workers are becoming superfluous; you hate your job, your boss, hate the servility of what you do, and how you do it, the pettiness of the tasks involved, and yet you want to keep your job at all costs. Maybe there's a point at which we can all be pushed over the edge, "set-free" as Marx said, or voluntarily take the jump ourselves, only to discover other aspects of ourselves and other ways to fill in the hole, make a little money, maintain our dignity and pride, and survive off what André Gorz calls a "frugal abundance." *Voici* the economic "rationality" of *Système D*, a streetwise rationality that isn't taught at any Harvard Business School.

We still hear voices on the Left bawling for full employment, and others are still battling for a return to decent jobs for decent pay and decent benefits. Fredric Jameson makes it clear that Marx never advocated any full employment policy.[27] Nowadays, decent jobs are the rare exception, the very rare exception, so exceptional that it's safer to bet that there is no such thing as decent jobs anymore. If the Left thinks otherwise then it's backing the wrong horse, channeling its energies in the wrong direction, one that's going backward and not forward. In a certain sense, the politicization of postwork society is already apace, receiving wider acknowledgment. If capitalists can do without workers, it's high time for workers to realize that they can do without capitalists, that they can devise work without capitalists, even work without the state. And that they can even build urban spaces for themselves, "occupy" urban spaces, construct and reconstruct not only a post–salaried work culture but a "postcity" culture as well. This, perhaps, is Henri Lefebvre's most brilliant and enduring insight, seemingly overlooked by all latter-day interpreters and critics: "Work doesn't end in leisure," he says at the climactic point of *La pensée marxiste et la ville*, maybe at the climactic point even of Marxist thinking about the city, "but in non-work. The city doesn't end up in the countryside but in the simultaneous supersession of the countryside and the city, which leaves a void that the imagination fills, with its theoretical projections and predictions." "What," Lefebvre asks, "constitutes non-work and the non-city?" "The urban," he tells us, defined by "encounters, gatherings, centerings and de-centerings." The supersession of work and the city has absolutely "nothing in common with what has been formerly voiced."[28]

There's something daringly radical and futuristic about this vision adapted from Marx, from his journeyman postulations with Frederick Engels in *The German Ideology* to his maturity in thoughts on the supersession of capitalism in the *Grundrisse*. Whatever way you look at things, there's no looking back now, even if, glancing over your shoulder, you feel the tug of what came before trying to harness you, trying to lull you backward, trying to entice your return through nostalgia. The supersession of capitalism, Marx insists, comes about *through* capitalism, by running through its corridor of flames; any postcapitalist society has to mobilize the heat and energy of capitalism and maximize and muster up all the generalized possibility of its development of science and technology. Postcapitalist society will somehow resemble, in form and content, what capitalism has bequeathed us, what remains solid in the transition, even if all aspects of ownership, control, and functioning would be different after the transition. Those gigantic urban forms we have today would still be ours in the future. Here, again, there's no turning back, no breaking anything down, no reversion to quaint, archaic times when cities were like villages and less intimidating—both conceptually and existentially. The same leap of the imagination Marx makes with technology and generalized fixed capital, outlined in a dozen-or-so pages of the *Grundrisse* (699–713), becomes grist to Lefebvre in a daring leap of his urban imagination. The same forces that generalize the intellect also generalize the city; they generalize it so much, in fact, that the city is transformed into something postcity, just as the development of the productive forces are destined to eventually see off the concept of work itself. If *Capital*, as Jameson suggests, is really Marx's manifesto of unemployment, then it's also a manifesto of a society of unemployment that generalizes urbanization. To clarify the stake, we can again paraphrase Jameson: to think of all this in terms of a kind of global unemployment and urbanization rather than to see it as tragic pathos is, I believe, to be recommitted to the invention of a new kind of transformatory politics on a global scale.

IV. Nonwork and the Postcity: Encounters on World Market Street

Mike Davis is right about one thing: a good deal of the urbanization of the future will be constructed out of crude brick, straw, recycled plastic, cement blocks, and scrap wood; and, for the moment at least, this urban form will continue to coexist alongside glass and steel and spectacle architectural forms. The latter, if not physically flimsy, are just as figuratively flimsy, especially when they have to withstand the economic tsunamis periodically sweeping through the global economy. Together, glass and steel, as well as prefabricated breeze-block, comprise the secondary circuit of capital; those Pollockesque skeins that we have perceived within our different way of seeing urbanization flow with the charged energy of Système D workers and their burgeoning habitats. These workers are literally building their urban society, both economically and physically, *producing space*, as Lefebvre would say, implicating themselves not by *conceiving* space in glass and steel but by practicing space as a life-and-death *lived* experience.

While it would be dangerously irresponsible to push too far the limits of Système D at work, and bidonvilles at home, makeshift work and makeshift homes nonetheless have a handy way of becoming more solid communities; lacking services one day only to find adaptive and inventive ways to install services another day; creating from a "slum" life-form a "normal," everyday life-form. Out of an ostensible disorderly "rabble" emerges an orderly neighborhood that somehow works for its denizens. The same vitality at work gets translated into the vitality of nonwork, of neighborhood building, of vernacular knowledge in the face of general intellectual knowledge. The seemingly most "primitive" precapitalist construction techniques reside within an overabundance of the most advanced capitalist construction and work techniques; never, apparently, the twain shall meet. Should they ever meet—should the fault line ever get reconciled between the internationalization of the economy, on the one hand, and the marginalization of everyday life tearing apart the urban fabric, on the other—we'll know that some sort of *political encounter* has occurred, that some seismic tremor or volcanic eruption has "taken hold." The terrain of its taking hold, of its taking shape, will be the urban scale; all "swerving" will doubtless *depend*, depend on numerous factors and conjunctures, on affections finding affinities, on a Here Comes Everybody congealing and gelling at a felicitous moment, on bodies coming together *here* as well as *there* simultaneously or almost simultaneously. At that imaginary point, economic self-empowerment would encounter political collective-empowerment, and the favelas as well as Wall Street, the malls as well as main streets, will all get occupied and democratized by an inexorable and an insatiable *swarming*, by a sheer numbers-game asserting the generalized force of a political subjects–game, channeling itself virtually, connecting itself really, a giant planetary web of communication and just-in-time self-organization.

In *Magical Marxism*, near the end, I suggested this swarming, this Here Comes Everywhere, would be an encounter *in* the city, a collective spirit expressive of the Right to the City. I thought the formula might be thus: HCE=RTTC; a global protest movement of the future would fight for its Right to the City, do so as a "cry and demand," exactly as Lefebvre identified. Now, I no longer think the Right to the City is, or should be, the banner under which a universal dreaming collective might assemble. Now, I think its unfolding, its coming together, its expressive collective desire, needs to be more open and expansive, reclaiming nothing other than its own impulse toward *democracy*, pushing outward onto the world, into a world without nation and without borders; into another way of seeing, of perceiving a mongrel world with a mongrel politics. One of the many interesting things that emerges from Neuwirth's *Stealth of Nations* is how this mongrel quality marks today's workers of the world. Even in China, *pace* Mike Davis, a mongrelization is in motion; about 300,000 Africans now live full-time in Guangzhou alone. Near its central station, in the Sanyuanli neighborhood, there are so many Africans that the district has become known as "Chocolate City"; elsewhere in Guangzhou, Arabs, Argentinians, Turks, and Filipinos have all come to hustle as Système D workers, a bottom-up globalization that's never included in official statistics because it all takes place off the record.

The cross-border global flows of Système D migrants and immigrants is now a "global back channel" (Neuwirth's term), meaning urban streets are, by definition, world market streets, streets that open themselves onto the world and along which the world comes to them. Down these streets, at these global bazaars, "the world" and "the city" meet one another in a passionate embrace; where "the city" ends and "the world" begins is anybody's guess. Everything is so integrated that what is the world and the city no longer makes any definitional sense: there's no "in" and "out" anymore. *New York Times* flat-earther columnist Thomas Friedman recently wrote about the mismatch between a CEO's vision of the world and a politician's; the article is surprisingly suggestive for leftists. "Politicians see the world as blocs of voters living in specific geographies," says Friedman, "and they see their jobs as maximizing the economic voters in their geography. Many CEOs, though, see the world as a place where their products can be made anywhere and sold everywhere. . . . In their businesses, every product and many services now are imagined, designed, marketed and built through global supply chains that seek to access the best quality at the lowest cost, wherever it exists. They see more and more their products today as 'Made in the World' not 'Made in America.' Therein lies the tension. So many of 'our' companies actually see themselves now as citizens of the world. But Obama is president of the United States."[29]

Can people on world market street adopt the same kind of global perspective as a CEO, as a citizen of the world, rather than, say, a Chinese worker? Can they, we, develop common notions based on a shared global existence? Is it possible to see oneself as a little cog in a great big expansive universe, yet see this great big expansive universe as clearly as the little cogs?; or to imagine oneself in the whole world, not just in one bitty corner of the world? (Thomas Friedman says that one day there'll be no more "developed" and "developing" countries, only HIES—High-Imagination-Enabling Countries—and LIES—Low-Imagination-Enabling Countries. Maybe this vision might one day work for people rather than just for capital?) To encounter others doing likewise, seeing oneself likewise, seeing the world likewise? To literally "make" oneself *as* the world? From such a standpoint, the terrain for any postwork politics, or even for any global citizenship, would be somewhere beyond the factory gates, beyond the old city limits, somewhere *within* global everyday life, inevitably along world market street, in urban society. To be sure, the "cry and demand" of a postwork, post-city politics won't likely be any cry and demand at all, since "words" as such are unlikely to be expressed. Rather than words giving rise to any encounter, what would get expressed would depend on the encounter itself.

Lefebvre says capitalism, from its very inception, "announced the complete urbanization of society."[30] It was, still is, a revolutionary process, expelling from the immediate activity of production millions and millions of people, transforming the countryside, disrupting agrarian life, forcing people to flood into cities. But that is history—the use and abuse of history. Now, not only those involved in immediate production have been "set free" from capitalist work but white-collar service workers, too, have been set free, including former salaried workers. Now everybody has somehow been set free from the city: they've been "liberated," as it were, *by* urban society. The meeting of downsized workers and upsizing cities has fueled itself, fed off itself. The conjoining of both has resulted in the creation of a thoroughly urban society: a nonwork and postcity society. Now a contingent, itinerant, surplus population, a "butterfly" population, a "floating" population (after Marx), flits between work, flits between places, floats in and out of spaces of marginality, avoiding clear flight paths and steady linear movement. Indeed, the whole trajectory of this butterfly population can't be accounted for within conventional steady-state aerodynamics, let alone within conventional steady-state economics.

With planetary urbanization, a planet-full of people can no longer find steady work or steady homes, and a huge unwieldy inertia persists, an inertia based on a sort of *hypertrophy*. It's not that urban regions are too big, or that there are too many people, but more that within current modes of societal organization we have a society that overreaches itself—not so much through technology as technocracy, not so much through overpopulation as *overbureaucratization*, a "double dependence," we've heard Lefebvre call it, between *technocracy* and *bureaucracy*, between corporate and financial monopolization of bureaucratic techniques *and* bureaucratic monopolization of financial and corporate techniques. For society to change, a collective force possessing a similar inertia must be mustered up: either huge numbers of people have to be concerned or, if the numbers are relatively small, enormous time for incremental change must be allowed.

In Isaac Asimov's sci-fi imaginary *Foundation*, there's a back flow in the historical geography of his galactic urban empire, Trantor; Lefebvre hints at it in *The Right to the City* but doesn't elaborate.[31] So here's my take on it: The back flow for Asimov, the necessary inertia, comes with so-called psychohistory, the brainchild of his central protagonist, mathematician Hari Seldon, who formulated psychohistory to predict the future in statistical fashion. Trantor's rulers became very interested in Seldon because they felt he could help them predict the future, intervene in the future, make the future theirs. Seldon soon became one of the most important men in the galaxy and assumed the role of First Minister under Emperor Cleon I's rule. For the scientist Asimov (he had a Ph.D. in chemistry), psychohistory was modeled off the kinetic theory of gases: molecules making up gases move about in absolutely random fashion, in any direction, in three dimensions and at a wide range of speeds. Nobody can predict the behavior of a single molecule. Yet as a mass of molecules, as gases, you can somehow describe what the motions would be on average, and from there work out the gas laws with an enormous degree of predictability.

Asimov applied this notion to human beings. (In Asimov's *Foundation* saga, there's no alien presence, no nonhuman life, save humanly made robots: his vision of the universe is all the more interesting because it is all-too-human.) All of us have free will, all of us as individuals exhibit behavior and act in ways that defy predictability. Still, for vast numbers of people, for diverse societies, for *mobs* of people, Asimov's Seldon suggests some sort of predictability is possible, like it is for gases. Thus psychohistory is "mob analysis," predicting mob behavior as intruding, intervening in historical contingency. The politics of mobs, then, is like the kinetic theory of gases; and the idea has considerable salience not least because it reveals something about the prospect of group encounters intervening in the historical-geographical logic of urbanization, intervening in a world without work or cities. Although here, maybe it's not so much psychohistory as *psychogeography* that resembles mob analysis, implying any densifying of human behavior, any human agglomeration (like urbanization), will likely create at a certain time and in a certain space a gathering of people that resembles a gathering of gases, a certain coming together of movement and stasis, of particle and wave. And this encounter will possess its own kinetic energy; sometimes negative energy, like indiscriminate rioting (British urban areas witnessed this not so long ago), but also positive energy, its own Brownian motion, perhaps generating an energy that's enough to alter the course of history (and geography).

In *Gold*, Asimov's final collection of fiction and nonfiction writings, the aging sci-fi godfather ruminates on the genre and futuristic world he'd created. He gives us a little more background to his concept of "psychohistory." Readers now have a clearer insight into what he had in mind. There were two conditions, Asimov says, "that I had to set up in order to make psychohistory work, and they were not chosen carelessly. I picked them in order to make it more like kinetic theory."[32] "First," he says, "I had to deal with a large number of human beings, as kinetic theory worked with a large number of molecules." It had to be a Galactic Empire, a big, complex world, a huge world, with a huge population, like a universe in which planetary urbanization has taken shape. Second, "I had to retain the 'randomness' factor. I couldn't expect human beings to behave as randomly as molecules," Asimov says, "but they might approach such behavior if they had no idea as to what was expected of them. So it was necessary to suppose that human beings in general did not know what the predictions of psychohistory were and therefore would not tailor their activities to suit."[33]

Yet as time went on, with fifty-odd years' hindsight, weird things happened in the field of science and society, Asimov says. Mathematicians began to get interested in a branch of science we now call "chaos" theory, where randomness meets underlying order, and where order unleashes a certain kind of randomness. "Imagine, then," Asimov notes, "how exciting it is for me to see that scientists are increasingly interested in *my* psychohistory, even though they may not be aware that that's what the study is called and may never have read any of my *Foundation* novels." Meanwhile, within the human world, one Asimov fan sends the great writer a clipping from the journal *Machine Design* (April 23, 1987), relaying the following info:

A computer model originally intended to stimulate liquid turbulence has been used to model group behavior. Researchers at Los Alamos National Laboratories have found that there is a similarity between group behavior and certain physical phenomena. To do the analysis, they assigned certain physical characteristics such as level of excitement, fear, and size of the crowd to model parameters. The interaction of the crowd closely paralleled the turbulent flow equations. Although analysis cannot predict exactly what a group will do, it reportedly does help determine the most probable consequence of a given event.[34]

Asimov's Hari Seldon had hoped psychohistory might be developed in the next century, and that was already 22,000 years into the future. "Is this," wonders Asimov, "going to be another case of my science-fictional imagination falling ludicrously short?"[35] Maybe we no longer need turbulent flow equations to tell us about the kinetic energy of the crowd, about its fears and level of excitement, about its size and politics. Maybe the combustible energy of the crowd, of this mob, expresses a radical eruption, not a random explosion, a volcanic happening rather than unannounced anarchy; since here, somehow and somewhere, we have underlying regularity, a gaseous encounter with inner structuring order.

CHAPTER SIX

Revolutionary Rehearsals?

The crowd sees the city around them with different eyes.
John Berger

To be on anew and basking in the panaroma of all flores of speech.
James Joyce

I. Encounters in Transition

The spark that triggers any irruptive, swerving encounter is like that first Jackson Pollock *drip*: suddenly the paint falls onto the giant canvas; things explode at ground level, on the floor, in the street; dense skeins of black and white swirls disrupt the field of vision; brown and silver nebulae dazzle; paint is layered on swiftly, like meteorites flashing across a white void. There's neither beginning nor end here; entering is via some middle door, with no meaning other than a pure intensity, a flow of pure becoming. Standing in front of a huge Pollock masterpiece like *One, Number 31* (1950), or *Autumn Rhythm* (1950), is an experience filled with the same dramatic (and unnerving) intensity as standing amid a huge crowd at a demonstration or occupation, amid a huge mob on the street or in a square. There's violence and beauty, and the same spontaneous energy that both incites and terrifies; the same splattering of colors and entangled lines are there before you but now they're direct extensions of your own body. Now you're in the canvas. Those swift, dripped lines that run right across the canvas somehow flow through you and become frenzied gestures of your own self, yourself in the crowd, the crowd in you. You forget all, tear yourself away from all, are present *here* and *now*; passions are expressed rather than illustrated.

During such intense *mob* moments, such moments when people encounter one another, "the instant of greatest importance," a thinker like Henri Lefebvre reckons, "is the instant of failure. The drama is situated within that instant of failure: it is the emergence from the everyday or collapse on failing to emerge, it is a caricature or a tragedy, a successful festival or a dubious ceremony."[1] Therein lies the problem: The encounter "wants to endure," Lefebvre says, needs to endure, has to endure. "But it cannot endure (at least, not for very long). Yet this inner contradiction gives it its intensity, which reaches crisis point when the inevitably of its own demise becomes apparent."[2] One moment leads to another, and a politics of encounter erupts when moments collide, when affinities take hold. But how can the intensity of the encounter be sustained, how can it be harmonized with a continuous political evolution, with a politics of transformation, one that endures over the long haul? How to ensure that this encounter in everyday life—this spontaneous lived moment—assumes a mutation of world-historical significance?

The question assumes considerable gravity as well as grace (as Simone Weil might have said) for any would-be revolutionary. In fact, it lays down the stakes of what it means to be revolutionary in the first place; to want to initiate a clear and clean *break* with existing reality, wanting to break on through into another reality, into another realm, into another mode of production. Needless to say, the theme is first and foremost *political* not theoretical, answerable only through practice, not radical thought. But the issue of *break*—the idea that the revolutionary encounter or series of encounters unleashes a transition into something distinctively *new*, that it can punctuate different eras, signal a rupture between an old and a newer epoch—has been debated among Marxists ever since the beginnings of Marxism. Lefebvre says "the urban" is itself revolutionary, and, as such, the revolution would consequently be urban. In a single line, that summarizes the gist of *The Urban Revolution*.

And yet within that line lurks something else. By "revolution," Lefebvre says, "I refer to transformations that affect contemporary society. . . . Some transformations are sudden; others gradual, planned, determined. But which ones?" "It is by no means certain in advance," he says, "that the answer will be clear, intellectually satisfying, or unambiguous."[3] Lefebvre reckons that the urban revolution—the arrival of urban society—is a complex mix of *organicism*, *continuism*, and *evolutionism*, something both determined and contingent, a radical break and a gradual morphing, something real and virtual, "the actual" and "the possible" encountering one another. The seeds of urban society, for instance, were sown in the city. The medieval town harbored the emergence of the industrial city, and within one its other could be glimpsed. The transition from one to this other is borne by a historical process *and* a political praxis; it is both preexisting and a new creation. Periodization, in other words, looked upon retrospectively, is a lot messier and nondetermined than it might first appear. History spirals rather than unfolds linearly; and within its process, continuity and evolution can sometimes mask the inner ruptures associated with revolutionary transition.

If all this was the tale of the past—of the past considered retrospectively, of what happened during the transition from feudalism to capitalism and from the industrial city to urban society—then what's to say it wouldn't mark what might come *prospectively*? What might constitute the transition from capitalism to postcapitalism? Doubtless Louis Althusser would concur: in the existing order, he might have said, we already have the germ of another order, and encounters within this order are somehow the stepping stones, if not the building blocks, of this new order. We know that Althusser philosophized "the encounter" in the 1980s; he'd also tried to theorize in the 1970s (with Etienne Balibar) the question of the transition from one mode of production to another. What Althusser and Balibar actually said then is pretty similar to Lefebvre's own take. The "transition from one mode of production to another," wrote Balibar, "can therefore never appear in our understanding as an irrational hiatus between 'periods,'" but is instead "the result of their conjunction"; "the problems of the transition and of the forms of the transition from one mode of production to another are problems of a more general synchrony," not "diachrony."[4] "It seems that the *dislocation* between connections and instances in transition periods merely reflects," Balibar concluded, "*the coexistence of two (or more) modes of production in a single 'simultaneity,' and the dominance of one of them over the other.*"[5]

A decade on from these words, Althusser returned to the problem of "dislocation" and "coexistence" in transition periods. But he began to pose things in a different way and in a different language. He started to use the language of the encounter, probing the existence of human freedom even in the realm of necessity, and asking how an agglomeration of atoms gets induced, in a chain reaction, by an initial serve and encounter, positing in the process a kind of materialist contingency of the world. All questions of origin are rejected, origins of feudalism, capitalism, and, presumably, socialism or communism, too, especially the type that's yet to come. What we have is a piling together, certain combinations conjoining, the welling up of a strange order from the very heart of disorder, to produce a new world. Never is there a definitive break, a complete rupturing or total severing; never will a wholly new reality emerge from the destruction of the old reality. Only a transformed, reworked reality will prevail, a new unity of existing and yet-to-exist elements, all taking hold in surprising ways, in contingent ways, in ways that *depend*. For Marx, the rise of capitalism happened largely by chance, as an encounter between the owners of money and of proletarians stripped of everything but their labor-power. "It so happened," says Althusser, "that this encounter took place, and 'took hold,' which means that it did not come undone as soon as it came about, but *lasted*, and became an accomplished fact."[6] The operative words, of course, are "lasted" and "did not come undone." An encounter that lasts, that doesn't become undone, relative to one that fades, that is undone, might give us a new vocabulary for understanding the meaning of revolutionary "success," of what "real" social change constitutes, as well as how we might identify revolutionary rehearsals from the real performance, real swerving from feigned swerving.

II. Encountering the Crowd in the Encounter

In Isaac Asimov's version of "psychohistory," he thinks we can render more determinant and predictable the history that Althusser and Lefebvre announce as contingent. Asimov suggests there's something more *knowable* about "mobs" in history than individuals in history; "human conglomerates," as he calls them, exhibit behavioral patterns on a par with gases. The psychodynamics of the crowd, of the mob in history, came under scrutiny at the end of the nineteenth century by French social psychologist and sociologist Gustave Le Bon, who, in *The Crowd: A Study of the Popular Mind* (1896), likewise linked the crowd's unstable and constantly volatile nature with the natural sciences, especially with *luminiferous ether*; the crowd for Le Bon was a heady collective potion, a dangerous vaporous brew that shifted about en masse like the Nietzschean herd. In *Mein Kampf*, Hitler picked up on Le Bon's ideas about the crowd losing its mind, about being openly susceptible to demagogues; apparently, Le Bon's text was Mussolini's bedtime reading as well. The dangers of mass politics, of mass manipulation and fascist politics, are all too evident in Le Bon's book, which utters a stark warning that crowds can swing to the Right as well as to the Left, that human encounters can create darker contingent histories.[7]

Le Bon is very clear that in the crowd the *conscious* human personality vanishes and with it the voice of reason and reasonableness. "The crowd," he says, "is always dominated by considerations of which it is unconscious: the disappearance of brain activity and the predominance of medullar activity; the lowering of the intelligence and the complete transformation of the sentiments; the transformed sentiments may be better or worse than those of individuals of which the crowd is composed; a crowd is as easily heroic as criminal."[8] The crowd, in a word, is a *contagion* and, like all contagions, Le Bon thinks, "it is a phenomenon of which it is easy to establish the presence, but that it is not easy to explain. It must be classed among those phenomena of a hypnotic order. . . . In a crowd, every sentiment and act is contagious, and contagious to such a degree that an individual readily sacrifices his personal interest to the collective interest. This is an aptitude very contrary to his nature, and of which a man is scarcely capable, except when he makes his part of a crowd."

Much of what Le Bon says about the crowd recalls the character Umberto in *G.*, John Berger's Booker Prize–winning novel from 1972. Early in the story, Umberto, father of the book's eponymous antihero (himself eventually done in by the crowd), remembers a terrifying childhood encounter with a revolting crowd; the focal point here is the 1898 Milan workers' uprising, occurring only two years after Le Bon's crowd monograph. Umberto has a kind heart, but he's a conservative with reactionary tendencies. He hates crowds: the crowd is at best remote and abstract, Umberto says, and at worst insane and rabid. A sane man should always see himself apart from the masses, apart from the crowd; he should always see himself as an exemption from the rest of the world. "Such a crowd is a solemn test of a man," Umberto muses. "It assembles as a witness to its common fate—within which personal differentiations have become unimportant. . . . It has assembled to demand the impossible. Its need is to overthrow the order which has defined and distinguished between the possible and the impossible. . . . In face of such a crowd there are only two ways in which a man, who is not already of it, can react. Either he sees in it the promise of mankind or else he fears it absolutely."[9]

In the crowd, Umberto says, the self is overwhelmed by the uncontrollable weight of the collective: individual identity, personal differences, character quirks are all unimportant when one gives oneself over to the crowd. When one joins in the crowd, one hands over something intimate inside oneself, one loses something. One gives oneself over to a giant entity assembled to demand the impossible; and the discrepancy between its demands and the impossibility of ever meeting those demands inevitably leads to violence. Inevitably, too, the crowd is mad, mad as hell, raving mad. So the promise of mankind, says Umberto, isn't easy to see in a crowd: every particular face, every set of eyes, congeals into a singular abstraction. A single pair of eyes, met in the crowd, is enough to reveal the extent of vacant possibility, of palpable impossibility. One is justified to fear the crowd, Umberto thinks; one is justified to fear its feral fate.[10]

Berger creates Umberto to test out his own concept of the crowd in history, Berger's own idea of the revolutionary potential of the collective and of romantic revolution. In *G.*, Berger gropes—gropes conceptually, gropes experientially—for an ideal of the individual within a common praxis: he gropes for what Jean-Paul Sartre labeled a "constituted dialectic" of history, a very different reasoning from Le Bon's about crowds and groups in history. The constituted dialectic, says Sartre in *Critique of Dialectical Reason*, is one in which "the individual cannot achieve the common objective on their own, but they can conceive it, signify it, and, through it, signify the reorganization of the group. . . . Individuals integrate themselves into the group and the group has its practical limit in the individual."[11] Berger puts it similarly in *G.*, though more romantically: "The crowd sees the city around them with different eyes. They have stopped the factories producing, forced the shops to shut, halted the traffic, occupied the streets. It is they who have built the city and they who maintain it. They are discovering their own creativity. In their regular lives they only modify presented circumstances; here, filling the streets and sweeping all before them they oppose their very existence to circumstances. They are rejecting all that they habitually, and despite themselves, accept: Once again they demand together what none can ask alone: Why should *I* be compelled to sell my life bit by bit so as not to die?"[12] (Emphasis is mine: suddenly, the crowd becomes vital for the efficacy of "I," for one's self-development.)

The most compelling passages on crowds in *G.* became actual reenactments of Berger's theoretical essay, "The Nature of Mass Demonstrations," first published in *New Society* when crowds of young men and women piled onto Europe's and America's streets in the spring of 1968. In this discussion, Berger hints of his research on the 1898 Milan uprising, when the cavalry charged the crowd and butchered a hundred workers, wounding many hundreds more. Berger reverses some of Le Bon's logic, arguing that rather than numb sensibility, in a crowd people become *more sensitive* as individuals, more feeling and thinking: for participants, "numbers cease to be numbers and become the evidence of their senses, the conclusions of their imaginations."[13] It's equally a question of individual representation: "The larger the demonstration," Berger says, "the more powerful and immediate (visible, audible, tangible) a metaphor it becomes for their total collective strength. I say metaphor because the strength thus grasped transcends the potential strength of those present, and certainly their actual strength as deployed in a demonstration. The more people are there, the more forcibly they represent to each other and to themselves those who are absent" (248). Berger is convinced that crowds of people in demonstrations can be distinguished from crowds in riots or even in revolutionary uprisings. The aim of a crowd in a demonstration is essentially *symbolic*; they are rehearsals, he says, for revolution, not strategic rehearsals, or tactical ones, but "rehearsals of revolutionary awareness" (247).

A mass demonstration is certainly a spontaneous event, Berger thinks; and yet, no matter how much it is spontaneous, it is equally something *created by individuals*. People literally come together to create a function, to protest, to express themselves; they're not responding to a function like a crowd of shoppers.

The crowd at a demonstration acts rather than reacts; or, if they react, it's only to react to what they have already done, to how their actions have been received by the powers that be. In any mass demo, at any mass occupation, demonstrators and occupants—the demonstrating and occupying crowd—"simultaneously *extend* and *give body* to an abstraction" (248). (In a more contemporary lexicon, we might say they *extend* and give a material *body* to a *virtuality*.) "Demonstrators interrupt the regular life of the streets they march through or of the open spaces they fill. They 'cut off' these areas, and, not yet having the power to occupy them permanently, they transform them into a temporary stage on which they dramatize the power they still lack" (248). "Demonstrations are protests of innocence," says Berger. The crowd at a mass demonstration, a mass encounter, or a mass occupation expresses political ambitions before the political means necessary to realize them is created.[14] The revolutionary in the crowd, as well as the revolutionary crowd, has to learn how to wait, how to symbolically rehearse, how to translate their inner force into an external common and transformative praxis. One has to test oneself in the collective and strategic drama of the historical performance itself, in the encounter that is destined to *last*, that *will not be undone.*

III. Smart Mobs and Flash Crowds

There's something about the political crowd today, something that's a lot *smarter* than the crowd of yesteryear. Those crowds at mass demonstrations had no power in the drama of the moment, no power to coordinate, no power to maneuver in the face of authority's assault. The crowds that Berger describes in *G.* have plenty of passionate individuals, united around a cause, who have identified a common enemy; yet they have no way to speedily round up the troops, no means to react like the army or a horseback cavalry. The crowd always had a logic and a rationale to its actions, and to its reactions, but when it came to offensive practice, the revolting crowd could never match the media power of its antagonists, the lines of communication of the ruling classes. In *Magical Marxism*, I recall the moment in Gabriel García Márquez's *One Hundred Years of Solitude* when the revolutionary freedom fighter, Colonel Aureliano Buendia, signals to his friend Gerineldo Márquez to "get the boys ready." "We're going to war," the colonel says. "With what weapons?" Márquez wonders. "With theirs," the colonel replies—with new corporate communication technologies, he might have said, turning them against their antagonists, mobilizing them as spontaneous radical weapons.[15]

Foremost here is the cell phone, now a redoubtable weapon for communicating *sur place*, on the spot, spontaneously. Young people raised in the culture of cell phones no longer make appointments or arrangements weeks in advance like older folks. By calling around, by passing the message on, by sending emails on the hoof, by providing graphic camera images, they organize themselves, rendezvous, communicate, and express themselves, *just-in-time*. Ditto in politics, whose tactics, crowd politics, and mass actions now dance to a different tactic: digital media have collapsed space and diminished the time of organizing, of shifting civilian troops around, of supplying reinforcements when and where needed. Now, spontaneous encounters can be managed and orchestrated via SMS updates, shared photos, Twitter streams, and on-location reports of movements, street closures, and police actions. These give protesters continuous and almost instantaneous updates about "swarming tactics" on the streets, crucial for outsmarting centralized police radio systems and for dodging "security bubbles" and heavy police presences. Younger participants here see themselves as second-generation, post-Seattle "Smart Mobbers," after Howard Rheingold's catchy thesis, the virtual communities guru whose influential book, *Smart Mobs: The Next Social Revolution* (2002), has become staple reading for disaffected computer geeks who've transformed themselves into intrepid hackers and connected citizens now morphing into the emergent Occupy movement. Smart Mob keywords are: "mobile communication," "pervasive computing," "wireless networks," and "collective action."

Digital media activism might even be ushering in a new "Fifth International," a qualitatively different form of leftist organizing and politicking from yesteryear's internationals, traditionally pioneered by party-based socialists and rank-and-file unionists. The current "informatized and globalized capitalism," writes Peter Waterman, the coiner of the "Fifth International" thesis, is a capitalism different in form and content from that pervasive during the era of the "International Working Men's Associations"; today, modes of solidarity and styles of praxis require other means and incorporate new nonaffiliated and nonaligned protagonists.[16] A newly forming, looser coterie of smart and concerned citizens, spanning the entire globe and dialoguing in many different languages, are thus finding their collective lingua franca in the growing array of informational technology acronyms like SMS, BBM, PDA, GPS, GPL, XML, and so on. And they're drawing upon their dazzling expertise to create an anarcho-communist subculture of politically minded hackers and virtual radicals whose activism and communication culminates as a palpable mega-underground finding its mass voice.

This fluid mix of online and offline activism and deliberate downshifting is a contra-capitalism germinating within actually existing capitalism, an auto-organization negating the system from within as it tries to invent an alternative community from without. The tactics, the actors, and the weapons are now all different from the past. This recentering and decentering of urban politics is diffusing and infiltrating within the social body of society, catalyzing a recomposition of that society. Experiments in other modes of life are getting explored within this new community of occupiers, within the interstices of a society whose monopoly and centralization of the means of production have reached a point at which they're incompatible with the socialization of labor. New technology has created ever more complex and diverse divisions of labor and, historically, capital has appropriated this as a source of relative surplus value. Technology's prowess, Marx says, rests in its ability "to increase the productive power of the individual, *by means of cooperation*," by creating a new productive power, "which is intrinsically a collective one."[17] But this cuts both ways: collective and cooperative power, hastened as it is by planetarization and informatization, opens up new potentialities for revolt and resistance; and Marx knew it.[18] The "unavoidable antagonism," he says, is that "as the number of cooperative workers increases, so too does their resistance to the domination of capital."[19] And it's an unavoidable antagonism that is broadening the terrain for any member of the neo-proletariat, for any mega-underground occupier, for any HCE, creating an expanded and more concentrated urban network for a different kind of cooperation, with new powers of desire and imagination within collective sharing.

What might be most revolutionary about the smart mob today is its speed, its gaseous flow, its rate of dispersal and cloud formation, the manner in which it flashes here and there. The smart crowd is equally the *flash crowd* that displaces itself with unnerving effect, indeed like luminiferous ether. What first began as science fiction now seems ominously real, if not Reality TV then certainly the reality of You Tube. In 1973 the Californian sci-fi writer Larry Niven wrote a compelling short story, "Flash Crowd," without any sign of alien life other than those feral rioters portrayed by mainstream TV networks. Niven takes us to futuristic Los Angeles, when Wilshire Boulevard is a pedestrian walkway and LAX is a quiet backwater terminal. Air and car travel have been superseded by teleportation and with it the whole space-time of the metropolis has changed. Swipe your credit card at any "displacement booth," dial the right coordinates for your voyage, and, with the rapidity of a voice during a phone call, you're in New York or Las Vegas or Rio. What's amazing in this super high-tech LA is how freeways and driveways have all grassed over; concrete strips are left for bicycles; wider spaces are for helicopters carrying cargo too large for displacement booths; and parking lots are mini golf courses.

Niven's central character in "Flash Crowd" is Jerryberry Jansen, an investigative journalist for CBA, a major network TV channel. He's a kind of gumshoe reporter, a roving "newstaper" who keeps his eyes and ears close to street, on the lookout for a good story, a newsworthy primetime TV story. Without quite realizing it, he suddenly finds himself at the Santa Monica Mall just as a riot breaks out, and he is in the heat of the drama as a mob starts to loot stores. It even looks like he's fanned the flames of the riot by poking his camera in people's faces: so intent on capturing a good story, he creates a good story. Crowds pour in, seemingly from nowhere, and Jerryberry videos the exploding scene, holding his camera aloft over the bobbing heads of people, who are manically smashing big display windows and helping themselves to assorted wares. "A young woman pushed herself close to Jerryberry," says Niven. "Her eyes were wide; her hair was wild. A kind of rage, a kind of joy, made her face a battlefield. 'Legalize direct-current stimulus,' she screamed at him. She lunged and caught the snout of Jerryberry's camera and mike and pulled it around to face her. 'Legalize wireheading!'"[20]

Before you know it, the rioters swarm and take over the entire mall. The cops manage to secure its perimeter and their helicopters fly overhead, but for a long while they are unable to control an angry mob of looters intent on after-hours shopping. Sirens wail; a CBA helicopter gets shot down; two men are carried away on stretchers. "Most of the street lights are out," Niven says. "Those left cast monstrous shadows through the mall. Orange flames flicker in the windows of a furniture store."[21] The explosive growth of the mall riot takes the enforcement agencies by surprise. When the drama finally quells and people go home, fingers point at Jerryberry, the supposed perpetrator: Did he start the riot? Just how did it all start? The news channel boss fires him. But Jerryberry wants answers himself, and he goes on a personal investigative quest for the truth. "Hell, I know what caused the mall riot," one interviewee tells him. "The news program, yes. But the long-distance displacement booths did it, too. Control those, and we could stop that kind of riot ever happening again."[22]

Hitherto, displacement booths were never questioned. After all, LA no longer had traffic jams, airlines, slow mail, smog, air pollution, or even slum landlords. You didn't have to live near your job or your welfare office now; job hunting, crowding, gridlock, all that's a thing of the past, the ancient past. With displacement booths nobody needs streets, either. People move like electrons in a tunnel diode, coursing at the speed of light, faster than the speed of light even. Electrons can and do actually dematerialize, and they can rematerialize elsewhere; in quantum physics they do it all the time. Einstein showed us how quantum mechanics is essentially *nonlocal*; disturbances from one source of the universe, he knew, instantly affect other distant parts. Einstein called it "spook action-at-a-distance," but he questioned it and ended up thinking it absurd and hence quantum theory wrong.[23] Yet quantum theory proved Einstein wrong; and later on physicists began hinting at the possibility of superneutrinos, particles inside electrons that might travel faster than the speed of light, which meant that long-distance teleportation was possible, effects become causes (not the other way around), and relativity theory was mistaken. "For ten minutes," a displacement booth expert tells Jerryberry, people become "a kind of superneutrino."[24] Still, there's a downside: displacement booths and teleportation "imply instant riots . . . instant getaways, instant smuggling," new forms of social unrest, and, maybe, just maybe, new forms of social protest and people mobilization, too.

What's significant, then, is CROWDS—crowd formation, mobs that travel from crowd to crowd, "looting where they can." The new crowd is the *flash crowd*, a veteran cop tells Jerryberry; flash crowds couldn't have formed that quickly, he says, before long-distance displacement booths. "It's a new crime," the cop sighs, "makes me almost sorry I retired."[25] From now on at the first word the police get of a flash crowd, of a mall riot–type crowd, the emergency switches are thrown at headquarters and they close down the displacement booths in the vicinity. "Our whole problem is that rioters can converge on one point from all over the United States," the cop laments. What we now have, he cautions, are "permanent floating flash crowds," a new phenomenon, a new threat—permanent floating populations who might now encounter each other at dramatic, unprecedented speeds and scales.[26]

Needless to say, the reality of teleportation is something futuristic; hypothetically possible, maybe, yet still sci-fi, still in the realm of conjecture, the maximum speed limit yet to arrive. Yet it's easy to see how even the limited, "slower" digital technology of today alters the speed and scale of crowds, of combustible looting crowds like Niven's flash crowd but also of protesting, combustible political crowds, of "spook action-at-a-distance." A text message is sent calling for an occupation, and instantaneously it might reach 10 people, then 20, then 50, and soon 500 or even 5,000 people. The audience multiplies exponentially, the virtual distance diminishes, and the physical crowd becomes viral, present, a movable feast; small inputs have potentially dramatic large-scale outputs. And when a crowd is dispersed, when it becomes physically separated as in past times, now it can still somehow remain connected and stay virtually wired as a wirehead, or maybe, even, a fused group.

IV. From Flash Crowds to Fused Groups

If he'd ever read Larry Niven's short story, Jean-Paul Sartre would have probably called the "flash crowd" a "gathering" or a perhaps a "group in series," a not-yet-consummated "fused group." The fused group lies at the heart of the *Critique of Dialectical Reason*, Sartre's magisterial work and his own favorite, which tried to critique dialectical reason in the name of a better dialectical reason, one that better informed and explained revolutionary practice. It's one, too, that worked out a constituted dialectic in which *individuals become the living temporalizations and spatializations of the group*. Thus the constituted dialectic represents Sartrean dialectical reason, a dialectical intelligibility that "explains the practical relations of individual functions within an organized group."[27] In this dialectic, the individual becomes a willing, conscious component of the revolutionary crowd; people constitute the dialectic itself, and they encounter one another as individuals within this dialectic, within its fused group, within its group in fusion.

For Sartre, the becoming of this dialectic follows distinctive steps: from alienated individuals to a "series" of individuals; from serial "gatherings" to groups; and from groups that encounter each another, that bond with one another, to become fused groups and a so-termed third party. The passage from one phase to another marks, for Sartre, the passage from revolutionary rehearsals to the real thing—to the veritable storming of the Bastille. This key moment of the 1789 French Revolution is fleshed out by Sartre to shed light on what constitutes revolutionary success and failure, and why. On July 14, 1789, insurgents blasted into the Bastille in an explosive assault that had been gurgling within Parisian everyday life. People's serial behavior had slowly been replaced by a new dimension of collective praxis. In seriality, individuals relate to one another inertly, passively, like the way individuals relate to one another in a line or queue, unified yet divided. In the seriality of 1789, the city of Paris was the field of the practico-inert, the passive staging of a puppet theater in which ordinary Parisians were the puppets. But as the people started to arm themselves against Louis XVI and his monarchy, defensive violence was unleashed, a spate of violence and looting—common action without either common organization or active totalization. Still, ever so steadily, the people got *active*, negated their own inertia and became conscious of themselves against an enemy, matching a group interiorization with an exteriorization. From initial passive seriality, when people allowed themselves to be represented by a crooked and corrupt assembly, a collectivity began to organize itself and to recognize itself in its actions and violence, in its contestation and spontaneity *against* that assembly. "The gathering," says Sartre, "perceived its reality as an organized being."[28]

As such, the fused group began to emerge, founded upon the dissolution of serial gathering. First, the group melded as a collective process of negation; soon a "positive determination of praxis" (357) really fused it, gelled it as well as ignited it. Typically complexly, Sartre says that "a fused group is in fact still a series, negating itself in re-interiorizing exterior negations; in other words, in this moment there is no distinction between the positive itself (the group in formation) and this self-negation (the series in dissolution)" (356). All actions thereafter represented "a constituted praxis, in and against the passive field." The culmination of the fused group, says Sartre, is when the unity of its participants creates a new combination, an inventive fusion of people who represent themselves both as an "I" and a "we," a unity of me and you, of you and me — especially of you and me *against* them. The net product is a distinctively new synthesis, a Sartrean "third party," in which "I, myself" becomes at the same time "we, the people."

Again, Sartre puts it smartly yet intricately, also rather beautifully: "Through the third party, in effect, practical unity, as the negation of a threatening organized praxis, reveals itself *through* the constellation of reciprocities. From a structural point of view, the third party is the human mediation through which the multiplicity of epicenters and ends (identical and separate) organizes itself directly, as determined by a synthetic objective."[29] At such point, the people are a short step from being capable of blasting into the Bastille, that black, threatening fortress in Paris's Saint-Antoine district, the symbol of repressive power, not only a prison with local inmates but a bastion with cannons that needed seizing. With the storming of the Bastille, this fabled, fused third party "interiorized as a fantom possibility of producing itself in the field of freedom."[30]

There is much that's brilliant and suggestive in Sartre's account of the fused group from *Critique of Dialectical Reason*, of "fantom possibilities" in the field of freedom; there's much that equips any latter-day freedom fighter and occupier, much that can inform our social–media organized praxis and how we can reveal ourselves, express ourselves, through a "constellation of reciprocities." Maybe, unsurprisingly, there are also a few things that need updating in Sartre's thesis, because somehow they don't quite go anymore. The major qualm is the idea of a fused group smashing the state, breaking into it like eighteenth-century insurgents raiding the Bastille, dismantling it and then taking things over. Any postcapitalist experiment will always be in the course of transition, always in the course of adaptation, always resisting something in order to affirm itself, always negotiating its own internal power-play alongside its will to empower itself. The act is rarely ever finished. In its search for autonomous self-affirmation and self-organization of everyday life, any fused group must wedge itself into state power, must create a *breach* within the interior of the neoliberal state's integration of political and economic life. Head-on confrontation, the sense of *smashing* something, probably won't create this breach, nor will the state be broken in any hammer blow.

Marx himself spoke of "breaking state power," of "smashing the state," when, in the autumn of 1870, Parisian workers tried to break French state power. Marx was skeptical about whether they'd succeed in this desire; he said any attempt to smash the state was the "folly of despair." Yet the following spring, during the Commune, a worker and citizen uprising became a vivid reality, and Marx changed his tune, greeting this spontaneous proletarian revolt with generosity despite its unfavorable auguries. As Lenin put it in *State and Revolution*, Marx wasn't only enthusiastic about the heroism of the Communards, who, he'd said, had "stormed heaven"; he equally regarded the event as a historic landmark in revolutionary practice, as a key experiment in advancing world proletarian revolution everywhere. It was a lesson to analyze and from which tactical lessons could be gleaned. Moreover, around the time of the Paris Commune, Marx wrote a letter to Kugelmann (April 12, 1871), in which he claimed: "If you look up the last chapter of my Eighteenth Brumaire, you will find that I declare that the next attempt of the French Revolution will be no longer, as before, to transfer the bureaucratic-military machine from one hand to another, but to *smash* it, and this is the precondition for every real people's revolution on the Continent. And this is what our heroic Party comrades in Paris are attempting."[31]

Lenin drew a similar conclusion: "To smash the bureaucratic machine," he said, "briefly expresses the principal lesson of Marxism regarding the task of the proletariat during a revolution in relation to the state." Still, despite Lenin and Marx's noble analytical intentions, *smashing* the bureaucratic state's financial machine is something no social movement is ever likely to achieve these days. The Communards discovered as much the hard way; they were, according to Lenin, working their way toward this goal of smashing the state, but they never quite reached that end. Maybe Lenin was asking too much—or too little—of the proletarian revolution? Because *smashing* doesn't seem quite right anymore: it's too impossible a practice and too simple an analysis. So rather than talking about smashing the state, perhaps it's more accurate to refer to making a breach within it, subverting it, as in a decoupling from the state's "official" domain to weaken its grip on civil society and loosen its political and bureaucratic straightjacket. This seems to me a much more fruitful choice of vocabulary in the contemporary age. A liberated, autonomous realm is one in which new communes bloom and the realm of the possible—another possible world—might be glimpsed. But it's a zone that must somehow be enlarged, must spread itself out, *horizontally*, made bigger and stronger on all sides and more resistant in its own self-affirmation at the core.

The Sartrean passage from seriality to third parties, from gatherings encountering one another to create a new heightened sense of unity and fusion—all of this continues to speak bundles about what needs to be done. Sartre says a "gathering" (*rassemblement*) is some form of collectivity, a series of people capable of constituting a group. "Groups," accordingly, aren't so much people standing behind each other in a cinema line as "an ensemble each of whose members is determined by the others in reciprocity."[32] Sartre doesn't say it but what makes fusion happen within a group is when something "takes hold," and here the idea of the encounter intervenes, and creates this swerving of history and geography. Its temporality is a shifting, nonlinear time-frame, a mix of real time and eternal time, a praxis taking hold synchronically and diachronically. Otherwise put, it takes time for self awareness and common notions to emerge, for adequate ideas to develop, and for constellations of people to invent and discover reciprocities. The gathering gathers momentum, digitally connects, and forms smart mobs and flash crowds on the street; then the encounter begins and leads to new encounters, to new acts of fusion, to new speeds and tactics.

Around that point, the geography of the fused group becomes transformed, too, in special and important ways. Before the encounter, before the fused group took hold, "the city," we might say, and its spaces were just there, simply latent, passive terrains of the practico-inert. I say "city" because these spaces existed like dead labor in redundant fixed capital, objectified in the landscape, smacking of alienation, of nonlife, of plain-old bricks and mortar, of concrete and steel. As Sartre says, the free group organizes to combat the "passive action of the practico-inert" (556), of the city as alienating objectification. For urban spaces to come alive, they need to be occupied and taken over by dynamic social relations between people, there and elsewhere in other urban spaces, bringing those to life as well, thus creating a living, organic spatiality that isn't so much a "constituent objectification" as a "constituted subjectivation," the "opposition and identity of the individual and the common."[33] "The crowd," John

Berger said, "sees the city around them with different eyes," sees itself in urban space, making this space, a decentered yet fused urban realm, in which, finally, they are participants and not pawns—citizens yearning to breathe free.

V. A Note on Radical Fusion: Collideorscapes, Wormholes, and Minor Space

Should an encounter *really* take hold, *really* gel, the Sartrean fused group would doubtless be a kind of political superstring theory realizing itself, a transformative conjoining around a collective boson. Like particle physicists today, we know theoretically and mathematically from our radical hypotheses that this collective reality exists, even if we have never yet witnessed it empirically. We are 99 percent sure that the figures stack up, that those in the boson will be the 99 percent. If that ever happens—when it happens—we will see before our eyes a beautiful *collideorscape*. The notion of the encounter is perhaps the central motif of James Joyce's *Finnegans Wake*. Here the *collideorscape* marks for Joyce something of a "collide and escape," a coming together, a kaleidoscope of sorts, a coincidence taking hold, a shaking up of things to give form to another reality, an escape into a changed perception, into another stage of liberation. So the *collideorscape* is a portmanteau word for a new portmanteau politics.[34] And in this portmanteau politics the spatial question won't go away: it'll always be the battleground for political struggle, the center stage of any encounter, of any *collideorscape*, of any fused group dissolving the city's practico-inert.

The vocabulary is strange here: it's meant to be, because we're trying to define a different object, trying to develop a new way of seeing and naming it—not only as an emergent planetary urban space but as an emergent political subject, too, trying at once to retheorize this new spatial object and nascent active subject. Yet we must tread carefully with any naming; we don't want to close things down and button things up (as Sartre said). Instead we want to define this conjuncture in its indefinite becoming, in its possible becoming. Revolution is a process, not only an end point; it can't only be an outcome, a finished product, something done forever. If dialecticians posit reality as movement and contradiction, as "the laws of motion," why would this apply only to capitalism? Would the motion stop, postcapitalism? That's why the Joycean terminology is so provocative and evocative: It flashes up a mental image, even a mental map, without offering definitive road directions. The Joycean *collideorscape* is another way of expressing the elusive conjoining of a *praxis* and a *process* that Sartre identified, that he was so adamant had to be conjoined, and that he'd suggested might resemble a "constellation of reciprocities." For Joyce, just as for

Sartre, this *collideorscape*, this "constellation of reciprocities," would sound (and smell!) like a "panaroma of all flores of speech."[35]

What might this *collideorscape* look like, how might we see it, imagine it? The imagery, the pictorial representation of resistance, the sight of a politics of the encounter unfolding in our mind's eye, might once again come from abstract expressionism, from for example, Jackson Pollock's 1950 canvas *Number 32*, currently hanging in Dusseldorf's Kunstsammlung Nordrhein-Westfalen. Pollock's patterning depicts the very act of *fusion*, of people becoming the Sartrean "fused group." Like all of Pollock's best art, it's not so much what he meant in his paintings as what it means for you when you encounter his paintings, what it does for you: all metaphorical and inspirational potential resides firmly in the eye of the beholder.

Only two colors make up Pollock's masterpiece *Number 32*, a painting he rated among his greatest: canvas white over which skeins of jet black swirls are splattered—bold black skeins. One is struck by the energy and vitality that radiates from this composition, from a blackness that seems to permanently oscillate; if you verge too close, it sucks you into its spiraling vortex. Energy enters via thin whirls and curves, puddles and dribbles, wiggly threads of splattered black. Yet there are points of convergence—snowflakes and dendrites—where the black paint thickens and is nodal, highly charged. Modest inputs here spiral inward and release enormous outputs, energy that pushes outward, a diffusion unleashing a quantity-quality reaction, a critical mass of power, the radical geography of mass encounter. What goes on in a Pollock canvas like *Number 32* isn't so much a picture as an event; every boundary between art and life collapses. In this imagery we not only glimpse radical fractals but also the physicists' concept of the *wormhole* coming to life, as illusive shortcuts and tiny trails toward liberation express themselves before our very eyes, letting us slip through.[36]

Wormholes create new regions of planetary urban space, blaze new spatial territories and a new political space-time dimension, with new *minor spaces* that secretly link and make bridges, or subterranean tunnels, between social movements everywhere. Do they exist in our cosmic universe? Do they exist in our social cosmos? Let's wait and see if wormholes *conclude* and *complete* the encounter, transmitting *messenger particles* that unite all struggles across the planet. Charged particles transmit negative, repulsive energy, frequently saying to other particles, "move apart"; yet every particle also has an opposite charge, with powers of attractions that say "come together." In our contemporary, ever-expanding urban universe, little loops of energy generate incredible force; they literally make the world go around, light it up with electricity, create a different kind of blue. It's time for political struggles to really energize this new planetary charge, to convert it into unprecedented cosmic singularity—into a new *concrete* expressionism and a passage into an almost-unimaginable parallel urban realm.

Wormholes are little troubling spaces that create vortexes within the macrospace of planetary capitalism. These wormholes create trouble because they spell ruptures and rifts within the plane of capitalist immanence. In the wormhole the specific gravity of the world market no longer applies; there the air and light are fresher and brighter. Wormholes bring rain to the arid zone of neoliberal desertification. Lefebvre calls the most troubling space within our actually existing terrestrial universe *abstract space*. By abstract space, he means a space infused with power and a certain notion of order and rationality. Abstract space is an essentially colorless and featureless space, formal and quantitative, Lefebvre says: it erases all distinctions that derive from nature and originate in the *body*. But abstract space isn't what it seems. It isn't what its name directly implies: there is nothing abstract here, abstract in the sense of something existing purely conceptually, in the mind. Indeed, abstract space is deeply material, deeply and troublingly *real*; it is really embodied in a space like the world market, embodied in glass and steel, in concrete, in social relations and institutions, in security zones, in assorted trade agreements, in the kind of vision of the world that is plotted at places like Davos each year when the World Economic Forum meets. Abstract space thus has very real social existence, just as interest rates and share prices do; real ontological status; and real, objective expression in specific buildings and places, in activities and modes of market intercourse over and through space.

Abstract space bears an uncanny resemblance to Marx's notion of *abstract labor*, even if Lefebvre ventures much further than Marx, for whom "abstract" operates as an explicitly temporal category. Marx, remember, holds that qualitatively different (concrete) labor activities get reduced to one quantitative (abstract) measure: money. Making a shirt is the concrete labor of a tailor whose use value is sanctioned by the market price for shirts, that is, its exchange value. At such a point, what is concrete, useful, and particular becomes abstract, money-driven, and universal. Similar things happen to space. There is no actual separation as such, no concrete space here and abstract space over there. Rather, it is much more a prioritization, a societal prioritization of the *conceived*, of *representations of space* over directly lived and perceived space, over the space of ordinary everyday life. In *The Production of Space*, Lefebvre insists that all of us "make" space; but all of us can't make that space in the same way, nor on the same terms, especially in terms of power. With the notion of "representations of space," Lefebvre underscores the dominance of the space that pivots around how assorted professionals, technocrats, and wealthy people envision the world, the world we are forced to live in. They have the power and knowledge to make their abstract representations real-life representations, both concrete and ideological; they can make space everywhere subject to their own signs and codifications, their own grandiose plans and world-historical paradigms.

For Lefebvre, the antidote to this abstract space of representation is *differential space*, a space that prioritizes *lived* difference, that emphasizes bodily difference, heterogeneity, and perceiving and feeling as much as thinking and conceiving—or else it wouldn't want to make the absolute Cartesian separations between these interrelated realms. We might say that differential space is an *affective* and *affecting* space, felt and heard, seen and directly experienced through the senses, implying, says Lefebvre, an intimate relationship to one's *body*. Curiously, in *The Production of Space* there are as many index entries for "the body" as there are for "Karl Marx" and "Marxism." *The Production of Space* is, then, very much the production of bodies in space. Bodies affect and get affected by space. Bodies are located in space, and they are associated with other bodies to produce space. Space is produced through bodies encountering other bodies. By walking down the street, encountering other people, we produce the social space of the urban. But this lived experience of the body, this active human agency, is never completely free: it is bound within a pregiven abstract space by a built landscape that provides the context for our daily lives, by activities and processes that take place, as it were, "behind our backs," because they operate in ways, and at larger spatial scales, beyond the immediacy of our everyday lives. (Sartre calls this phenomenon, this instantiation of abstract space, the "practico-inert.") In this way, bodies are troubled by abstract space; yet, at the same time, they can also create trouble for abstract space.

Lefebvre uses the term "differential space" as a practice that can intervene in the production of abstract space. He uses it, in other words, as something both metaphorical and practical, as something here in what we already have now, yet also as something *normative*, too, something that ought to be and might be here soon. But it's possible to give this idea of differential space another spin, relabel it as a space that makes trouble, a space we can deem *minor space*, something emerging *within* a wormhole. This notion of "minor" isn't taken from Lefebvre but from Gilles Deleuze and Félix Guattari, from their book on Kafka, "For a Minor Literature" (*pour une littérature mineure*, or "Toward a Minor Literature" as it's translated in English).[37] What we are talking about here is *minor space*—subversive, intrusive, interventionist, troublesome space, troublesome for the dominant order, for "major" abstract space—much as Deleuze and Guattari invoke Kafka as the destabilizer of canonical "major" literature.

Deleuze and Guattari's book on Kafka is a weird one; all Deleuze's books with Guattari are rather weird, weirder than they were when he wrote on his own. But if we are to mobilize their central argument about what defines "minor" literature, we can get some way into defining "minor" space. Thus there are three components to minor space, just as there are for minor literature, and each relates very pressingly to "the body":

(1) Instead of a "deterritorialization" of language (Kafka, a Jew, writing in German, in Catholic Czechoslovakia), minor space involves a deterritorialization of the body. The deterritorialization of the body in minor space means that the body's relationship with abstract space is disruptive, out of place, displaced, the wrong body, the wrong color, the wrong gender, the wrong shape, a body that perhaps finds itself awkwardly embedded in a borderland territory. The deterritorialized body is a body that stands its ground, that takes to flight or fight. It's important to remember that deterritorialization isn't *placelessness*: bodies can be rooted in a place, can even yearn to be rooted, in the sense that they are forcibly nomadic because they have no desired place (e.g., Palestinians on the West Bank). Something like a deterritorialization of the body occurs in that strange, liminal reality found in virtual space, one that circulates online but which sometimes finds itself reterritorialized offline, somewhere in a place. In minor space, being out of place might be a state of perpetual becoming. Bodies in minor space aren't homogeneous, aren't either/or as much as both and neither. They don't fit easily into any dominant whole; the body in minor space is what is left over after all the sums have been done, after everything has seemingly been accounted for by the established order. The deterritorialization of the body in minor space is an affirmation of residue, of remainders, of the radicality of the irreducible, even if the notion of "minor" here in no way implies the quantitative few: we are talking about a social, cultural, and political minority who are maybe a quantitative majority, the 99 percent, for example.[38]

(2) A connection of the individual body to a *political immediacy*. The deterritorialized body is the political body. Everything in minor space, like Deleuze and Guattari's minor literature, is political—often willy-nilly. It is a microspace that lodges itself somewhere and some-

how into the power relations of abstract macrospace, challenging, in some way or another, the authority and legitimacy of those power relations. In Judith Butler's essay "Bodies in Alliance and the Politics of the Street," written when bodies occupied Zuccotti Park,[39] she uses Hannah Arendt's notion (from *The Human Condition*) that all political acts require a "space of appearance." People *appearing* collectively defines politics and the public realm: "it is the space of appearance in the widest sense of the word," writes Arendt, "namely, the space where I *appear* to others as others appear to me, where people exist not merely like other living or inanimate things *but make their appearance explicitly*."[40] "To rethink the space of appearance," Butler says, pushing Arendt further, "in order to understand the power and effect of public demonstrations for our time, we will need to understand the bodily dimensions of action, what the body requires, and what the body can do, especially when we must think about bodies together, what holds them there, their conditions of persistence and of power." Butler is surely spot on in urging us to understand "the bodily dimensions of action"; yet does Arendt's idea still stand for how bodies would politically function in minor space? Somehow the "space of appearance" doesn't seem quite right. For the politics of the body in minor space isn't defined by appearance so much as *by opacity and anonymity, by clandestinity and dissimulation, by invisibility*. One of the most radically challenging themes emerging from *The Coming Insurrection*, authored by the suggestively provocative "Invisible Committee," is precisely this notion of clandestinity, of invisibility, of how apparent absence can unnerve the powers that be.[41] The power of *surprise*, of secret organization, of rebelling, of demonstrating and plotting covertly, of striking invisibly and in multiple sites at once, is the key element that the Invisible Committee affirms for confronting a power whose firepower is always vastly superior. To be explicitly visible, *to appear explicitly*—in a maneuver, in organizing, in an occupation—"is to be exposed, that is to say above all, vulnerable."[42] Here black ski masks and Guy Fawkes masks become emblems of veritable nobodies, of invisible underground men and women, of people without qualities who want to disguise their inner qualities. These people shun visibility in public and have little desire to be the somebody the world wants them to be. Bodies in minor space are expressive bodies, yet they are also bodies weary of revealing too much of themselves, which is why they may wear disguises and masks: bodies reveal their true identities by dissimulating their faces, by disguising themselves, by transgressing where these bodies are supposed to be and how they are supposed to act and look. Bodies in minor space scramble and blur the dominant, "major" cartography of abstract space, doing so as they sometimes blur and scramble their own bodies.

(3) It is no surprise, perhaps, that the third characteristic of minor space is that everything it does, everything it needs to do, takes on a *collective value*. The body in minor space utters a language of *collective expression*; it is therefore an affective and affecting body, in a space that implicitly and explicitly constitutes a *common* action, making collective enunciations. It is a space that tries to produce something concrete, in an active solidarity, in spite of its skepticism of the dominant order. Minor space is political and collective because it knows that, at the level of individuality, the lone body is a fragile body, and hence the expressiveness of the body always needs to be voiced as a collectivity. We might say that minor space is expressive of those "common notions" that Spinoza outlines in *Ethics* and that Deleuze makes so much of in his book on Spinoza's "Expressionism." A body's structure is a composition of its relationships to other bodies. Hence a common notion is something that bonds us biologically and mentally, corporeally as well as cognitively; a body expressing a common understanding, sharing common ground; and bodies expressing naked life despite outwardly disguised and clothed dissimulation. All common notions we understand as agreeing with our body and our mind, with our collective bodies and minds, in a necessary complementarity between bodily feeling and conceptual understanding.

Occupy, of course, has all the credentials for creating a minor space, and embodies its central criteria: the deterritorialization of bodies, bodies out of place, present where they shouldn't be, absent from where they should be, bodies being themselves and somebody else (Guy Fawkes) and expressive of a common collective—the 99 percent—as they enunciate a new sort of political discourse that doesn't demand anything. No body present here wasn't there before, as James Joyce might have said: "Only is order othered." Minor space thus *others order*, and does so by making no claims, no rights' claims; it shows rather than tells, expresses sentiment rather than theory. Which perhaps raises the question: Would the sum of all minor spaces constitute something of an alternative "major" space? Perhaps. To express doubt here isn't to be necessarily pessimistic. It's rather to suggest that minor space is intrinsically defined by its *negative capability*. That's not to say, either, that minor space isn't creative or affirmative: it can be absolutely creative and affirmative, both artistically and practically, aesthetically and politically. But it is a creative/lived act that draws sustenance from its *oppositional* status. It tries to create something positive, but its determination is one of negation; it is negation that gels the different minor spaces together—"all determination is negation," said Spinoza (Letter #50 to Jelles). Spinoza's phrase is something else than Hegel's famous urging "to look the negative in the face and tarry with it."[43] The former's reasoning suggests that all fusions come together because a negative energy forces open the wormhole, that each encounter is an expression of dissatisfaction. However, while each encounter creates its own minor space through negativity, the conjoining of each space produces something positive, something affirmative that goes beyond living permanently with the negative. The sum is the magical power of *positivity*. The math is simple: the multiplication of negative integers stacks up into a positive whole number. Such is the creative tension, an affirmation and assertion of our own minor-hood, and no less inspiring for that. On the contrary, I think we have just cause to celebrate our becoming minority, to fete our own collective joyfulness in a sad world.

CHAPTER SEVEN

Imaginary Pragmatics and the Enigma of Revolt

> Nowhere had he seen officialdom and life as interwoven as they were here, so interwoven that it sometimes even looked as if officialdom and life had changed places.
>
> **Franz Kafka**

To celebrate our becoming a minority, and to posit an *almost-unimaginable* parallel urban realm, only opens the door, likely a backdoor, to the faint possibility that there *is* an imaginary parallel urban realm out there, one yearning to be *invented*.[1] In any flight through the wormhole to another political space-time dimension, into a minor space, physicists will tell you that enormous amounts of negative energy are required to force that hole open, to keep it open, and to permit a time-space crossover to take place. Negative social energy, of course, is a lot of disgruntled and discontented people, fusing themselves together, sometimes fighting one another, oftentimes knowing better what they don't want than what they do. Negative energy is repulsive in the sense that it's necessary to keep the wormhole from collapsing, from caving in under gravity, under the oppositional energy of an enemy intent on closing things down. But it's equally clear that for blazing another cosmic future, a new terrestrial one here on earth, a good deal of positive energy is required, too, energy that's not only destructive but creative, an affirming power rather than that which simply denounces.

To create the almost-unimaginable, imagination is pretty crucial. One needs an active sense of *experimentation*, of experiments with society as well as with concepts, of moving beyond simple or even complicated "critiques of capitalist political-economy" and something that expresses only critical negativity. Experimentation gives a deeper sense to Marx's eleventh thesis on Ludwig Feuerbach about changing the world. The point, rather, should be to experiment with the world, people experimenting with how they live in the world, experimenting with what that world might be, experimenting with how they might construct an alternative urban life and how they might make that realm for themselves. To say all this isn't to voice a utopian yearning: experimentation isn't to rally around utopianism, not that that is necessarily bad. It's more that what needs developing is, for want of a better label, an *imaginary pragmatics*, something neither utopian nor pragmatic as such.

Imagination is vital stuff here. But it's been serially lacking in the Left's militancy, in what it wants and how it might get it. It's hard to know whether the Left's past inefficacy is because it lacked imagination or whether its inefficacy has throttled its imagination, doused the flames of the Left's imaginative drive. Some combination of both is probably the case. By imagination, I love Sartre's citation from *The Imaginary* (1940), which I mobilized as an epigraph to *Magical Marxism*: "*the act of the imagination is an act of magic.*" "It is an incantation," says Sartre, "destined to make the object of one's thoughts, the thing one desires, appear in such a way that one can take possession of it." Needless to say, "there's always," Sartre qualifies, "in that act something of the imperious and infantile, a refusal to take account of distance and difficulties."[2] Perhaps it's just as well: otherwise nothing would happen, nothing would get done, nothing would even be ventured. Thus the word "magic" in *Magical Marxism* is closely linked with imagination, with imperious desire, with "infantile" yearning to do something else, to invent something else, to do it *now*, not when the time is right (and ripe), or not when analysis says the moment is pregnant and that the productive forces have reached such and such a level of maturity. There's another quote I like relating to the imagination. It's by Spinoza, from *Ethics*: "Humans strive to imagine only those things which increase their power of acting."[3] So imagination means setting in motion something pragmatic, something around which one can *act*, a concrete praxis, a magical act, like an occupation becoming viral, using imagination to spark people's imagination.

But let's be clear about what "imaginary pragmatics" is and isn't. It's not, for instance, a pragmatism of compromise, which is what most pragmatics is; it's not a pragmatics of the moment, a status quo pragmatism. Instead, it's an imaginative form of action and activism that constantly tests out and overcomes its own limits, pushes beyond its own limits, and experiments with itself and the world. It's not that ideas get tested with reality to see if they work (the classic definition of pragmatism) but rather to see if an experimental idea can be tested with one's own imagination to find out whether it can be *made true*. Sartre always liked to insist that imagination is something *lived*, but also *lived-beyond*. You don't know in advance what's going to work and what isn't. So you *experiment*. If it works, it pulls *unreality* on, makes it *real*; real politics follows imaginary politics. The experiment is frequently geared toward self-expression, often collective self-expression, to a becoming and a growing, and there's no logical order, no a priori rationality involved here; and, of course, there are plenty of hazards en route. For that reason, it seems mistaken to ask what are "feasible" parallel urban visions to current neoliberal excesses; it's time for the Left to voice something excessive, mobilize around something not-yet-feasible, and get going on a project that might make it work. What we need is something *unfea-sible*, not necessarily parallel to what "they" do, but superimposed upon what they do, inscribing and reinscribing for ourselves something else; swarming over what they do; creating our urban realm and minor spaces within, above, below, and beyond what they do, beyond their reality; and doing it in another dimension that they can't access and have no security clearance to access.

One of the great inspirations for *Magical Marxism* was Garcia Marquez's *One Hundred Years of Solitude*, which makes us believe that people are followed by butterflies, live for over a hundred years and can levitate up to heaven. In *One Hundred Years of Solitude*, the patriarch of the spectral city of Macondo, José Arcadio Buendia—a city, remember, that came to him as a "supernatural echo in his dream"—says he could never understand the sense of a political contest in which adversaries agree upon the rules. Moderation usually means losing before you've even begun to fight. Why be feasible? José Arcadio Buendia had two aspects of his personality indispensable for the Left: *practicality* and *un-bridled imagination*, twin powers making for an almost inexhaustible magical source and force. Indeed, *practicality* and *imagination* are two aspects of José Arcadio's personality that animated his spirit of social initiative. He was forever forward-looking, never dwelt on the past, and his insatiable curiosity and desire for adventure convinced friends and comrades to cross the distant mountains, to try to found a new city, a new urban reality. Through sheer will and hope of a better life to come, they kept going, kept hacking through the jungle. The imagery, the metaphor, is uplifting.

Garcia Marquez's *One Hundred Years of Solitude* gives us a different, "magi-cal" language to frame things, to perceive reality. It led me to believe that the modus operandi of Marxists should be, after José Buendia's wayward revolu-tionary son, Colonel Aureliano Buendia, "*to sneak about through narrow trails of permanent subversion.*" The Left has to construct its own minor trails to sneak through, trails that make Marxism constructive and positive—make it inven-tive and experimental, probably clandestine, initially gurgling covertly within the interstices of bourgeois society. Aureliano Buendia is a personality dear to the Left's heart: waging thirty-two battles for the liberal revolutionary cause, he lost every one of them! And yet losing these political battles never impeded his grand existential quest, his grand existential war, which Aureliano won hands down every time over his rightist antagonists. In engaging in struggle, in individual and collective struggle (including the struggle with himself), he forged a new subjectivity, a new radical spirit for himself. In experimenting and acting in the world, in engaging with the world politically and practically, we, too, discover others who are doing likewise and, in the bargain, we transform ourselves. It's not so much that people organize and then act, as, *by acting*, people discover other people, and then they begin to organize themselves; and here, again, why limit ourselves to actuality, to the what *is*, to something rational? Let's invent our own concept of reality, another reality.

What might this mean today? For a start, imaginary pragmatics within the urban context doesn't mean building more buildings, let alone more spectacular buildings. It means more occupations. In the United States alone, there's already a surfeit of vacant buildings and vacant lots resulting from overspeculation, abandonment, and mortgage foreclosures. In Baltimore, there are 42,000 vacant housing units (14 percent of its housing stock) and 17,000 vacant lots; Philadelphia has 60,000 vacant housing units; St. Louis, 6,000 vacant buildings. In 2011, a New York–based grassroots organization, Picture the Homeless, estimated there were 3,551 vacant buildings and 2,489 vacant lots citywide. If these vacant units were redeveloped and rehabbed, there's a capacity to create nearly 200,000 new dwellings for those in need.[4] That's a lot of steady work for architects and urbanists without anybody ever building anything new again for years and years. But of course it's not architectural and developmental will that's needed or indeed lacking: it's political will. In recent years, even prior to the Occupy movement, we've seen glimmers of this political will stirring within civil society, rekindling with a different modus operandi from before, expressing itself more militantly. Born out of a sense of frustration and bewilderment, often verging on disbelief—disbelief over what corporate and financial power is getting away with—disgruntled citizens started to collectively organize. Soon this organizing took shape in the form of groups like Picture the Homeless (founded in 1999 and still run by homeless people) and the nationwide alliance Take Back the Land.[5]

Take Back the Land borrows its organizing and mobilizing techniques from Latin American social movements, especially Brazil's Landless Rural Workers' Movement (MST), with direct-action occupations of land and vacant lots, to claim and reclaim for ordinary people abandoned and foreclosed properties and land across America. "Since the fall of 2008," the movement says, "the US Government has purchased millions of foreclosed properties from banks through the Troubled Asset Relief Program (TARP). These acquisitions bailed out the financial industry, which was literally on the verge of collapse. The concrete result of the TARP bailout has been the transfer of $1.5 trillion in public wealth into the hands of private institutions and individuals (in the form of bonuses) to preserve their fortunes. While taking money from everyday workers and handing it over to huge, too big to fail, financial institutions helped forestall the collapse of the world's financial markets, it has not prevented the displacement and dispossession of millions of ordinary families—disproportionately low-income and women of color. In short, the banks have been saved, but people have been abandoned."[6]

Take Back the Land's battle cry says it all: "OCCUPY, RESIST, PRODUCE." The latter notion to "produce" gives the movement a dynamic, inventive, and *active* edge, something that affirms self-organizing and experimentation, something that moves in, occupies, resists, and defends. Yet it creates, too, makes things happen, new things, produces a new reality out of the ruins of the old bankrupt reality. The movement has a three-pronged agenda, a different groove from the activism of old: (1) The issue is fundamentally about land, particularly community control of land, and especially control of land by black communities. (2) The government is an integral part of the problem; ordinary folk can't depend on it for offering solutions. (3) Development isn't about buildings or technology; it's about lives and actual people. We might say that the land in question—the spatial question, if you like—is about a "landscape of affect," an emotional landscape in which people don't express themselves necessarily in words but in feelings (rage, anger, sadness, love) and, especially, in *action*: through activity, through collective hustle. That way the physical and social landscape around them isn't so much a Sartrean practico-inert as a substance of their own everyday lives, a dynamic urban realm expressive of human passions.

More recently, Take Back the Land's activism has connected with Occupy, dialoguing with them, allying with them, and forming out of the mix a twin-track campaign: #OCCUPY and LIBERATE. On the face of it, these two banners seem similar, even indistinguishable; yet there are significant differences, says Max Rameau, who is seeking to "upgrade" each respective organization. He wants to show how each track can perform unique and critical functions, how strategic thinking can shift the alliance onto a higher plane of immanence. #OCCUPY, Rameau points out, "has mobilized mainly, though not exclusively, disaffected young and impacted working and middle class whites"; LIBERATE comprises mainly low- and middle-income people of color. #OCCUPY's "primary frame is the economic system and the injustice it produces"; LIBERATE, meanwhile, "frames issues in terms of land control and use (such as housing, farming, and public space)." #OCCUPY targets "those symbols, institutions, and persons responsible for perpetrating the economic crisis—the 1%—through the 'occupation' of public and private spaces"; LIBERATE's base "is the victims of the crisis, who are protected via land liberation and eviction defense."[7]

Needless to say, although #OCCUPY and LIBERATE are importantly distinguishable, they complement one another, reinforce one another, and cover one another's backs. "Two intractable images of the housing crisis," Rameau says, "include the banks responsible for this financial mess and the homes from which families are evicted." On each flank, war can be waged, fighting the banks, protesting and occupying them on their own turf, while liberating the spaces these banks have foreclosed, taking control of *our* turf in the 'hood. Both #OCCUPY and LIBERATE, Rameau says, defiantly occupy the 1 percent and liberate the 99 percent, forging dual tracks and parallel visions—resulting in mutually supportive fused groups.

Take Back the Land and #OCCUPY strike as solider platforms to launch offensives, solider, maybe, than that of the Right to the City. As I've suggested throughout this book, it's time good-guy activists give up on "rights" and refrain from making rights claims. I know this might seem troubling to a lot of dedicated people who see "rights" as fundamental mobilizing platforms as a strategic masthead to defend people, protesting against arbitrary arrests and unlawful imprisonment and against state-sanctioned torture, wars on terror, and so forth. The idea of "human rights," after all, appeals to our *humane* sensibilities, to what it means to suffer as a *universal species*, and all that understandably touches, moves, and angers people where and whenever abuses are inflicted. So in abandoning that terrain, one might ask, don't we lose all firm ground from which to engage in a struggle for social justice?

Quite the contrary: the radical ground is much shakier and looser when you invoke "rights" and is more likely to cave in under your feet. As the French historian Marcel Gauchet said in 1980, "*les droits de l'homme ne sont pas une politique*" ["the rights of man aren't a politics"].[8] In other words, when rights are so flagrantly and frequently abused, so blatantly and brutally denied, and all done so serially and seemingly at all times, then as a lever for political engagement the "rights" agenda stirs only the bleeding hearts of liberals; it tends to fall on the deaf ear of reactionaries, especially those intent on bullying and business. One could even argue that in our post-9/11 militarist age, with its Washington-inspired consensus of freedom and democracy at 30,000 feet, rights have been subverted by the Right; the language of human rights, then, is likely to backfire or else get fired back.[9]

Disentangling *our* rights (good guys) from *their* rights (bad guys) is hazardous terrain indeed, the more so when one has recourse to a universal benchmark to adjudicate. What *is* the criterion that demarcates our rights from theirs?

Aren't universal rights more like Plato's concept of justice from *The Republic*: those that are advantageous to the stronger? Maybe the Left should sober up and forget about asking for rights, for the rights of man, for human rights, for rights to the city. These are the emptiest of empty political signifiers: too abstract and distant a metaphysical concern, too conciliatory and "reasonable" a political program. Indeed, when anybody makes a rights claim from below, it's as if they're asking for something, pleading for something, demanding something, *asking somebody to grant something*. The claim implies a sympathetic interlocutor, a higher interlocutor, an honest and impartial interlocutor, but it's not clear who that is. In our society, the interlocutor is willy-nilly a person, a government, or an institution in and with power, a higher court of justice who judges. But why ask *them* for something one hasn't got? Why make a pleading claim? Why speak in a conciliatory tone? (José Buendia wouldn't have been impressed!) Why not just act and affirm? Why not just *do* without asking, *take* without making claims to anybody? Why not just take back what has been dispossessed, occupy, and take control of what one wants yet lacks?

The big problem with rights is that they are founded on an implicit principle of *recognition*, on a theory of recognition, on the *mutual acknowledgement* of adversaries. "It is only by being 'recognized' by another, by many others, or—in the extreme—by all others, that a human being is really human, for himself as well as for others." So spoke the Marxisant Russian émigré Alexandre Kojève, in his famous seminar on Hegel's *Phenomenology of Spirit*. Kojève, from the Left, was instrumental (and culpable) in emphasizing the question of recognition, using Hegel's great idealist tome to deepen Marxism metaphysically, bedding his logic down in the "master–slave" dialectic, or what Hegel labeled the conundrum of "Lordship and Bondage."[10] "Man was born and History began," Kojève says, "with the first Fight that ended in the appearance of a Master and a Slave."[11] Universal history is, for Kojève, "the history of the interaction between warlike Masters and working slaves," and liberation necessitated a "struggle for recognition," a "dialectic of the Particular and the Universal in human existence." On the one hand, the slave can't be content with attributing a value to himself alone. He wants his *particular* value, his own worth and dignity, to be recognized by everyone—that is, *universally*, and above all by the master, who doesn't deign to recognize him or his rights. On the other hand, the master likewise yearns for universality, but similarly can't have it so long as he oppresses his other, the slave, the serf, him or her who is dispossessed and who doesn't acknowledge their master's authority.

Thus an inextricable antinomy ensues, "two opposed shapes of consciousness," according to Hegel in *Phenomenology*: "one is the independent consciousness whose essential nature is to be for itself, the other is the dependent con-sciousness whose essential nature is simply to live or to be for another."[12] The master and slave sit on either side of the great metaphysical fence. But they can recognize themselves only by mutually recognizing one another. So long as the master is opposed to the slave, so long as mastery and slavery exist, Kojève says, "the synthesis of the Particular and the Universal cannot be realized, and human existence will never be 'satisfied.'"[13]

The analogy with the rights question is maybe obvious. The realization of rights ceases to be a dream, says Kojève, ceases to be an illusion, an abstract ideal, "only to the extent that they are *universally recognized* by those whom I recognize as worthy of recognizing them."[14] That is how human rights (and human freedom) are granted: they're acknowledged, recognized, by the power-ful and the weak alike, both of whom become mindful of one another as people, as human beings, as Beings with shared consciousness and self-consciousness. And that is what is problematic with this appeal, with this theory of recognition, even if Kojève was savvy about two things: the supersession of this existential impasse requires a *Fight* (always capitalized for Kojève) and this Fight could, of course, only be enacted through *Action* (again capped), through active struggle. (Having truth claims conditioned by action and struggle meant Kojève, here at least, remained very Marxist.) But why should this fight and this activism base itself on mutual recognition?

Marx never saw it like that. In *Capital*, in the "Working Day" chapter, he gives his own account of how any right might be enacted and how it might be granted. The dialogue he constructs, barely four pages long, between the capi-talist and laborer around the length of the working day, vividly demonstrates how questions of rights have no universal meaning, no foundational basis in institutions, nor are they responsive to any moral or legal argument or theory of recognition. Questions of rights are, first and foremost, for Marx, questions of *social power*, about who *wins*, almost Nietzschean in going beyond good and evil. "The capitalist takes his stand on the law of commodity-exchange," Marx says. "Like other buyers, he seeks to extract the maximum possible benefit from the use-value of his commodity. Suddenly, however, there arises the voice of the worker, which had previously been stifled in the sound and the fury of the production process: 'The commodity I have sold you differs from the ordinary crowd of commodities in that its use creates value, a greater value than it costs. That is why you bought it. What appears on your side as the valorization of capital is on my side an excess of expenditure of labor-power.'"[15]

What the capitalist gains in labor, Marx says, by putting his employee to work for as long and as hard as possible for the maximum duration of the working day, the worker loses "in substance" through damage to their health and well-being. "Everybody has a right to their property," the UN Declaration of Human Rights (1948) has it, and no one can be deprived of this inalienable right. "The capitalist," Marx says, sticking tight to the UN's credo, "maintains his right as a purchaser when he tries to make the working day as long as possible, to make two working days out of one. On the other hand, the peculiar nature of the commodity sold implies a limit to its consumption by the purchaser." So the worker responds in kind, and likewise clings on to the UN's Declaration: "the worker maintains his right as a seller when he wishes to reduce the working day to a particular normal length."[16] Consequently, here, Marx concludes, is an "antinomy of right against right, both equally bearing the seal of the law of exchange," both equally bearing the seal of the UN's Declaration of Human Rights. As such, for Marx, "between equal rights force decides."[17] Hence the struggle for rights isn't something granted from above, nor acknowledged through the courts; neither is it granted through *mutual recognition*. Instead, for those who have no rights, rights are something that must be taken, that involve struggle and force, a Fight. Thus one must certainly fight for one's rights, but Fight without asking for these rights to be granted; nobody is going to recognize the displaced, the banished, and the dispossessed apart from the displaced, the banished, and the dispossessed themselves. What has been taken must be reclaimed, by force, reclaimed through practical action, through organized militancy, through spontaneous subversion, through encountering others doing likewise. That is the only means through which one creates a Marxian truth, obtains a Marxian right: through force.

And that is why Marx avoided using the language of rights. There are no rights, no rights to the city, no rights to this and that. We, the people, have no rights as such. There is nobody to recognize what we lack, no mutual recognition, no mutual conciliation, no expectations of anybody granting us anything. And so we should begin again with no expectations, expecting nothing, demanding nothing, taking without asking, taking without being recognized, taking back that which has been dispossessed, and building something else in its stead. Work together, for sure, in mutual recognition of fellow-traveler slaves—the 99 percent—but not with the masters; create alliances with people who have no rights; work with architects and activists, with ordinary people and specialists, with people with common sense and those with a sense of scale. Together, we can develop *common notions* around *adequate ideas*. Common notions are different from universal rights; they're more pragmatic, more concrete, more changing and changeable, deduced and negotiated, relevant to a specific problematic and to a specific group—to a fused group.

And if we don't need to build buildings, we *do* need spaces for new *encounters*, spaces in which people can encounter one another and where new affinities can be met and forged, where new, futuristic magical desires can reanimate urban spaces. Already such spaces are emerging in strange and unforeseen places, in the interstices of planetary urbanization, in minor spaces. In an inexorable drive to urbanize the world, those sprawling strip malls that once went up in rapid succession in the United States are just as quickly folding in succession. "As retailers crawl out of the worst recession since the advent of malls," the *New York Times* recently noted, "many are realizing they are overbuilt and are closing at a fast clip." These strip malls are being stripped down and reinvented for new uses, for planetary urbanized uses, which is to say as community farms and spaces for small organic holdings, as new green spaces and creeks and parks.[18] (The prospect takes us back—or else propels us fleetingly forward—to Larry Niven's sci-fi fantasy of LA's Wilshire Boulevard grassed over for pedestrians.) What's getting invented here is new, smaller-scale retailing and nonretailing within overaccumulated and devalued giant retailing. Devalued spaces now revalorize as the downtowns the suburbs never had, as Main Streets on the edge with green space. Creative destruction, at last, might allow for nonpatented creativity.

The prospect of planetary urbanization begetting its other, creating alternative "nonurbanized" spaces *precisely because* of urbanization, wasn't lost on Isaac Asimov. One aspect of Trantor's hypertrophy, he knew, was that if steel domes canopied everywhere and everything, and if high-tech urbanization and postindustrialization meant zilch arable land for cultivation, whither the planet's food? Where would the behemoth's food actually come from? Where are the farms for food production, the real farms, not just the corporate factory farms? Asimov recognized Trantor's vulnerability, its destabilizing dependence: feeding itself. For much of its reign, Trantor had to import its food from outlying planets and was reliant on extraterrestrial suppliers. Later, we begin to hear of strange organic food production existing within its cavernous neighborhoods, like those of the sector Mycogen, in Corbusian buildings, some underground, others vertical and overground, a flourishing of Steiner-style "microfarms with secret yeast supplies."

This was bio-agriculture that mixed high-tech automation with low-tech "primitive" labor. Hari Seldon remembered "stepping out into a narrow corridor, on each side of which were large thick glass tanks in which roiled cloudy, green water full of swirling, growing algae, moving about through the force of the gas bubbles that streamed up through it. They would be rich in carbon dioxide, he decided."[19] A vivid example, maybe, of what nowadays might be seen as an emerging "vertical farm" movement, which holds that it's more economically and ecologically viable to cultivate plant life within skyscrapers and in vertical spaces—within, as it were, the very bowels of planetary urban life. Climate-controlled "glass houses" (as John Hix's canonical text documented) aspire to feed urban populations in more energy-efficient production systems, with less pesticide usage and runoff water pollution, taking advantage of new hydroponic and aeroponic technologies. The theme merits airtime, debate, and development, since there are a lot of vacant floors awaiting cultivation the world over.

These are modest instances of what might be described as *morphing encounters*, gradual changes that have an evolving and emergent possibility; they signal change, to be sure, but change within disrupted continuity. These transformations represent a constantly adapting landscape and system within the confines of existing social relationships. This is a kind of evolutionary reformism that posits change incrementally, over the longer timescale, an almost-inevitable historical change as human beings respond and adapt to shifting contextual circumstances. (We might wonder whether the recent transformation in Egypt, after Mubarak's ousting, constitutes such a morphing encounter. Only time will tell.) Meanwhile, within these morphing encounters we also find *punctuating encounters*: extensive and intensive associations between people that jar and intervene unexpectedly, that produce sudden changes and sudden jumps that *last*, that burst things asunder, that create grand historical transformations—revolutionary transformations in which nothing is ever the same again. These kinds of encounters induce a "speedism" that produces and reclaims spaces, spaces that fulfill democratic yearnings; these include physical offline spaces as well as those dramatized by online networks between people, new urban kaleidoscopes, and *collideorscapes*.

Participants here fuse not only as a singularity sharing their passions and affirming their hopes but also as a force that creates its own historical space. It's not in space that people act: *people become space by acting*. They *are* space. (Jackson Pollock claimed he *was* nature.) In these punctuating encounters, entire spaces become performative spaces; nobody is merely watching or performing for somebody else: everybody is creating an event, an *invironment*, by transforming the relationship between people, by communicating in space, by transforming space, by engaging in a scenic dialogue with a space. In an invironment the "performance" itself engineers and creates the spatial relations as well as the behavior of every participant; that, in turn, leads to more fluid encounters in which the performance is somehow controlled by the shifting spatial configuration. Invironments are spaces that literally *erupt* as street drama—as dramatic street theater. The efficacy of this street drama will necessarily depend on the performative activity of creating a space, a space in which actors and spectators unite to know each other as one. Sheer relationships, group rituals, collective rhythms, and repetitions define elemental connections in space as well as fusions between crowds of people and their individual bodies. Separations are overcome and, for a moment, for an instant, for an instant that lasts, a punctuating encounter is glimpsed. The moment lasts because it is an encounter that draws people *forward*; the encounter doesn't decompose, doesn't fall apart into something that took place historically, yesterday, last week, the year before or fifty years ago. With an encounter that lasts nothing is the same ever again: it catapults people into a process of *becoming*, of becoming something different.

The advent of Occupy over the past year or so has provoked an epistemological rift in the ontological morphing of our social, political, and economic life—that subtle, creeping shift of our being in the world. Something decidedly different has unleashed itself, revealed itself, gotten created, and it is something different from the past, different from 1968. A lot of people have drawn similarities between the Occupy movement and 1968; I'm not so convinced. Things, I've argued in this book, are different today: the *tactics* and *tempo* of struggle have changed, the *terrain* of struggle has changed. The world has changed, too, changed enormously since 1968, since the flower power 1960s, and it has changed in very significant political ways. These changes have had their own punctuating refrains. In 1967, on the cusp of student protest, The Doors sang, "We want the world and we want it *now*." Exactly a decade on, in 1977, a decade vilified by fiscal crisis and economic slump, the Sex Pistols bawled, "NO FUTURE! NO FUTURE FOR YOU AND ME!" And then, not quite a decade on again, in 1984, during the backend of Ronald Reagan's first term and in the thick of Thatcherism, Michael Jackson and his USA for Africa harmonized, "We are the World." A strange, almost inexplicable act of incorporation and co-optation, of universal reabsorption, had taken place. From wanting the world in 1967, there was no world worth having in 1977: it could all go to fuck. Only then, as we hobbled into the 1980s, we were told that now, somehow, we were the world. That same "no future" had been thrown back in our faces: we were this no future, this TINA, and we've been living with it ever since.

That infamous Orwellian year of 1984 isn't a bad starting point to reflect upon this rift. In 1984 in his famous essay, "Postmodernism, or, the Cultural Logic of Late Capitalism," Fredric Jameson announced, among many other things, something significant: "the abolition of critical distance," the Left's "most cherished and time-honored formula."[20] Henceforth critical distance finds itself, perhaps for the first time ever, thoroughly outmoded and impotent. There's no longer any without, only within, no repositioning of ourselves *beyond* what we progressives are critically analyzing, critically struggling against; now there is no way for us to get critical leverage on the beast whose belly we're all collectively inside.

This lack of outside—or reframing of what inside and outside might now constitute—likewise preoccupied Salman Rushdie in 1984. In "Outside the Whale," Rushdie provided a thicker, more humane texturing to what Jameson awkwardly affirmed, taking on George Orwell at the same time. In "Inside the Whale" [1940], Orwell suggested there was an outside to this grubby profane world of ours, a safe haven somewhere, at least an outside for intellectuals who can find warm wombs, proverbial Jonah whales, within their texts and art. Inside this outside, great art is incubated, Orwell said, great art and literature that says bundles about our corrupt and venal political and economic system. But Rushdie had none of this: "The truth is that there is no whale. We live in a world without hiding places; the missiles have made sure of that. So we are left with a fairly straightforward choice. Either we agree to delude ourselves, to lose ourselves in the fantasy of the great fish . . . or we can do what all human beings do instinctively when they realize that the womb has been lost forever—that is, we can make the very devil of a racket."[21]

So maybe 1984 signaled the real end to the 1960s, sealed its fate. The year 1984 meant the end of the without, the end of critical distance, the end of 1968. Or maybe it meant the end of continuing its tradition using the same mindset, with the same frame of reference, and the same militancy. Making a racket 1960s-style no longer seems tenable today, no more seems the required politics to tackle this beast that had absorbed us within it, wholescale and wholesale, lock, stock, and barrel. Something else is needed than the desperation of Zoyd Wheeler, Thomas Pynchon's hippie antihero from *Vineland*—which, remember, was also set in 1984—leaping through plate glass windows, breaking on through to the other side, trying to cling on to his government stipend as a mental degenerate. Beneath the cobblestones there's no longer any beach; and if there is, its waters are now too polluted to permit nude bathing.

Our urban world is a different place from what it was in 1968. It permits different hopes and dreams, poses different threats and possibilities. Paradoxically, today's neoliberal reality is more easily critiqued than ever before using basic Marxist tools. At the level of analysis, it has never been simpler to adopt a classical Marxist stance *and be right*. And yet, at the level of political practice, that analysis seems far too facile, far too futile to lead us anywhere constructive. There's little in this analysis and ensuing critique that leaves us with any guides as to political practice, to practical struggle, to how we might *act* on this knowledge. One of the difficulties is that the world we think about, the world that functions through a particular economic model, is classically *Capital*-ist in the sense of Marx's great text; yet the world we have to act in, the world we progressives have to organize in, is tellingly Kafkaesque. Marxists know how to analyze and criticize this reality; indeed, we know that all-too-well, sometimes a little too well for our own good! But we know less about how to act, how to construct a practical politics from the standpoint of this theoretical knowledge. There's no direct correlation between the two. We have yet to resolve what I shall call *the enigma of revolt*.

The present conjuncture is Kafkaesque to the degree that castles and ramparts reign over us everywhere. These castles and ramparts are usually in plain view, frequently palpable to our senses, even inside us, yet at the same time they're distant and somehow cut off, somehow out of reach and inaccessible; and their occupants are evermore difficult to pin down when we come knocking at their doors, providing we can find the right door to knock on. Kafka was better than Marx at recognizing the thoroughly modern conflict now besieging us under capitalism. Marx understood the general dynamics of the production of castles and the trials this system subjects us to. But he understood less about its corridors of power and how its organizational bureaucracies functioned. Marx understood the difficulty of waging war against a process. However, he wasn't around long enough to imagine how this process would one day undergo administrative (mis)management—how it would not only get chopped up by massively complex divisions of labor but also beget even more massive bureaucratic compartmentalizations, done by unaccountable and anonymous middle-managers.

Kafka knew how modern conflict wasn't just an us against other people class affair but an us against a world transformed into an immense and invariably abstract total administration. The shift Kafka makes between his two great novels, *The Trial* (1925) and *The Castle* (1926), makes for a suggestive shift in our own supranational administered world. In *The Trial*, Joseph K., like a dog, stands accused in a world that's an omnipotent tribunal, a sort of state-monopoly capitalist system. In *The Castle*, the protagonist K. populates a world that has suddenly shrunken into a village whose dominating castle on the hill seems even more powerful and elusive than ever before. Perhaps in this village with its castle we can now glimpse our own "global village," a world shrunken by globalization, a world in which the psychological drama of one man confronting a castle is now really a political parable of us all today—as we have to conceive a collective identity to resolve the dark gothic mystery we ourselves have scripted, an urban mystery in which we are simultaneously inmates and warders. "Direct dealings with the authorities was not particularly difficult," K. muses,

> for well organized as they might be, all they did was guard the distant and invisible interests of distant and invisible masters, while K. fought for something vitally near to him, for himself, and moreover, at least at the very beginning, on his own initiative, for he was the attacker. . . . But now by the fact that they had at once amply met his wishes in all unimportant matters—and hitherto only unimportant matters had come up—they had robbed him of the possibility of light and easy victories, and with that of the satisfaction which must accompany them and the well-grounded confidence for further and greater struggles which must result from them. Instead, they let K. go anywhere he liked—of course only within the village—and thus pampered and enervated him, ruled out all possibility of conflict, and transported him into an unofficial, totally unrecognized, troubled, and alien existence. . . . So it came about that while a light and frivolous bearing, a certain deliberate carelessness was sufficient when one came in direct contact with the authorities, one needed in everything else the greatest caution, and had to look round on every side before one made a single step.[22]

K. marvels at a world that sounds eerily like our own: "Nowhere had he seen officialdom and life as interwoven as they were here, *so interwoven that it sometimes even looked as if officialdom and life had changed places*" (53, emphasis added). It follows now that progressives need the greatest caution in everything we do; we need to look around on every side before we can make a single step. The gravity of the situation isn't lost on any of us. But the gravity of this situation nonetheless "pampers" and "enervates" us, too, and tries to rule out all possibility of conflict by absorbing us into its "light and frivolous bearing." It has *integrated* us into *its* reality, a reality that satisfies all our unimportant wishes and desires; it has integrated itself into us as an apparently *non*alien force.

In our own times, the Kafkaesque castle has become the Debordian "integrated spectacle," a phenomenon that permeates all reality. If the dynamics of *The Trial* exhibited the traits (and the leakiness) of the "concentrated" and "diffuse" spectacles that Debord outlined in *The Society of the Spectacle* (1967), then *The Castle* is late-Debord and tallies with the *Comments on the Society of the Spectacle* he'd make twenty-one years later. "When the spectacle was concentrated," Debord says, "the greater part of the surrounding society escaped it; when diffuse, a small part; today, no part."[23] The society of the castle and of the integrated spectacle is like a vast whirlpool: it sucks everything into a singular and unified spiraling force, into a seamless web that has effectively collapsed and amalgamated different layers and boundaries. It has created a one-world cell-form of planetary urbanization. Erstwhile distinctions between the political and the economic; between urban and rural; and between form and content, conflict and consent, politics and technocracy have lost their specific gravity, have lost their clarity of meaning. Integration functions through a *conflating* process of co-optation and corruption, of reappropriation and reabsorption, of blocking off by breaking down. Each realm now simply elides into its other.

Where K. goes astray, and where his quest borders on the hopeless, is that he's intent on struggling to access the castle's occupants; he wants to penetrate the castle's bureaucratic formalities and the "flawlessness" of its inner circle. K. struggles for a way in rather than a way out. Using all the Cartesian tools of a land surveyor, he confronts the castle on the castle's own terms, on its own ostensible "rational" frame of reference. K.'s demands, consequently, are too restrictive and too unimportant, too conventional and too self-conscious. He wants to render the world of the castle *intelligible* as opposed to rendering it *unacceptable*. Instead of trying to enter the inner recesses of our castle, of unpacking its meaning, of demystifying its fetishism, instead of trying to find doors to knock on and people to make *rational* complaints to, we need to rethink this enigma of revolt under planetary urbanization and to rethink it on our terms, not theirs—not on the castle's terms, not on the terms of any "logic of capital."

For, in truth, there is no more an *enigma of capital*. We have David Harvey to thank for that; he's already done the steady work, revealed to us that now there can no longer be any fetishism within neoliberal capitalist society.[24] Marx exposed bourgeois sleight of hand and revealed for people the hidden world of capitalist alienation, demonstrating the "root" cause of their subjugation and domination. But today people around the world don't need Marx to reveal the root of their misery, to correct the lacunas in their vision of everyday reality: they know it all too well themselves. They're bludgeoned by a system that's all too obvious to them, that's based on raw, naked, and highly visible power, on brute force that doesn't need unmasking by anyone. This ruling class wallows in the obviousness of its shenanigans because it knows that its opposition is too weak and feeble to stand up to its power.

Thus there is no enigma of capital, at least not for us. It's *their* enigma. For us, *their* circulation, production, and accumulation by dispossession are not enigmatic: they are obvious, blunderingly obvious, bludgeoningly obvious, an obviousness based on pure power, on obvious power. If there is an enigma, it is how this power is administered, how it's controlled, how its controlling center has become "occult" (as Guy Debord said). The enigma before us is an administrative conundrum of how to struggle *within* this total administration, under whose writ politics and economics, the public and the private, state and non-state have all become indistinguishable—indistinguishable in the traditional way we understood these categories. Public spaces are now privatized, public services are privatized, the public is now private; entrepreneurs become politicians, politicians get entrepreneurial; billionaires head up agencies whose budgets dwarf even the biggest supra-international organizations; what was once public is now private. The public realm of what Manuel Castells labeled "collective consumption"—goods consumed collectively, like transport and utilities infrastructure, hospitals, schools, public spaces, and so on—hasn't so much been abandoned by the state as sold off at bargain prices to private capital. Not only has the state retracted from paying for items of collective consumption but these items have actively been dispossessed, revalorized for profit. The plot thickens, too, as elsewhere public goods become publicized private billboards. In financially strapped urban areas of America, like in Baltimore, efforts to raise the municipal coffers now mean firetrucks are emblazoned with glossy corporate ads; in Philadelphia, subway riders now bear travel cards with McDonald's ads; Kentucky Fried Chicken logos embellish manhole covers and fire hydrants in urban Indiana; pizza chains advertise on public school buses.[25] So it goes, on and on, the medium is the message.

We have to rethink, accordingly, the whole nature of what is the public realm in this age of privatization and neoliberalization, a privatization that Marx saw, in the *Communist Manifesto*, coming way back. Bourgeois society, he reminded us, would "leave no other nexus between man and man than naked self-interest, than callous cash payment." Bourgeois society would "drown the most heavenly ecstasies of chivalrous enthusiasm, of philistine sentimentalism, in the icy water of egotistical calculation." Bourgeois society would "resolve personal [and public] worth into exchange value." Bourgeois society would rip away halos of every sort, convert all erstwhile hallowed and holy realms, including the public realm itself, into another money realm, into another means to accumulate capital. Marx leaves us with the bleak task of picking up the pieces of what "the public" realm might still mean.[26]

We need to redefine its context, redefine not a public realm that is collectively owned and managed by the state but a public realm that is collectively run and managed by the people, irrespective of who actually owns the damn thing. The public realm must somehow be *expressive* of the people, expressive of their *common notions*, common notions that Spinoza always insisted were not universal notions or some form of universal rights. Spinoza was dead against an abstract conception of universality, which he said is an *inadequate idea*. Common notions are general rather than abstract, general in their practical and contextual applicability. From this standpoint, when something is public, its channels for common expression remain open, negotiable, and debatable, political in the sense that they will witness people encountering other people, dialoguing with other people, arguing with other people. In the urban realm these public expressions will likely be more loudly heard and intensely felt. When the whole world has been privatized, I'm certain that the public realm will be defined by this idea of a common notion, of a common practice, of acting and expressing rather than simply being there. As I've suggested, twenty-first-century public spaces are urban public spaces not for reasons of their pure concrete physicality, nor because of tenure, but because they are meeting places between virtual and physical worlds, between online and offline conversations, between online and offline encounters. That is why they are public: because they enable public discourses, public conversations to talk to each other, to meet each other. They are public not because they are simply there, in the open, in a city center, but because these spaces are made public by people encountering one another in these spaces.

One of the most interesting things about the Occupy movement, about why it is potentially so radical as well as so potentially flawed, is that it has reframed the whole nature and language of revolt and expression. For a start, it doesn't make any demands and has no designated leaders. It has unnerved the enemy because it has tried, inadequately for the time being, to utter a different vocabulary of revolt. It does everything that Kafka's K. tried not to do. K., after all, was obsessed with demanding his rights—"I want no favors from the castle, I want my rights"—and also obsessed with cracking the secret *interior* of the castle, of gaining entry. He became so obsessed with the castle that he'd begun to internalize its logic, and he was suffused by its logic to the extent that he could only think via its logic. Above all, he wanted clarity, wanted to clear up that which was unclear. It was the wrong question to ask. K. needed to *embody* the castle, to get into the castle, to penetrate its ramparts; he sought out its *physical* presence and its representative: Klamm. K. had to humanize the castle somehow and wanted to deal with it on personal terms.

Thankfully, the Occupy movement does none of those things. In fact, it doesn't pose questions to anyone in particular, doesn't personalize its grievance; instead, it indicts the system and has tried to infiltrate the capillaries and arteries of power as an *abstract* entity, an abstract space. And if protagonists occupy space somewhere, these spaces of occupation are curiously new phenomena, too, neither rooted in place nor circulating in space but rather an inseparable combination of the two. The efficacy of these spaces for any global movement is defined by what is going on both inside and outside these spaces, by the here and the there. It's a dialogue between inside and outside that knows all the while that the dichotomy represents only different moments within a unity of process, a la Marx's "Introduction" to the *Grundrisse*. Marx's famous schema of how capitalist production begets distribution, how distribution begets exchange, exchange consumption, consumption more production, distribution more exchange, exchange more distribution, distribution more production, and so forth, now has to be a vision of *the circulation of revolt*, of its production and virtual circulation, of its emotional and empathetic exchange, of its consummation, and of how all this hangs together in some complex, enigmatic global flow of counterpower.

And if there is a theoretical project here, it is mapping these flows of revolt, figuring out how to make urban theory more *affective* and *effective*. *Affective*, in the sense that it touches us as human beings, affects us sensually, makes us joyous and angry, compassionate and caring, pissed off and performative; *effective*, not through understanding these emotions, but by putting these emotions into practice, making them matter in action, through action. How can we not so much organize this action as *coordinate* this action, coordinate it horizontally, manage the radical fusions between people in specific places, in their minor spaces. Within this project there is no going backward, no invocations of old truths or of old desires for a clear-cut public sector as the antidote to private greed. It is too late to go back now; the yearning for a steady job, as in the good old days, with benefits, belonging to a union, and with old forms of vertical organization, done through representative bodies via old labor institutions, do-good city municipalities—all that seems quaintly nostalgic. More than anything else, there are no more *expectations*, no system to count on, no bosses or governments to guarantee anybody a living.

Now, we are left with bare life, with the naked truth: how to resolve the enigma of urban revolt ourselves; how to do so without safety nets, without the welfare state, without paternal capitalism; and how to do it without subsidization. (The revolution will never be funded, of course, even if it might yet get televised on You Tube!) An all-new vocabulary is required to resolve this enigma, a new way of seeing, a new structure of feeling. The enigma of revolt is tantamount to discovering (or inventing) a superstring theory of urban revolution, making it empirical, real; a radical Higgs boson whereby some secret dimension unites all hitherto dissociated struggles, an unknown dimension of space-time, an unknown patterning of minor space. But the passage to this alternative political reality isn't achieved through analyzing what *they do*, what capital does, as much as analyzing what *we do*, especially what we might be able to do *inside* what they do, *beyond* what they do. It involves a change of heart as well as of tack. It involves an effort to address pragmatically and programmatically that great Sartrean question: *Is struggle intelligible?* It equally involves an effort to address pragmatically and programmatically that great Kafkaesque question: *How do we escape the Castle within us?*

NOTES

PREFACE *The Personal and the Political*

1. Some of Muschamp's outspoken pieces from the *New York Times, New Republic,* and *Art Forum* have been compiled and edited by Muschamp's successor at the *Times,* Nicolai Ouroussoff. See *Hearts of the City: The Selected Writings of Herbert Muschamp* (New York: Alfred Knopf, 2009). "Hearts of the City" was the title of Muschamp's unfinished autobiographical book, poignant sections of which trail off in Ouroussoff's edited collection.

2. Herbert Muschamp, "Something Cool," foreword to Andy Merrifield, *Henri Lefebvre: A Critical Introduction* (New York: Routledge, 2006), xi.

3. I am referring to *Metromarxism*'s and *Magical Marxism*'s respective front covers.

4. Cf. James Joyce, *Finnegans Wake* (London: Faber & Faber, 1966), 42), "The great fact emerges that after that historic date all holographs so far exhumed initialled by Haromphrey bear the sigla HCE and . . . to his cronies it was equally certainly a pleasant turn of the populace which gave him as sense of those normative letters the nickname Here Comes Everybody. An imposing everybody he always indeed looked, constantly the same as and equal to himself and magnificently well worthy of any and all such universalization." Recall, too, that HCE—Humphrey Chimpden Earwicker—Joyce's dreaming protagonist, is himself a city builder. I will be returning periodically to Joyce's old Earwicker, to HCE, throughout the text.

5. Fredric Jameson, "Postmodernism, or, the Cultural Logic of Late Capitalism," *New Left Review* 146 (July–August): 53–92.

6. Muschamp, "Something Cool," xii.

7. Ibid., xiii.

8. Cf. Lefebvre, *Logique formelle, Logique dialectique* (Paris: Anthropos, 1969).

9. This impulse, as we'll see in a later chapter, defines Louis Althusser's "philosophy of the encounter," his "aleatory materialism," his postbreakdown investigation into the nature of revolutionary determinacy and contingency. Althusser claimed aleatory materialism is Marx's nonteleological materialism, steering him away from Hegel and bringing him closer to Epicurus and especially Spinoza. Spinoza, Althusser says, rejects all questions of Origin, all questions of End, and posits a transcendental contingency of the world in which everything *depends.* As for Epicurus (who, remember, was the subject of Marx's doctoral thesis), he imagined the formation of the world as atoms falling parallel to one another in a prehistoric void—falling as rain. It rains and no drop touches the other until the parallelism is broken, until "an infinitesimal swerve" occurs, until an inexplicable "clinamen" supervenes, without apparent cause, inducing the encounter, the piling up and the consequent birth of the world. The contingent encounter that gave rise

to the world—the clinamen inducing this coming together—is likely how a new birth of the world will take hold today or how any new transformation will occur. Hence, so far as "the encounter" goes, Lefebvre and Althusser, apparently polar-opposite Marxists, have more in common than one may have first imagined. (The two men had something else in common: both wrote classic texts of "confessional Marxism," *Le somme et le reste* [1959] and *The Future Lasts a Long Time* [1989].)

10. Henri Lefebvre, *Le droit à la ville* (Paris: Anthropos, 1968). In this text, either because of author or production carelessness, Asimov's famous planet is called "Trentor." Unfortunately, the error/misprint is repeated in Elizabeth Lebas and Eleonore Kofman's sloppy translation of "The Right to the City" in *Writing on Cities* (Oxford: Blackwell, 1996). I will, accordingly, cite from both the French and English versions throughout this text, using my own translations of the former. Asimov (1920–1992) himself began his *Foundation* series as a trilogy, but he ended up writing seven books. For over forty years he continued to build upon what is still the greatest sci-fi epic ever written. Beginning in 1951 with *Foundation*, Asimov polished off the final *Forward the Foundation* only days before his death. Asimov was actually born in Russia the year Isaac Babel wrote his civil war *Red Cavalry* stories. Asimov came to the United States as a young child and was brought up in Brooklyn; he lived all his professional life in Manhattan, where, as an agoraphobic, he seldom ventured off the island. In Trantor, one can feel the claustrophobia that obviously comforted Asimov; everyday life there took place largely underground, beneath a giant ceiling of millions of steel domes. In his career, Asimov penned over 400 books—short stories, novels, scientific treatises, and nonfiction commentaries—making Lefebvre, with his 68, look like a slacker.

11. See Lukasz Stanek, *Henri Lefebvre on Space: Architecture, Urban Research, and the Production of Theory* (Minneapolis: University of Minnesota Press, 2011), 187.

12. Andy Merrifield, "The Sentimental City: The Lost Urbanism of Pierre MacOrlan and Guy Debord," *International Journal of Urban and Regional Research* 28, no. 4 (2004): 930–940.

CHAPTER ONE *The Final Frontier*

1. Isaac Asimov, *Foundation* (London: Voyager Paperback, 1955), 11.

2. Isaac Asimov, *Foundation's Edge* (London: Granada Publishing, 1983), 62.

3. Remember that Lefebvre's "cavalier style" in *The Right to the City* is cued with an epigraph from Nietzsche: "With serious things, one needs to be either quiet or speak with grandeur, which is to say, with cynicism and innocence."

4. Robert Bononno's translation renders passive Lefebvre's active understanding of urbanization. "Society has been completed urbanized," he begins the University of Minnesota Press's 2003 edition. "We will start from a hypothesis [*Nous partirons d'une hypothèse*]," Lefebvre says. "The complete urbanization of society [*l'urbanisation complète de la société*]." The nuance seems to me important. For the purposes of this book, I will use both the French and English versions of Lefebvre's great urban

text. Citations from the French edition, like those from *Le droit à la ville*, will be my own.

5. Henri Lefebvre, *La révolution urbaine* (Paris: Gallimard, 1970), 7.

6. See Ricky Burdett and Deyan Sudjic, eds., *The Endless City* (London: Phaidon, 2007).

7. E. Soja and M. Kanai, "The Urbanization of the World," in Burdett and Sudjic, *The Endless City*, 54–69.

8. X. Chen, "Shanghai: The Urban Laboratory," in Burdett and Sudjic, *The Endless City*, 118–124.

9. T. Brinkhoff, *The Principle Agglomerations of the World*, http://www.citypopulation .de (retrieved 1/10/2011).

10. Louis Wirth, "Urbanism as a Way of Life," *American Journal of Sociology* 44, no. 1 (July 1938): 2. It's worth mentioning, alongside Wirth, the French geographer Jean Gottmann, one of the first prophets of planetary urbanization. In his classic *Megalopolis* (Cambridge, MA: MIT Press, 1961), Gottmann recognized how the United States' Northeast seaboard region, stretching from Boston all the way down to Washington, D.C., represented a new superurbanized form, no longer a city but a metrozone that was even devouring the standard notion of "region." According to Gottmann, "the oyster had opened its shell" and would never be the same oyster again. "Megalopolis" was Gottmann's attempt to name this prototypical form of city life, to understand rather than judge it either good or bad. Gottmann's book merits a close reread because there are insightful chapters on changing urban employment compositions, shifts within service occupations themselves (not just tertiary activities but "quaternary" sectors), and the strange emergence of "megalopolitan agriculture," cultivated in a zone neither traditional city nor traditional countryside. Gottmann took the terminology "megalopolis" from the Greek, from an ancient Peloponnesian dream-city that never materialized in its day; though, as Gottmann said in 1961, this immense urban dream has finally come true.

11. *Le droit à la ville* (Paris: Anthropos, 1968), 83.

12. *The Urban Revolution* (Minneapolis: University of Minnesota Press, 2003), 57.

13. "It is seeing which establishes our place in the surrounding world," John Berger says in his groundbreaking text on art criticism, *Ways of Seeing* (Harmondsworth, UK: Penguin, 1972), 7; "we explain that world with words, but words can never undo the fact that we are surrounded by the world. The relation between what we see and what we know is never settled. Each evening we see the sun set. We know that the earth is turning away from it. Yet the knowledge, the explanation, never quite fits the sight."

14. See, especially, chapter 1 of *The Urban Revolution* and chapter 4 of *The Production of Space* (Oxford: Basil Blackwell, 1991). Lefebvre also devotes considerable attention to the passage from the feudal (commercial) city to the capitalist (industrial) city in another 1970s book: *La pensée marxiste et la ville* (Paris: Casterman, 1972) (see chap. 2, 39–41, 45–69). The argument is interestingly bedded down in Marx and Engels's *German Ideology* (London: Lawrence & Wishart, 1970).

15. Karl Marx and Frederick Engels, *The Communist Manifesto*, Penguin Deluxe Edition (New York: Penguin, 2011), 67.

16. Karl Marx, *Capital III* (New York: International Publishers, 1967), 333.

17. Karl Marx, *Grundrisse* (Harmondsworth, UK: Penguin, 1973), 408.

18. Karl Marx and Frederick Engels, *The Manifesto of the Communist Party*, Penguin Deluxe Edition (New York: Penguin, 2011), 68.

19. Karl Marx, *Theories of Surplus Value—Part III* (Moscow: Progress, 1975), 253.

20. Marx, *Capital—Volume One* (Harmondsworth, UK: Penguin, 1976), 140.

21. Spinoza, *Ethics*, Part I, Proposition X, Everyman Edition (London: Everyman, 1993), 9.

22. C. Cernuschi and A. Herczynski, "Cutting Pollock Down to Size: The Boundaries of the Poured Technique," in E. Landau and C. Cernuschi, eds., *Pollock-Matters* (Boston: McMullen Museum of Art, Boston College, 2007), 73–85.

23. Clement Greenberg, "The Crisis of the Easel Painting," in Greenberg, *Art and Culture* (Boston: Beacon, 1961), 155.

24. David Harvey, *The Limits to Capital* (Oxford: Blackwell, 1982), 413–430.

25. Jean Gottman, "Introduction: The Opening of the Oyster Shell," in Jean Gottman and Robert Harper, eds., *Since Megalopolis: The Urban Writings of Jean Gottmann* (Baltimore: Johns Hopkins University Press, 1990), 3–20.

26. David Harvey, *The New Imperialism* (New York: Oxford University Press, 2003), especially chapter 4.

27. Marx, *Capital I* (Harmondsworth, UK: Penguin, 1976), 875.

28. Eminent domain is compulsory acquisition of land by the state. It is the sequestration of land by the government that often displaces low-income populations. Once, seemingly long ago, this act of public expropriation was done in the name of some greater common good, like commandeering land that would eventually be used for public services and/or public utilities. Now, it expresses the public sector seizing land and then giving it away at discount prices for upscale private reappropriation, letting private economic interests cash in on what is effectively legalized public subsidization—legalized looting. Many urban areas the world over have seen the greatest land grab in history, when big corporate money obtains at practically no cost large swaths of land for redevelopment.

29. Isaac Bashevis Singer, "The Spinoza of Market Street" in *The Spinoza of Market Street and Other Stories* (Toronto: Ambassador Books, 1958), 6–7.

30. In a curious sense Pollock's paintings suggest these two seemingly different vantage points: the outer space cosmos of stars, planets, galaxies, and meteorites; and the equally mysterious and magnificently kinetic disorderly world of the urban everyday. In another sense, Pollock's pictures portray something inconceivably small, too—the reality of protons and electrons and subatomic particles—which likewise seem part of our inner self. (Pollock's paintings, John Berger once said, "are like pictures painted on the inside walls of his mind.")

31. According to Althusser, the metaphor expresses spatial verticality because capi-

talist society for Marx is an edifice with "floors"; each floor needs all the other floors so the building can remain upright. World market street, however, would operate more in a *horizontal* sense, as a lateral web of social relations, with each street existing relatively autonomously vis-à-vis other streets on an immanent planetary plane.

32. Louis Althusser, *Essays in Self-Criticism* (London: New Left Books, 1976), 129.

33. The notion of "seeing" here is both literal and metaphorical, perceptual and something more than perception. Seeing, of course, is crucial in Spinoza's own Pantheist thought—hardly surprising given Spinoza's lens-polishing predilections. For Spinoza, polishing lenses was equivalent to polishing propositions, removing the opacity from truth, letting it be clearly glimpsed, like cataracts being peeled away. Jorge-Luis Borges said that when Spinoza polished his crystal lenses he polished a vast crystal philosophy of the universe, which are touching words coming from a blind man. "He grinds a stubborn crystal," wrote Borges in his famous sonnet "Spinoza." "The infinite map of the One who is all His stars." Another man of seeing, John Berger, is likewise another Spinoza fan. In the recent *Bento's Sketchbook* (London: Verso, 2011), Berger isn't so much devoted to Spinoza the lens-polisher/philosopher as to Spinoza the drawer, the Spinoza who for most of his shortish life carried a small sketchbook. The point to remember in all these interpretations is how "vision" has a specific meaning for Spinoza; it doesn't solely emanate from the intellectual as it expresses a certain perception, an intuitive sort of reason, seeing things *sub specie aeternitatis*—"in view of eternity."

34. *Le monde diplomatique*, May 1989, 16–17. Lefebvre's essay has since had two reruns, both times in *Le monde diplomatique*'s bimonthly magazine, *Manière de voir*. The first was a special edition, "*Banlieues: trente ans d'histoire et de révoltes*" (no. 89, October/November 2006); the most recent is "*L'urbanisation du monde*" ["The Urbanization of the World"] (no. 114, December/January 2010 2011).

35. Removal can be forced and brutal, like under Brazil's military regime (1964–1985), which displaced thirty million family and tenant farmers from the land, reenacting the barbarism of eighteenth- and nineteenth-century English Enclosure Laws. Or it can be more indirect, like slashing import tariffs on specific commodities and providing generous subsidies for export trade, leaving smallholders to the vagaries of the world market. Elsewhere, "incorporation drives" are more subtle and progressive, "accompanied as they are by an intensification of communication and exchange of goods, persons and ideas between the rural neighborhoods and the urban centers" (Andrew Pearse, "Metropolis and Peasant: The Expansion of the Urban-Industrial Complex and the Changing Rural Structure," in T. Shanin, ed., *Peasants and Peasant Societies* [Harmondsworth, UK: Penguin Books, 1971], 76). Here rural localities begin to conform to urban cultural norms and economic aims; soon they're institutionally incorporated; credit and technical services are offered, developing new forms of dependency; obsolescence then ensues in certain sectors of the rural economy. As Pearse says (77) in what remains one the best accounts of the expansion of the "urban industrial complex" into rural areas, henceforth "agricultural productive effort and investment are justified by urban rewards."

CHAPTER TWO *Here Comes Everybody*

1. James Joyce, *Finnegans Wake* (Harmondsworth, UK: Penguin, 1976), 32. When Joyce lived in Zurich, he and Carl Jung got together a few times; Jung was convinced that Joyce was schizophrenic. Always skeptical of psychoanalysis, Joyce himself refused to let the Swiss psychologist psychoanalyze him. Later on, desperate about his daughter Lucia's mental condition, he relented and agreed to allow Jung to analyze her. The sessions, however, proved disastrous and Joyce soon broke off contact with Jung. In several places of *Finnegans Wake*, the psychologist is satirized: in using "*Jungfraud*" instead of *jungfrau* (the German for young woman), Joyce puns both Jung and Freud; he saw them equally as "frauds." In truth, the Joycean unconscious, with its patterns of raving and instinctual behavior, resembles more Deleuze and Guattari's "desiring machine" from *Anti-Oedipus*; Joyce, remember, was Guattari's hero.

2. Joyce, *Finnegans Wake*, 261.

3. Ibid., 32.

4. Clay Shirky, *Here Comes Everybody: The Power of Organizing without Organizations* (New York: Penguin, 2008).

5. Ibid., 31. In a somewhat different guise, imaginative positivity and creativity were major themes in my *Magical Marxism* (London: Pluto Press, 2011).

6. Malcolm Gladwell, "Small Change: Why the Revolution Will Not be Tweeted," *New Yorker*, October 4, 2010.

7. Marx, *Grundrisse* (Harmondsworth, UK: Penguin, 1973), 99.

8. Henri Lefebvre, *La proclamation de la Commune* (Paris: Gallimard, 1965).

9. Henri Lefebvre, *The Explosion* (New York: Monthly Review Press, 1969); Lefebvre, *L'irruption, du Nanterre au sommet* (Paris: Anthropos, 1968).

10. Henri Lefebvre, "The Urban in Question" in Elizabeth Lebas and Eleonore Kofman, eds., *Writings on Cities—Henri Lefebvre* (Oxford: Basil Blackwell, 1996), 209.

11. Lefebvre never quite lived long enough (he died in June 1991) to witness how suburban areas the world over have transformed themselves. This is especially the case in the United States, where what was once low-density sprawl has filled itself in to become high-density sprawl, a sprawl that defines newer urban forms—Joel Garreau calls them "Edge Cities"; Ed Soja, "Exopolises," or "Post-Metropolises." Incredibly, the quintessential stretched out, decentered, and dissociated city of Los Angeles is now America's densest metropolis, with the largest expanse of areas with over 10,000 people per square mile, nudging ahead of New York. Once-decentered suburban forms have recentered into new centers; polycentric forms have sprouted new community coalitions (and not only rich, reactionary NIMBY types). Theorists such as Roger Keil point out that these suburban borderlands and edge-city peripheries are now central in a congealed and legitimate urban form of the future. It is not that sprawl is good: it is that it is here to stay, and not all bad, and it is also the life form in which ecological struggles must now unfold. Roger Keil, "Frontiers of Urban Political Ecology," in Matthew Gandy, ed., *Urban Constellations* (Berlin: Jovis Verleg GmbH, 2011), 26–29.

12. Lefebvre, "The Right to the City," in Lebas and Kofman, *Writing on Cities*, 126.

13. Lefebvre, "Engels et l'utopie," in *Espace et politique* in *Le droit à la ville* (Paris: Anthropos, 1968), 217; cf. *Metromarxism* (New York: Routledge, 2002), 42–48.

14. Peter Marcuse, "The Right to the Creative City," paper presented at a conference on "The Limits to the Creative City," University College London Urban Laboratory, Hub Westminster, London, July 29, 2011.

15. This last remark may be a backhand rejoinder to Marshall Berman, who'd ended *On the Town* (London: Verso, 2009), his paean to Times Square, by ontologizing Times Square, suggesting Times Square since its inception in 1901 has expressed a deep human desire for urban life, for bright lights and the big city, for our right to participate in the spectacle, for "our right to party," as Berman puts it (paraphrasing the Beastie Boys): "*You gotta fight for your right to party!*" "Whatever this fight consists of," says Berman (225), "it may be the only way we can translate the Enlightenment idea of 'the right to the city' into twenty-first century Times Square." For an interesting glimpse of Marcuse's own conception and ongoing problematization of RTTC, see the special issue of the journal *City: Analysis of Urban Trends, Culture, Theory, Policy, Action* 13, nos. 2–3 (June–September 2009).

16. "In March 1964," writes Mark Tushnet in his compelling "Critique of Rights," "five black men tried to use a segregated public library. When they were denied service, one sat down in a chair in the reading room while the others stood quietly nearby . . . In December 1982, a group of homeless men pitched tents in Lafayette Park across from the White House. At night their lack of any place to sleep other than the tents brought home to the public the terrible consequences of its penny-pinching. Can anyone seriously think that it helps either in changing society or in understanding how society changes to discuss whether the black men and the homeless men were exercising rights protected by the First Amendment? It matters only whether they engaged in politically effective action. If their action was politically effective, we ought to establish the conditions for its effectiveness, not because those conditions are 'rights' but because politically effective action is important" (Mark Tushnet, "Critique of Rights," *Texas Law Review* [May 1984]: 1370–1371).

17. Bob Colenutt, "The Contemporary Politics of Rights in UK Urban Development," paper presented at The Limits to the Creative City Conference, July 29, 2011.

18. Tushnet, "Critique of Rights," 1363.

19. See *http://usf2010.wordpress.com* (accessed October 22, 2012).

20. David Harvey, "The Right to the City," *New Left Review* 53 (September–October 2008): 40.

21. Manual Castells, *The Urban Question: A Marxist Approach* (London: Edward Arnold, 1977), 90.

22. Castells, *The Urban Question*, 90. The emphasis is mine, underscoring a citation from *The Urban Revolution* that is important and one to which I will return in chapter 3.

23. Manual Castells, "Is There an Urban Sociology?" in C. Pickvance, ed., *Urban Sociology: Critical Essays* (London: Tavistock, 1976), 57.

24. Louis Althusser, *Lenin and Philosophy and Other Essays* (London: New Left Books, 1971), 155.

25. Lefebvre himself knew this well. Remember how much of his thinking about radical urban politics sprang from rural everyday life, especially from seasonal festivals and raucous, Rabelaisian blowout feasts (*ripaille*). Lefebvre's own disposition was a strange urban-rural mix. When describing his physiognomy in *La somme et le reste* (Tome 1), he spoke of his long, angular, urban face—his head of Don Quixote; yet his stocky body was peasant-like (*trapu*), he said, resembling Sancho Panza's (*La somme et le reste* [Paris: La nef de Paris, 1959], 242). Lefebvre was proud of this curious combination. He lamented the destruction of the countryside almost as much as he lamented the destruction of the traditional city, even though he knew that in both instances there was no going back.

26. Régis Debray, *Revolution in the Revolution? Armed Struggle and Political Struggle in Latin America* (New York: Grove Press, 1967), 77. Emphasis added.

27. Jean-Paul Sartre, *Critique of Dialectical Reason—Volume One* (London: Verso, 1976), see, especially, 45–48; 318–321.

28. John Berger, *Lilac and Flag: An Old Wives' Tale of the City* (London: Granta Books, 1990), 47.

29. The term is Lefebvre's, from *La métaphilosophie* (Paris: Editions de minuit, 1965), 77.

CHAPTER THREE *The Urban Consolidates*

1. This bourgeois scramble for solidity takes on a regionality, evident in the recent "Eurozone crisis." Many capitalists now want the European Central Bank to intervene, to provide a "firewall" addressing the volatile liquidity of financial markets. They want stabilization to let the European Union and its member states implement austerity measures.

2. Henri Lefebvre, *Le droit à la ville* (Paris: Anthropos, 1968), 110.

3. In his "Painter of Modern Life" essay (Charles Baudelaire, *The Painter of Modern Life and Other Essays* [London: Phaidon Press, 1995]), Baudelaire was referring to the painter Constantin Guy as "the man of the world," "the lover of universal life" who loved to go incognito, who "wants to know, understand and appreciate everything that happens on the surface of our globe." Baudelaire's thesis can be applied to many contemporary metropolitan dwellers, irrespective of gender. They're all people of the world, "people who understand the world and the mysterious and legitimate reasons behind all its customs," identifying themselves in thought with all the thoughts that are moving around them. The crucial point about Guy is that he is *not* blasé; Guy hates blasé people and he himself is passionately engaged with the world, passionately curious about the world. He tries to establish his dwelling in the ebb and flow of life, in the fleeting and infinite.

4. Henri Lefebvre, *The Urban Revolution* (Minneapolis: University of Minnesota Press, 2003), 174.

5. Ibid., 118.

6. Manuel Castells, *Communication Power* (Oxford: Oxford University Press, 2009), 34.

7. Lefebvre, *The Urban Revolution*, 194–195n1.

8. Henri Lefebvre, *The Production of Space* (Oxford: Blackwell, 1991), 102.

9. Lefebvre, *The Production of Space*, 102. Emphasis added.

10. Ibid., 331.

11. In the early 1980s Lefebvre began to hint at this kind of citizenship, founding "Le groupe de Navarrenx," a dozen-or-so academics and fellow-travelers who met regularly at the retired philosopher's Pyrenean home. The result was a collaborative volume, *Du contrat de citoyenneté* (H. Lefebvre et al., eds., *Du contrat de citoyenneté* [Paris: Syllepse, 1985]), a collection of essays around "A New Right of Citizenship." Lefebvre kicks off the text with a discussion that blends Rousseau's *Social Contract* with a rights-conscious Karl Marx. This "New Right of Citizenship" is multifold: "The Right to Information"; "The Right to Free Expression"; "The Right to Culture"; "The Right to Identity in Difference"; "The Right to Self-Management"; "The Right to the City"; and "The Right to [Public] Services." Its demands are well taken; the problem, however, is that here as elsewhere in *Du contrat de citoyenneté* the argument is pitched at so high a level of abstraction that, while well-meaning, it may strike a reader as rather facile and hollow. In many ways, the argument attests to Marx's own suspicion with rights' questions: that rights are too conciliatory, too liberal and bourgeois a preoccupation, and that they cannot deal adequately with the property rights question, with the structural injustices and inequalities resultant of the normal functioning of our political-economic system. As many of us know only too well, human rights are flouted each and every day, despite the presence of the 1948 UN Universal Declaration of Human Rights. And when rights are flouted, *people are left with no right to ever reclaim their rights.*

12. *The Communist Manifesto* (New York: Penguin "Deluxe" Edition, 2011), 68.

13. Murray Bookchin, *Post-Scarcity Anarchism* (London: Wildwood House, 1974), 221. Bookchin and Lefebvre had a lot in common: both were committed Communists of sorts, chips off the old Communist bloc[k], and they had a mutual interest in romantic libertarianism. "Listen, Marxist!" Bookchin's well-known pamphlet from 1969, is a telling example of a love-hate relationship of an anarchist-ecologist and Marxist; Lefebvre, of course, was a Marxist urbanist with anarchist sensibilities. Both men bedded their politics in an urban context and knew how this deeply affected any privileging of a vanguard working class. "Are you an anarchist or Marxist?" a perplexed student once asked Lefebvre in the 1970s. "A Marxist, of course," the septuagenarian professor replied, "so that one day we can all become anarchists" (Lefebvre, cited in Edward Soja, *Thirdspace* [Oxford: Basil Blackwell, 1996, 33]). "All the old crap of the thirties," Bookchin says in "Listen, Marxist!" (173), "is coming back again—the shit about the 'class line,' the 'role of the working class,' the 'trained cadres,' the 'vanguard party,' and the 'proletarian dictatorship.' It's all back again, and in a more vulgarized form than ever." "This pursuit of security in the past, this attempt to find a haven in a fixed dogma and an organizational

hierarchy as substitutes for creative thought and praxis, is," for Bookchin, "bitter evidence" of how little many revolutionaries are capable of revolutionizing themselves, let alone society.

14. Marshall Berman, "Tearing Away Veils: The Communist Manifesto," in Karl Marx and Frederick Engels, *The Communist Manifesto*, Penguin Deluxe Edition (New York: Penguin, 2011), 10.

15. The reality of a decent, salaried job nowadays is, in Andrew Ross's faithful words, "nice work if you can get It" (cf. Ross's *Nice Work If You Can Get It* [New York: NYU Press, 2010]). Many people associate informal work, hustling a living in intermittent and menial self-employment, as the plight of the developing world; they don't realize that this is the increasing plight of *all* the world's laboring populations. Here it isn't so much the free market that's the issue as the "flea market" (Robert Neuwirth's term): odd-jobbing and exchanging and peddling what wares you have in a pushcart. In Italy, Spain, and Greece, almost a third of the laboring population earns a living through these means. Rather than being something peripheral to "formal" work, informal work is a vital revenue-earner for many countries' economies and, in certain instances, not a problem to postindustrial, postsalaried work life but the solution (see Robert Neuwirth's *Stealth of Nations: The Global Rise of the Informal Economy* [New York: Pantheon, 2011]). I will return to this theme and to Neuwirth's book in chapter 5.

16. André Gorz, *Farewell to the Working Class* (London: Pluto Press, 1982), 68.

17. Ibid., 68.

18. Berman, "Tearing Away Veils," 11.

19. Murray Bookchin, *The Rise of Urbanization and the Decline of Citizenship* (San Francisco: Sierra Club Books, 1987), 60. Unbeknownst to one another, Bookchin and Lefebvre tried to redefine citizenship and the city during the same mid-1980s period. The former saw the role of the city as politically instrumental; the latter seemed ambivalent about the city's role under planetary urbanization. Bookchin condemned urbanization from the standpoint of citification; Lefebvre problematized citification from the standpoint of urbanization. In 1995 Bookchin updated his 1987 text, renaming it *From Urbanization to Cities: Towards a New Politics of Citizenship*, and diluting his ecological component while affirming a "libertarian municipalism" as a buttress to uncontrollable urbanization. For a helpful discussion of the development of Bookchin's thought, see Damian White's *Bookchin: A Critical Appraisal* (London: Pluto Press, 2008).

20. Bookchin, *The Rise of Urbanization and the Decline of Citizenship*, 48.

21. Roger Keil, "Frontiers of Urban Political Ecology," in Matthew Gandy, ed., *Urban Constellations* (Berlin: Jovis Verlag, 2011), 29.

22. Keil, "Frontiers of Urban Political Ecology," 29.

23. Manuel Castells, "Neo-Anarchism," *La Vanguardia*, May 21, 2005, cited in White's *Bookchin: A Critical Appraisal*, 177.

24. Marshall Berman, *All That Is Solid Melts into Air* (London: Verso, 1988), 150.

25. Ibid., 153.

CHAPTER FOUR *The Politics of the Encounter*

1. Louis Althusser, *Philosophy of the Encounter, Later Writings, 1978–1987* (London: Verso, 2006), 197 (Althusser's emphases). This line of thinking about the transition from feudalism to capitalism had been first explicated in *Reading Capital*, by Etienne Balibar's chapter on primitive accumulation, with an "encounter" between contingent forces giving rise to the birth of capitalism; all of which demonstrates a theory of the encounter in unexpressed and implied terms. See "Elements for a Theory of Transition" in Louis Althusser and Etienne Balibar, *Reading Capital* (London: Verso, 1979).

2. Althusser, "The Undercurrent of the Materialism of the Encounter," in *Philosophy of the Encounter*, 167.

3. *Clinamen* is Lucretius's original Latin word, referring to the unforeseen deviation in linear trajectory, the unpredictable, random movement of matter; in English *clinamen* translates as "swerve."

4. Lucretius, *The Nature of Things* (London: Penguin Classics, 2007), 42.

5. Althusser, "The Undercurrent of the Materialism of the Encounter," 169 (emphases in original). Althusser draws a lot from the Roman philosopher and poet Lucretius, whose six books of *The Nature of Things* expound the earlier ideas of the ancient Greek Epicurus. It's hard not to believe that Althusser hadn't read Gilles Deleuze's *The Logic of Sense*, too, first published in 1969, because it gives a brilliant summary of Lucretius's *clinamen*. "The *clinamen*," Deleuze writes, "manifests neither contingency nor indetermination. It manifests something entirely different, that is, the irreducible plurality of causes or of causal series . . . the *clinamen* is the determination of the meaning of causal series, where each causal series is constituted by the movement of the atom and conserves in the encounter its full independence" (Deleuze, *The Logic of Sense* [London: Continuum Books, 2004], 306–307). For a nice recent take on Lucretius's famous swerve, a swerve that arguably gave birth to the Renaissance, to Enlightenment humanism, and to a new intellectual dawn, see Stephen Greenblatt's *The Swerve: How the Renaissance Began* (London: Bodley Head, 2011). As Greenblatt shows, out of Lucretius's gloomy falling rain came the radiant light of reason, rebelling against the crippling orthodoxies of the church and centuries of monastic darkness.

6. Althusser, "The Undercurrent of the Materialism of the Encounter," 193.

7. Ibid., 196.

8. Henri Lefebvre, *The Urban Revolution*, 32.

9. Ibid., 124.

10. Ibid., 125.

11. *V for Vendetta* (New York: Pocket Star Books, 2005), 4. I am citing from the film's novelization by Steve Moore (no relation to Alan), based on a screenplay written by the Wachowski brothers.

12. *V for Vendetta*, 73–74.

13. Kalle Lasn, cited in "Revolution Number 99," *Vanity Fair*, February 2012, 63.

14. James Carroll, "Youth Pushed to the Edge," *International Herald Tribune*, October 11, 2010.

15. Cf. James Joyce, *Finnegans Wake* (New York: Penguin, 1976), 21: "When mulk mountynotty man was everybully and the first leal ribberobber that had ever had her ainway everybilly to his love-saking eyes and everybuddy lived alove with everybiddy else." Everybuddy lived alove with everybiddy else, preventing everybully from taking over. The digital presence concerned with the occupied movement is formidable. As of November 2011, according to the *New York Times* (November 24, 2011), there were 1.7 million videos on You Tube, viewed a total of 73 million times, and more than 400 Facebook pages with 2.7 million buddies around the world. When the late Gil Scott-Heron sang "The Revolution Will not be Televised," he was rapping to another, older generation of militants.

16. Bill Wasik, "Crowd Control," *Wired*, January 2012, 112.

17. Gilles Deleuze, *Expressionism in Spinoza's Philosophy* (New York: Zone Books, 1990), 274.

18. Ibid., 290–291, emphasis in original.

19. Ibid., 294.

20. A recent World Economic Forum (WEF) report cited the Occupy movement among business leaders' and policymakers' "Top Global Risks" for 2012: "If not addressed," the report warned, they contain "the seeds of dystopia," "a place where life is full of hardship and devoid of hope." According to WEF bigwigs, Occupy exhibits a potentially damaging "backlash against globalization" and "the darker side of connectivity," as do cyberhacker groups like Anonymous, whose "motives for subversion can be as trivial as simple boredom"! (see www3.weforum.org/docs/WEF_GlobalRisks _Report_2012.pdf).

21. Jacques Derrida, "Specters of Marx," *New Left Review* 205 (May/June 1994), 45–46, emphases in original.

22. Henri Lefebvre, *La pensée marxiste et la ville* (Paris: Casterman, 1972), 68.

23. Karl Marx, *Grundrisse* (Harmondsworth, UK: Penguin, 1973), 705.

24. Lefebvre, *La pensée marxiste et la ville*, 68.

CHAPTER FIVE *The Planetary Urbanization of Nonwork*

1. Fredric Jameson, *Representing Capital: A Reading of Volume One* (London: Verso, 2011), 149.

2. Henri Lefebvre, *La pensée marxiste et la ville* (Paris: Casterman, 1972), 7.

3. Ibid., 45.

4. Karl Marx and Frederick Engels, *The German Ideology* (London: Lawrence & Wishart, 1969), 68–69.

5. Ibid., 69.

6. Lefebvre, *La pensée marxiste et la ville*, 30–31.

7. Ibid., 59.

8. Cf. André Gorz, *Métamorphoses du travail: la critique de la raison économique* (Paris: Gallimard, 1988); the text was translated into English as *Critique of Economic Reason* (London: Verso, 1989). See, also, Gorz's *Farewell to the Working Class* (London: Pluto Press, 1982); and *The Immaterial* (London: Seagull Books, 2010).

9. In *Megalopolis*, Jean Gottmann, from a non-Marxist standpoint, had already begun hinting at such a correlation. In many ways, he was much more up to speed then (1961) than Lefebvre himself. In *Introduction to Modernity*, published the same year as Gottmann's masterpiece, Lefebvre was still only testing the water with his explorations into capitalist modernity and urbanization. In "Notes on a New Town," he's preoccupied with French New Town development, which now seems like an archaic historical curiosity relative to the prevalence of megalopolitan development everywhere around the world. Gottmann identified a "quaternary family of economic activities," something different from simple "tertiary" service activity, because the quaternary sector involves "transactions, analysis, research, or decision-making, and also education and government." Older "city" divisions of labor were getting phased out, replaced by the rise of jobs requiring more intellectual training and responsibility, and these, said Gottmann, were the driving force of megalopolitan expansion (see Jean Gottmann, *Megalopolis*, 576–77).

10. Marx, *Grundrisse*, 700.

11. Ibid., 704–705.

12. Ibid., 705 (emphasis added).

13. Ibid., 705–706.

14. Needless to say, the social threats and political prospects of so-called immaterial labor and cognitive capitalism have prompted lively debate among Marxists and post-Marxists. All more or less agree, however, that cognitive capitalism marks the crisis of capitalism, not the resolution of its dilemmas. For more details, see my *Magical Marxism* (London: Pluto Press, 2011), especially chapter 5.

15. Apple made $13 billion in profits and $46 billion in sales during the final quarter of 2011 alone. Its iPads are made in Chengdu, China, by the Chinese company Foxconn whose starting pay for menial workers is $2 an hour, and workers live in crammed dormitories for which they are charged $16 a month (see John Lanchester, "Marx at 193," *London Review of Books*, April 5, 2012).

16. Slavoj Žižek, "The Revolt of the Salaried Bourgeoisie," *London Review of Books*, January 26, 2012, 9.

17. Marx, *Grundrisse*, 705.

18. Cited in Robert Neuwirth, *Stealth of Nations: The Global Rise of the Informal Economy* (New York: Pantheon, 2011), 18.

19. Ibid., 19.

20. Ibid., 179.

21. I've seen this one for myself, close up, at the Coalcalco rubbish dump in the northernmost reaches of Mexico City, in an urban milieu that's more Mad Max than anything else. Puny little donkeys are everywhere in Coalcalco, clip-clopping along stoically,

pulling rusty carts laden with bags of trash piled up high, sometimes bulging over the sides. They come by the dozen, in rapid succession, and donkey owners dispatch sacks of detritus into a deep crater in the earth. The carts come and go each weekday, off-loading 20 tons of trash a day, thanks to some 350 donkeys and as many horses who act as an ad-hoc refuse collection service, a stand-in for the formal one the municipality doesn't have. Residents in surrounding neighborhoods leave the family garbage in sacks outside their front doors and before long donkeys pass by to whisk them away. For their services, donkey proprietors receive a tip of several pesos and when the carts are full they deposit their loads at the town dump. A lot of these men were once farmers who worked the land, frequently their own land; yet now there's no rural land left, nothing green that hasn't been devoured by inexorable gray, by metropolitan expansion, by speculative metropolitan development.

22. Neuwirth, *Stealth of Nations*, 28.

23. Mike Davis, *Planet of Slums* (London: Verso, 2006), 19. More recently, Davis, with considerable hubris, has laid into what he takes to be "post-Marxist" camps, into those theorists who live in countries "where the absolute or relative size of the manufacturing workforce has shrunk dramatically" and who "lazily ruminate on whether or not 'proletarian agency' is now obsolete, obliging us to think in terms of 'multitudes,' horizontal spontaneities, whatever." "But this is not a debate," Davis says, "in the great industrializing society that *Das Kapital* describes even more accurately than Victorian Britain or New Deal America. Two hundred million Chinese factory workers, miners and construction laborers are the most dangerous class on the planet. Their full awakening from the bubble may yet determine whether or not a socialist Earth is still possible" (Mike Davis, "Spring Confronts Winter," *New Left Review* 72 [November/December 2011]: 15). Chinese workers and ex-workers will doubtless play their relative part in pushing toward a postcapitalist politics; but to posit them as "the most dangerous class" seems politically rhetorical as well as analytically dubious.

24. John Berger, *Lilac and Flag* (London: Granta, 1990), 49, 114.

25. Neuwirth, *Stealth of Nations*, 151–152.

26. Cf. Marx, *Capital Volume One*, 794–802.

27. Fredric Jameson, *Representing Capital*, 149. "Marx does not call for the correction of this terrible situation," Jameson says, "by a policy of full employment; rather, he shows that unemployment is structurally inseparable from the dynamic of accumulation and expansion [149]. . . . To think of all of this in terms of a kind of global unemployment rather than of this or that tragic pathos is, I believe, to be recommitted to the invention of a new kind of transformatory politics on a global scale" (151).

28. Lefebvre, *La pensée marxiste et la ville*, 68.

29. Thomas Friedman, "Made in the World," *New York Times*, January 28, 2012.

30. Lefebvre, *La pensée marxiste et la ville*, 137.

31. Cf. Lefebvre, *le droit à la ville* (Paris: Anthropos, 1968), 123–124.

32. Isaac Asimov, *Gold: The Final Science Fiction Collection* (New York: HarperPrism, 1995), 224.

33. Ibid.

34. Cited in ibid., 226.

35. Ibid., 227.

CHAPTER SIX *Revolutionary Rehearsals?*

1. Henri Lefebvre, *Critique of Everyday Life—Volume Two* (London: Verso, 2002), 351.

2. Ibid., 345.

3. Henri Lefebvre, *The Urban Revolution*, (Minneapolis: University of Minnesota Press, 2003), 5.

4. Etienne Balibar, "Elements for a Theory of Transition," in *Reading Capital* (London: Verso: 1971), 272, 281, 307.

5. Ibid., 307. Emphasis in original.

6. Louis Althusser, *The Philosophy of the Encounter: Later Writings* (London: Verso, 1978–1987), 197. Emphasis in original.

7. Asimov himself suspected as much, knew as much. In *Foundation and Empire*, he created the *mentalic* character "the Mule" who reaches inside the minds of individuals to adjust their emotional life, scuppering Hari Seldon's psychohistorical grand plan for the galaxy. Through the Mule's manipulation, people (as individuals and en masse) behave as before; they retain their sense of logic, their former personalities and memories. Yet their ability to desire and resist has been fundamentally altered, thus invalidating Seldon's assumption that no single individual could have a dramatic effect on big socio-historical trends.

8. Gustave Le Bon, *The Crowd: A Study of the Popular Mind* (1986), etext.virginia.edu/toc/modeng/public/BonCrow.html (retrieved March 8, 2012).

9. John Berger, *G.* (London: Hogarth Press, 1989), 10.

10. In his recent *Rebel Cities: From the Right to the City to the Urban Revolution* (London: Verso, 2012), David Harvey throws the metaphor back in the face of the ruling classes to reflect not on nihilistic and feral mobs of rioters and demonstrators but on capitalism's "feral" tendencies; on the "feral instincts" of its financial and political ruling class, "pontificating unctuously about the loss of moral compass, the decline of civility, and the sad deterioration of family values and discipline among errant youths" (156). They do so, says Harvey, while "feral bankers plunder the public purse . . . hedge fund operators, and private equity geniuses loot the world of wealth; telephone and credit card companies load mysterious charges on everyone's bills; corporations and the wealthy don't pay taxes while they feed at the trough of public finance" (156). Harvey's book is full of powerful language and telling critique, full of interesting insights for "anticapitalist" struggles; yet it is marred, subtitle notwithstanding, by the conflation of the right to the city with the urban revolution. Such conceptual confusion creates a political confusion that Harvey can't quite reconcile in his vision of practice, despite the surety of his scathing critique.

11. Jean-Paul Sartre, *Critique of Dialectical Reason—Volume One* (London: Verso, 1976), 524.

12. Berger, *G.*, 68–69.

13. Berger, "The Nature of Mass Demonstrations," reprinted in *John Berger: Selected Essays, ed.* Geoff Dyer (London: Bloomsbury, 2001), 247–248.

14. In 2008, in a theater in Ramallah, Palestine, under a curfew and with the menacing presence of the Israeli military, John Berger read aloud these passages on crowds from *G.* Amid charged and frayed emotions, he read to a crowd of Palestinian men, women, and children who identified themselves as kindred with the participants of 1898. "I had the impression," Berger said, "of having written the chapter for this precise moment in Ramallah, more than thirty-years later" (see Andy Merrifield, *John Berger* [London: Reaktion Books, 2012], 207).

15. Andy Merrifield, *Magical Marxism* (London: Pluto, 2011), 91.

16. Peter Waterman, "International Labor Communication by Computer: The Fifth International," Working Paper Series No. 129, Institute of Social Studies (iss), The Hague, The Netherlands, July 1992.

17. Marx, *Capital Volume One*, 443. Emphasis added.

18. Marx's discussion on "Cooperation" (*Capital Volume One*, chap. 13) is still worthy of inspection. It continues to say a lot about the relationship between technological advancement and collective human potentiality, and this not only in its capitalistic guise. "When the worker cooperates in a planned way with others," says Marx (447), "he strips off the fetters of his individuality, and develops the capabilities of his species." Why see this as exclusively a workplace affair?

19. Marx, *Capital Volume One*, 449.

20. Larry Niven, "Flash Crowd," in Niven, *The Flight of the Horse* (London: Futura Books, 1975), 105. In Niven's sci-fi, "wireheading" is a form of direct brain reward brought about through electrical stimulation; happiness is thereafter possible and pleasure an imaginable, feeling experience. In Niven's *Known Space* tales, a wirehead has had a brain implant fitted, a so-called droud, that stimulates ceaseless and addictive pleasure, usually to a wirehead's detriment, since everything else in their life gets deprioritized. Wirehead is also the name of an interactive video game from 1995.

21. Ibid., 107.

22. Ibid., 117.

23. Michio Kaku, *Parallel Worlds* (London: Penguin, 2006), 175.

24. Niven, "Flash Crowd," 123.

25. Ibid., 158.

26. Ibid., 163.

27. Sartre, *Critique of Dialectical Reason*, 505.

28. Ibid., 356.

29. Ibid., 367 (emphasis in original).

30. Ibid., 363.

31. Cited in *Karl Marx, Civil War in France* (New York: International Publishers, 1940), 123 (Marx's italics).

32. Ibid., 828.

33. Ibid., 559.

34. James Joyce, *Finnegans Wake* (Harmondsworth, UK: Penguin, 1976), 143. "What would that fargazer seem to seemself to seem seeming of, dimm it all? Answer: A Collideorscape!"

35. Ibid., 143.

36. Cf. Brian Greene, *The Elegant Universe* (London: Vintage Books, 2000), 264–265.

37. Gilles Deleuze and Félix Guattari, *Kafka: Toward a Minor Literature* (Minneapolis: University of Minnesota Press, 1986).

38. Henri Lefebvre uses the idea of residues and the *"irréducible"* in *Métaphilosophie* (Paris: Editions du minuit, 1965). Totalizing systems, he says, always "expulse" a certain residue; each residue constitutes its dialectical other, precious and essential in its irreducibility, in its implacability, in its refusal to sit down and comply. Philosophy, for example, "expulses" the everyday, festivals, and the ludic; technocracy expulses desire and imagination; bureaucracies expulses "deviancy" and subversion; reason and rationality expulse irrationality and spontaneity.

39. Butler's article is accessible at the online journal *Transversal*. See http://eipcp.net/transversal/1011/butler/en/ (accessed July 10, 2012).

40. Hannah Arendt, *The Human Condition* [1958] (Chicago: University of Chicago Press, 1999), 198 (emphases added).

41. The Invisible Committee, *The Coming Insurrection* (Los Angeles: Semiotext(e), 2009).

42. Ibid., 112. In the 1960s Allen Ginsberg had a habit of taking his clothes off at "Be ins" and political gatherings; he had a great desire to express his own *authenticity*. Nowadays, though, to be naked signals only vulnerability and/or a certain naiveté and stupidity.

43. G. W. F. Hegel, *The Phenomenology of Spirit* (Oxford: Oxford University Press, 1977), 19.

CHAPTER SEVEN *Imaginary Pragmatics and the Enigma of Revolt*

1. The citation in the epigraph to this chapter comes from Kafka's unfinished final novel, *The Castle*, one of the last books Henri Lefebvre (re)read (see *Conversations avec Henri Lefebvre* [Paris: Messidor, 1991, 23]). Perhaps Lefebvre thought Kafka's book was particularly pertinent for understanding the conjuncture in which we were told history had ended and to which there was now no alternative (TINA)?

2. Jean-Paul Sartre, *The Imaginary* (New York: Routledge, 2004, 125).

3. Spinoza, *Ethics*, Book III, Proposition XII (London: Everyman Edition, 1993, 92).

4. See *Picture the Homeless*: http://picturethehomeless.org/Documents/Flyers/city wide%20findings_Flyer.pdf.

5. Take Back the Land started out in Miami in 2006 when a handful of activists and homeless people seized control of a vacant publicly owned lot in the Liberty City section of the city, establishing, out of discarded plywood and packing palettes, tin roofs and

cardboard boxes, a self-run shantytown called Umoja [Unity] Village, housing fifty-three displaced residents. The village was held for six months before a mysterious fire burnt it to the ground. Nonetheless, these actions attracted sympathetic audiences nationwide, sparking a larger campaign against capital investment through gentrification, predatory loans, and enticing financial packages, on the one hand, and capital divestment through housing foreclosures, abandonment, and repossession, on the other. Take Back the Land received added lift from Michael Moore's film, *Capitalism: A Love Story*, which featured activist Max Rameau and highlighted the successes of the Miami occupations and eviction defenses.

6. See Take Back the Land, www.takebacktheland.org/index.php?page=about-the -take-back-the-land—movement.

7. Max Rameau, "Occupy to Liberate," see www.organizingupgrade.com/2011/11/max -rameau-occupy-to-liberate/.

8. Marcel Gauchet, "Les droits de l'homme ne sont pas une politique," *Le débat* 3 (July–August 1980): 3–21.

9. A case in point would be the anti-abortionist Christian Right's "Right to Life" campaign, with its belief that eggs are people, sacralizing the egg and the sperm against the "evils" of contraception.

10. Alexandre Kojève, *Introduction to the Reading of Hegel: Lectures on the "Phenomenology of Spirit"* (Ithaca, NY: Cornell University Press, 1980), 9. The French writer Raymond Queneau supervised the eventual book version of the classes taught at Paris's École des Hautes Études during the period 1933–1939, compiled from Kojève's scattered notes and draft papers. The late American conservative scholar Allan Bloom, immortalized in Saul Bellow's beautiful novel *Ravelstein*, edited and introduced the text. Bloom called Kojève "the most thoughtful, the most learned, the most profound of those Marxists who, dissatisfied with the thinness of Marx's account of the human and metaphysical grounds of his teaching, turned to Hegel as the truly philosophical source of his teaching" (viii). Turning to Hegel's liberalism doubtless made Marx seem a lot more palatable to anti-Marxist conservatives like Bloom. Kojève himself went on to become a French diplomat. He died in May 1968, just as radical students across the world were attempting to transform the master–slave dialectic out on the streets.

11. Kojève, *Introduction to the Reading of Hegel*, 43. All upper cases are in Kojève's original.

12. G. W. F. Hegel, *Phenomenology of Spirit* (Oxford: Oxford University Press, 1981), 115.

13. Kojève, *Introduction to the Reading of Hegel*, 58.

14. Ibid.

15. Marx, *Capital—Volume One* (Harmondsworth, UK: Penguin, 1976), 342.

16. Ibid., 344.

17. Ibid.

18. "How about Gardening or Golfing at the Mall?" *New York Times*, February 5, 2012.

19. Asimov, *Prelude to Foundation* (London: Voyager, 1988), 212.

20. Fredric Jameson, "Postmodernism, or, the Cultural Logic of Late Capitalism," *New Left Review* 146 (July–August 1984): 87.

21. Salman Rushdie, "Outside the Whale," reprinted in Rushdie, *Imaginary Homelands: Essays and Criticism, 1981–1991* (London: Penguin, 1991), 99.

22. Franz Kafka, *The Castle* (New York: Penguin, 1997), 52.

23. Guy Debord, *Comments on the Society of the Spectacle* (London: Verso, 1991), 9.

24. David Harvey, *The Enigma of Capital and the Crisis of Capitalism* (London: Profile Books, 2010).

25. "Your Ad Here, on a Fire Truck? Broke Cities Sell Naming Rights," *New York Times*, June 24, 2012.

26. Marx, *Communist Manifesto* (New York: Penguin, 2011), 67.

INDEX

abandonment (property), 117, 152n5
abstract expressionism, xvii, 7, 9–10. *See
    also* Pollock, Jackson
accumulation (of capital), 11, 15, 30, 39, 46,
    55, 69, 74, 76, 78–79, 129–30, 145n1,
    148n27; by dispossession, 11, 15, 69,
    78–79, 129–30; primitive, 11, 55, 145n1
activism, 18–19, 20, 24, 33, 47, 64–65,
    66, 71, 98–99, 115, 118, 121; strong-tie,
    19–20, 47, 66; weak-tie, 19–20, 47, 66
Adbusters (magazine), 61
aleatory materialism (Althusser), 54–57,
    135n9
alienation, 105, 129
Althusser, Louis, 14, 29, 55, 56, 74, 75, 93,
    94, 136n9, 138n31, 145n1, 145n5
anarchism, 45, 50, 143n13
Apollinaire, Guillaume, 15
Arendt, Hannah, 111
Asimov, Isaac, xviii, xix, 1, 2, 11, 49,
    72, 73, 123, 136n10, 149n7. *See also*
    psychohistory; Trantor, planet of
Assange, Julian, 60. *See also* WikiLeaks

Babel, Isaac, 136n10
Balibar, Etienne, 57, 93, 145n1
banlieues (France), 15, 22, 30, 50, 139n34
Bastille (storming of), 102–3
Baudelaire, Charles, x, 37, 51, 52, 142n3
Bellow, Saul, 152n10
Berger, John, 31, 32, 46, 81, 91, 95, 96, 97,
    106, 137n13, 138n30, 139n33, 150n14;
    G., 95, 96, 97, 150n14; *Ways of Seeing*,
    137n13
Berman, Marshall, 45, 46, 47, 51, 52, 141n15

Bloom, Allan, 152n10
Bohr, Niels, 7
Bookchin, Murray, 45, 48, 49, 50, 143n13,
    144n19
Borges, Jorge-Luis, 139n33
Bouazizi, Mohamed, 61, 62
Brown, James, xx
Buckmaster, Paul, xx
bureaucracy, 45, 61, 72, 88, 104–5,
    127–29
Bush, George W., ix, x
Butler, Judith, 111

Cameron, David, 25
capital: fictitious, 10–11; finance, 11, 25,
    26 27, 75, 77; fixed, 10, 71, 78, 84,
    105; primary circuit of, 10; secondary
    circuit of, 10 11, 15 16, 85
capitalism, 8, 11, 35, 74, 77, 87, 93–94,
    98–99, 127, 132, 145n1, 147n14;
    cognitive, 70–71, 147n14; immaterial,
    70–71, 147n8; unemployment and, 71,
    74, 82–84, 148n27
Carroll, James, 64
Castells, Manuel, 27, 28, 29, 34, 35, 37, 38,
    50, 60, 70, 130; *The Urban Question*,
    27, 29, 38, 141n22. *See also* networks
Castle, The (Kafka), 127, 128, 131, 133,
    151n1
centrality, 15–16, 21, 22, 24, 34, 35, 39–43,
    49, 63, 67; centralization and, 37, 42,
    99; dialectics of, 39–43
citification (Bookchin), 48–49, 144n19
citizenship, 16, 34, 42–44, 48, 87, 143n11,
    144n19

GEOGRAPHIES OF JUSTICE AND SOCIAL TRANSFORMATION